The Internet Marketing Plan, Second Edition

The Internet Marketing Plan, Second Edition

The Complete Guide to Instant Web Presence

Kim M. Bayne

Wiley Computer Publishing

John Wiley & Sons, Inc.

NEW YORK · CHICHESTER · WEINHEIM · BRISBANE · SINGAPORE · TORONTO

This book is dedicated to my mother, Rita, for teaching me to trust my heart, and to my father, Haaren, for teaching me to trust my head.

Publisher: Robert Ipsen
Editor: Carol A. Long
Associate Managing Editor: Angela Smith
Associate New Media Editor: Brian Snapp
Text Design & Composition: North Market Street Graphics

Library of Congress Cataloging-in-Publication Data:

ISBN 0-471-35598-4

Printed in the United States of America.

10 9 8 7 6 5 4 3 2

Contents

Acknowledgments

My decision to write *The Internet Marketing Plan* was inspired by enough individuals to fill an entire encyclopedia. Unfortunately, I can only scratch the surface in these pages. My thanks and appreciation to the following:

My husband, Bruce Davis Bayne, for patiently listening to my endless ramblings about minute aspects of the Internet, for putting up with my incredibly late hours during the writing of this book, and for never letting me forget how important it is to laugh

My daughter, Kaitlyn Ruth Bayne, for reminding me to take a break when I needed it most, for showing me how gratifying it is to learn new things, and for telling me to "put it on my Web page"

Tony Donohoe, for the inspiration to write by his example

The librarians and staff members of Charles Leaming Tutt Library at The Colorado College, for teaching me the values of and techniques for effective research, both online and otherwise

The late Professor Albert Seay, for recognizing that I had to find my own path, ruling passion and all

Richard Zech, for hiring me for my first in-house marketing communications position

The now-historical Colorado Marcom Network and its yearly editors conference Silicon Mountain Symposium, its founders, former members, and participating companies, for influencing my creation of HTMARCOM, the original listserv (e-mail discussion group) for high-tech marketing communications

Doug Mitchell, for his support in my career and for his never-ending entrepreneurial spirit

Kristin Zhivago and Mac McIntosh, for encouraging me to venture out on my own

Jim Sterne, for inviting me to join the faculty of his very popular Marketing on the Internet seminar series

The following individuals at Wiley Computer Publishing:

Carol Long, Senior Editor

Christina Berry, Editorial Assistant

Angela Smith, Associate Managing Editor

The rest of my immediate family and very close friends for helping me put things in perspective

About the Author

Kim M. Bayne is host of the internationally syndicated public radio talk show "The Cyber Media Show with Kim Bayne," an hour-long look at Internet use, marketing strategies and tactics, airing weekly on both traditional public radio and in streaming audio on the Web. As creator and producer of "Kim Bayne's Body of Experts," she hosts live online chat events with members of the Internet marketing elite. Since 1994, she has published "Kim Bayne's Marketing Lists on the Internet" (ISSN 1084-7391), the premier Web directory and in-print newsletter of marketing discussion lists, news groups, and forums.

As founder and moderator of the now-historical HTMARCOM, the original listserv (e-mail discussion group) for high-tech marketing communications, Ms. Bayne presented at Jim Sterne's ground breaking "Marketing on the Internet" seminars in mid-1994, the world's first Internet marketing seminar series. Online since 1981, her influence as an Internet marketing pioneer has been documented in more than two dozen books and numerous magazine articles, including "Online Marketing Handbook" by Dan Janal and "World Wide Web Marketing" by Jim Sterne. She has been featured and/or quoted in such publications as *Advertising Age, Business Marketing, CARN* (Corporate Annual Report Newsletter), *Interactive Age, Marketing Computers, PR News, Sales and Marketing Management, United Airlines' Hemispheres* and the *Washington Post.* She is a top-rated speaker at Internet conferences and seminars around the world on issues like "Using Traditional Media to Brand Web Sites" and "Developing A Successful Internet Marketing Plan." She has lectured in locations such as Hong Kong, the Philippines, Mexico and Canada, and on such prestigious campuses as the University of California Los Angeles.

A recipient of multiple association and industry awards in advertising copy writing, product marketing, public speaking, and Web content and design, Ms. Bayne possesses a well-rounded background in a variety of disciplines, including hands-on and management experience in every aspect of marketing communications on both the agency and client sides. Prior to her current career as a broadcast personality and print journalist, she held a variety of marketing positions with high tech manufacturers and advertising/PR agencies, including managing her own firm, wolfBayne Communications, a high tech marketing consultancy. As a veteran of corporate marketing campaigns, Ms. Bayne has been actively involved in the implementation of advertising, branding and corporate identity, collateral, direct response, media and public relations, and trade shows, to name a few areas of responsibility. Her technology marketing experience encompasses a broad range of computer and electronics products and services, including mass storage peripherals, ICs, software and board products.

Before entering the world of technology marketing, Ms. Bayne served as reference services coordinator and interlibrary loan para-librarian for the academic library of a small, Midwestern private college. After earning an undergraduate degree from her alma mater The Colorado College, she joined the staff of Charles Leaming Tutt Library, receiving on-the-job training in the use of traditional and on-line tools for academic and business research purposes. In addition, she received classroom instruction in computer-assisted retrieval through Denver's Bibliographic Center for Research. As an extension of her interlibrary loan responsibilities, she conducted on-line research for undergraduate, graduate, and faculty library patrons, through such services as Dialog Information Services and OCLC. Rarely far from a computer, her leisure time activities included exploring the world of bulletin board systems.

Ms. Bayne has written breaking news, trends analysis, opinion columns, case studies, and profile features for a variety of trade publications, including *Advertising Age, Business Marketing, Internet Marketing & Technology Report, Internet & Electronic Commerce Strategies,* and before its demise, *American Demographics' Marketing Tools.* Her columns of Web site reviews, Internet marketing advice and opinion appear in print and on-line editions of selected city/suburban newspapers and business journals. Her Masters degree is in computer resources management.

Introduction

When the first edition of this book was published, the climate for Internet marketing was very different. Much has happened in the past few years to change the e-business landscape. For one thing, the major players are no longer "pure Internet players." Companies like Amazon.com have seen the need to add traditional media into the marketing mix. Unable to ignore the Internet's potential growth any longer, most off-line marketing giants have finally added an Internet element to their business. So far, my view of the Internet as one piece of the overall marketing puzzle has stood the test of Web time.

In the early days of e-commerce, I wrote that the Internet had finally broken the glass ceiling for women. The great e-commerce equalizer had succeeded where years of well-intentioned, but ineffectual, equal opportunity programs had fallen short. The Internet still remains the best hope for someone interested in expanding and improving her market reach, but over the past few years, competition has grown dramatically fierce. As in the real world, large companies have acquired smaller companies, and everyone wants to align with a partner. Consequently, many commercial Web sites are a crowded collection of logos, banner ads, and links touting strategic alliances and parent companies. The Web is now just another mainstream den of big business.

It's no wonder that the Internet appears powerful, captivating, and dangerous to the novice online marketer. Even today, companies jump online without much forethought or are driven into the situation by outside forces. Customers ask for Web page addresses, colleagues brag about their latest online achievement, and competitors aggressively launch an in-your-face Internet campaign. Ad agencies, many who are new to the e-commerce game, routinely pitch Web development services. Internet service providers have upped the ante with direct mail and advertising campaigns offering Web hosting discounts and free e-mail access. All of these factors can and do force a marketer to make hasty decisions regarding a company's online presence.

Sometimes a marketer, such as yourself, uploads a quick-and-dirty Web page in response to all of this market urgency. You view your pro tem solution as merely a placeholder, just until you "get around to" dedicating the time needed to develop a good Web marketing program. As time passes and the pressure builds, so does the ad hoc Web site. Like a patchwork quilt, with leftover bits of fabric, you piece together your Web site. The final result: We've covered ourselves. That's about it. You virtually ignore the big marketing picture. And that's where most companies fail. The development of your Internet marketing presence shouldn't be an on-the-fly proposition just because technology makes it possible.

With *The Internet Marketing Plan* you will be able to create a coherent and integrated Internet marketing presence to enhance your overall general marketing communications program. *The Internet Marketing Plan* is a hands-on workbook, which includes discussions, tips, and techniques for combining traditional marketing concepts with new Web marketing methods. This book is chock-full of little anecdotes, worksheets, checklists, and brainstorming ideas. *The Internet Marketing Plan* book and CD-ROM set will help you create a blueprint that you can use to effectively design, implement, and evaluate your Internet marketing programs.

Who Should Read This Book?

Your job title might be vice president of marketing and sales or even trade show administrator. You might be responsible for your company's advertising, sales literature, public relations, or even every aspect of marketing communications. You now are responsible for your Internet marketing presence as well. This book answers questions for those of you who have amassed a lot of experience in traditional media but have little expertise in applying the Internet to your traditional marketing program. It also answers questions for those of you who have a lot of hands-on Internet experience, but little expertise in applying traditional marketing communications strategies and tactics to Internet tools.

Getting the Most out of This Book

The activities in this book include reviewing and comparing examples of how companies have created their Internet marketing presence. These exercises also include steps for deciding upon and inventing your own approach. During this process, you will take notes on information that is useful for your company to include—as well as to ignore—in your Internet marketing plan. Which brings me to the subject of how you might choose to read this book.

I'm not one to dictate how someone should read a book. It would be silly of me to expect everyone to read this one in the exact order in which it was conceived. After all, *I* read consumer magazines from back to front cover, for some unknown reason. Sometimes I just skip around and look at anything that happens to catch my fancy, which is pretty much how many people watch television, too.

If you're one of those people who likes to "surf," whether it be online, in front of the TV, or with this book, you'll still get a lot out of this. You may even decide to read it from beginning to end someday. Since I can't be sure how you'll approach *The Internet Marketing Plan*, I have included quite a bit of repetition throughout. By doing so, this book becomes a combination reference tool and workbook, one that you will be able to refer to repeatedly, long after your plan has been finalized.

How to Use This Book

Now that I've said all that, here is my *recommendation:*

1. Gather all the material you have that addresses how your company does business and markets its products.

2. Read the articles throughout the book.

3. Read lots of other articles in Internet and marketing publications.

4. Visit the Web sites included on the inetplan.htm bookmarks file.

5. Explore how successful companies present both image and information at their Web sites.

6. Learn by example.

7. Decide what works for your company and what doesn't.

8. Take copious notes.

9. Complete the worksheets in each chapter.

10. Draft each section of your Internet marketing plan.

11. Open a duplicate copy of the Internet Marketing Plan template found in Appendix A, which is a basic outline for your plan. Insert each section of the plan as you complete it.

How to Use the Worksheets, Forms, Checklists, and Questionnaires

Each of the forms in this book require you to perform one or more of the following actions:

- Perform research.
- Ask questions.
- Answer questions.
- Make choices.
- Write text.

Your choice to complete every worksheet is up to you. Decide for yourself how detailed you want your plan to be or how much time you have to devote to this process. You might even want to do an in-house survey of everyone's tolerance level before you embark on a 100-page tome.

It's simply not possible to cover all the variations in marketing plans that can exist in the world. There are variations for every type of marketer, company, product, or industry imaginable. In appreciation of this fact, I have included all of the forms that appear in this book on the accompanying CD-ROM. You can modify them to your heart's content. If you have spent quite a bit of time modifying or enhancing a form, you may wish to submit your version for inclusion in the next edition of this book. If I include your form, I'll credit your contribution in writing. Just e-mail *kimmik@wolfBayne.com* with your offer to share your form revision with other marketers like yourself.

How to Use the CD-ROM Included with This Book

Included with this book is a CD. The CD is provided for your convenience in drafting your Internet marketing plan. The CD contains the following files.

Spreadsheet

Included on this CD is a template labeled budget.xls, which is a spreadsheet containing a basic outline for your Internet marketing budget. This outline is only a skeleton, which you will complete with your own numbers. Open this file and insert costs as you go along. Format your worksheet according to your company's style, or invent your own. After you have completed drafting your budget, include it somehow in your Internet marketing plan.

Forms

Included on this CD are all of the forms you need to complete in order to write your Internet marketing plan. Illustrative tables and graphics appearing in the book are not included on the disk. For your convenience in locating, modifying, and/or printing out the forms, the disk files are labeled like the figures in the book. For example, Figure 3.6 is in the file labeled figure03-06.doc, in Microsoft Word format.

Bookmarks

Included on this CD is a bookmark file labeled bookmark.htm that you can either import into your Web browser software or access from your CD or hard drive by opening it as a file. If you decide to use it as a file, open your browser and select it by name, rather than open any other type of program. Using it as a file will also allow you to click on each of the links, as long as you are connected to the Internet.

The bookmark file is arranged by chapter and contains all of the URLs referenced throughout the book. It will save you time in locating various addresses on the World Wide Web.

All of the URLs referenced in this book and in the bookmark file were working at the time I submitted my manuscript for publication. Keep in mind that URLs change frequently on the Internet. By the time this book is published, some of the URLs will already be out of date. If a URL has changed and you find that you are no longer able to locate the corresponding Internet resource, I would welcome a note from you. Please e-mail me at kimmik@wolfBayne .com. I will catalog the new URL for any future editions of this book.

Creation: Building Your
Internet Marketing Plan

Writing the Internet Marketing Plan: An Introduction

(The Internet) has transformed how many people do business and continues to grow at an astounding rate.
Larry Kesslin, President, Let's Talk Business Network

Practically every traditional marketing project you undertake will have a beginning, a middle, and an end. You write copy for a piece of sales literature. You have it designed, typeset, and printed. Finally, you arrange for literature distribution. You'll probably experience this same exact project over and over again for the life of each particular product. Most important, the final result, the printed data sheet, brochure, or direct-mail circular, is a tangible piece of marketing evidence that you have indeed completed an activity. Not so with the Internet.

The nature of the Internet is volatile. It not only lends itself to frequent, sometimes hourly, updates and revisions, but it demands it. It's a work-in-progress that is constantly evolving. It is very rare that a Webmaster says with confidence that he or she has completely finished. If a Webmaster does say that, it may mean that he or she has gotten a better offer and starts the new job on Monday.

There will always be one more change that is worth making, regardless of how happy everyone is with the so-called final result. That is why creating a written Internet marketing plan is so important. An Internet marketing plan will improve your ability to manage your Internet marketing presence more effectively, not only for your own sanity but also for that of your company's.

What Is an Internet Marketing Plan?

In the world of traditional marketing, you propose or justify a new program or its continuation through its relationship to several different elements, including the company, its products, the market, a budget, and staff considerations. In order to execute successfully any type program at all, you need a plan. You need a detailed road map of sorts. An Internet marketing plan *is* that road map. That's where this book enters and your work begins.

The elements of an Internet marketing plan are not much different than the elements of a traditional marketing plan. Okay, in this book, they look practically identical. Why shouldn't they be? It's very simple. Without an Internet marketing plan that at least resembles something you've seen or worked with before, you've got a smaller chance that your marketing staff and management will understand what you're trying to accomplish. The Internet marketing plan (Appendix A) upon which this book is based includes these sections:

- Section One: Business Overview and Executive Summary
- Section Two: Applicable Internet Market Statistics
- Section Three: Marketing Communications Strategies
- Section Four: The Internet Marketing Task Force
- Section Five: Internet Marketing Program Implementation
- Section Six: Internet Marketing Budget
- Section Seven: Internet Marketing Plan Summary
- Section Eight: Supporting Documents

This book represents but one way to prepare your marketing plan. If you've written a plan before, then you have your own way of organizing the final document. For example, you could decide to move the section on creating a task force to the end. The choice is yours. Bottom line: Don't strain trying to find a new marketing plan format for the Internet when, after all, it's just media. Once you and everyone in your organization feel comfortable with using the Internet for marketing purposes, you can experiment with different ways to present your program.

If you absolutely have to have a sexy new way to present your Internet marketing plan, here's a good technique for impressing your colleagues:

Step 1. Edit each section of your plan down to bullets similar to a slide show outline.

Step 2. Convert each section into HTML with a 20-second refresh per page.

Step 3. Stick the plan on your company's intranet for everyone to see.

Step 4. Add an e-mail comment form for immediate feedback.

Step 5. Get back to work. You have a plan to execute!

One more thing: Keep the text of your plan as readable as possible. As you use new terms that may or may not be familiar to the readers of your plan, define them in the simplest terms possible. You really have nothing to gain by emulating someone intent on overwhelming staff members with a newly attained command of online vocabulary.

About Writing the Plan

Whether it is for traditional or new media, writing a marketing plan requires time, research, and patience. An Internet marketing plan, like the World Wide Web that it discusses, is a constantly changing document. The execution of that plan involves updating the plan's content and adapting to the changing marketplace and technology that drives the online world. Don't be surprised when you find yourself revising and adding new sections to the plan to improve it. After all, the Internet marketing plan is your working document for success.

How to Use This Book

- Read the articles.
- Look at the illustrations and figures.
- Visit the Web sites mentioned in the chapters and included in the accompanying bookmark file.
- Explore how each company used information to create or enhance its presence.
- Explore how your company can use this information to create or enhance its presence.
- Take copious notes.
- Complete the worksheet(s) and/or activities in each chapter.
- Open a duplicate copy of the Internet Marketing Budget found on the disk file budget.xls. Insert cost data as you discover it.
- Open a duplicate copy of the Internet Marketing Plan template found in Appendix A, which is a basic outline for your plan. Insert each section of the plan as you complete it.

How the Internet Marketing Plan and This Book Are Organized

Let's take a look at the different sections, which coincidentally are the outline for your own Internet marketing plan. This book is divided into two major parts.

Part One, Creation: Building Your Internet Marketing Plan

In Part One, you'll spend time gathering data that, in most cases, already exists in other forms. For this section, you'll need your company profile, your annual report, your marketing budget, your sales literature, and perhaps some reports by industry analysts that dissect your market. While you're at it, dig out the competitive literature you picked up at that last trade show. You'll need this when we get to the chapter on market statistics.

When you decide to address budget issues, enlist the help of your Internet services department, local computer store, and/or local Internet service provider. Pull out your address book with your ad agency's number or that of your local Web design boutique. While you're grabbing phone numbers, don't forget your company's internal extension list as well. Guess who you'll be calling to recruit for your Internet marketing team? Yep, your coworkers. At the very least, if they don't end up on your Internet marketing team, you can pick their brains. Believe it or not, their seemingly uninitiated ideas can help you sell your plan to as many people as possible. The chapters in this section include the following.

Chapter 2, Preparing the Business Overview and Executive Summary

You may have to ask management for the money to launch your Internet marketing program. In order to address this particular readership of your plan, this book includes how to tell the bigwigs (senior level executives and/or potential investors) who you are, where you've been, what you're doing, why you're doing it, and how to proceed from here. It's basically a history lesson drafted in business review terms.

Chapter 3, Analyzing Internet Market Statistics

In order to justify your Internet marketing program, you must gather lots and lots of information that proves your company should be there. You can do this in the following ways:

- Demonstrate the successful use of the Internet
- Demonstrate the successful use of the Internet in your market
- Demonstrate the successful use of the Internet in your market for your product or service

In this section, we'll point you to resources that will help you in this endeavor. And if you didn't get enough of browsing the Net for your initial answers, we'll spend even more time with you in the chapter on market research, just to keep you on your toes.

Chapter 4, Formulating Marketing Communications Strategies

An approach to your Internet marketing would be nice. In this chapter, we'll get you in the mood to start thinking of strategies and tactics you can use.

Chapter 5, Forming the Internet Marketing Task Force

Before you become overconfident about your Internet marketing venture, remember this: Anything that can go wrong, will. It's even more likely because of the continuously changing technical aspects of the Internet. That's why you're going to want to form an Internet marketing task force or team. You will have to decide whether you want to form your team before or after you put your plan together. Maybe management will even decide that for you. Regardless, the formation of your team will be one of the plan elements that will drive your budget as well.

Part Two, Implementation: Fitting the Internet into Your Marketing Communications Mix

In Part Two, you'll continue drafting portions of your plan, but you'll also take into account the actual activities associated with executing it. You'll also receive practical help in the actual implementation phase.

Eventually, you'll need to address how the Internet fits into your overall marketing communications program. Be ready to review everything you've done with traditional media up to now. Defining activities that relate to the rest of your marketing program will keep you from duplicating efforts or overlooking the obvious. You will soon realize how easy it becomes to leverage your other marketing programs when the Internet becomes part of the picture. The Internet marketing plan is no different. We'll apply the Internet to these selected marketing communications activities:

- Chapter 6, Designing Advertising and Direct-Mail Campaigns
- Chapter 7, Utilizing Collateral Materials/Sales Literature
- Chapter 8, Developing a Corporate Identity
- Chapter 9, Conducting Market Research
- Chapter 10, Executing Public Relations and Promotional Programs
- Chapter 11, Incorporating Sales Support Functions
- Chapter 12, Planning Trade Shows
- Chapter 13, Measuring Internet Marketing Results
- Chapter 14, Launching Your Internet Marketing Program
- Chapter 15, Planning Your Internet Marketing Budget

The marketing communications programs outlined in these chapters are only the tip of the iceberg. I know that you have responsibilities in other areas that I have failed to mention. Everyone in marketing always does. Marketing communications responsibilities differ by company, and I hope the areas outlined in this book will, at the very least, cover the average marketing communications agendas.

How Much Should You Write?

Most company executives do not have a lot of time to read lengthy documents. Sometimes your wonderfully crafted Internet marketing plan will become part of a larger, more extensive marketing plan for the company, a division, or an entire network of interconnected companies. Another marketing professional like yourself may have the task of editing plans down to the bare essentials, leaving out all your hard work and finely tuned prose. That's why it's important for you to keep your plan as concise as possible.

If at all possible, keep each section of your plan to one page or less. Supplement your written word with easy-to-read diagrams, charts, and schedules. Most of the information you wish to include in your Internet marketing plan may already appear in other company documents. Save time, money, and space. Refer to these other documents and get to the point about the Internet while you have the reader's attention.

General Internet Marketing Implementation Strategies

Now you know what you've gotten yourself into. Before you start putting your thoughts down on paper, it's time to create a unique state of mind with which to approach our Internet marketing plan. As marketers devise ways to fit the Internet into their traditional marketing communications mix, they must include both strategic and tactical approaches in their use of this exciting new medium. Along those lines, here are my favorite 10 strategies for Internet marketing. These apply whether you decide to use e-mail, the Web, FTP, newsgroups, or all of these.

Strategy 1: View the Internet as an Adjunct

When marketers embraced the Internet and started making advertising and promotion a reality, no one intended it to become the only element in your marketing mix. How many times have you heard company representatives say, "We don't have much budget. The Internet is cheap enough and print advertising is so expensive. Let's just put up a Web page and cut back on our other activities." Think about this. Did the rules of marketing change overnight when businesses discovered the Internet? For the sake of this argument, the answer is no.

Off-Line and Online Media Are the Perfect Couple

There exists a synergistic relationship between traditional media and online media. You must marry them in a complementary way. The Internet is not designed to be the only element in your marketing mix. Successful businesses still continue to plan well-rounded marketing communications campaigns. Successful businesses investigate every opportunity and shine like industry stars when they do. Marketers at these companies leave no stone unturned. They have used and will continue to use every available marketing vehicle that suits their particular needs.

This advice becomes all too clear when you realize that the Internet is one of those marketing elements that requires the presence of other marketing media in order to work most effectively. Think of it as throwing a holiday party. Sure, we all know it's New Year's Eve, but if you don't send me an invitation, how will I know *you* are having a celebration?

Old marketers' tales. Marketers sometimes claim that the Internet didn't work for them because no one visited their site. One Internet marketing myth says that putting up a Web page constitutes creating an Internet marketing presence. Yes, there are robots out there that search and catalog pages on the Web, but why leave your promotion to chance? Another Internet marketing myth claims that registering with online search engines will cover just about any promotion you'll ever need. Well, I already know that *you* don't believe any of that, because you're reading this book.

Most people won't know about or even notice your online presence unless they are already online looking for you or your type of product. How do you get them to notice your online activities? One way is by flaunting your presence in off-line media. I *love* to hear this statement after someone looks at a company brochure with the URL prominently displayed, "I didn't know they had a Web page. Great! I'll have to look at it the next time I'm online."

How Do You Spell Information?

Now let's take this one step further. You've become excited about the potential for creating a very powerful online presence. You've become less enthusiastic about the potential of your print advertising in trade publications. You're not too interested in spending time on your ad placement anymore, since you know that the Internet is the wave of the future. Mr. Bob Big Bucks, CEO, *doesn't* have time to get online, but he *does* influence buying decisions. How are you going to continue to reach him?

Companies who decide to eliminate a portion of their marketing program in favor of an Internet marketing presence may be selling their customers and clients short. The keyword here is *eliminate.* Ask your customers how many different ways they get their information before they purchase. They each tell a different story about how they gather their product and service features and benefits on a daily, weekly, or monthly basis. For example, I receive my consumer product news through print magazine ads, TV commercials, and coupons and offers in the Sunday paper. I receive my technical product information, such as that needed for my computer and its peripherals, through print manuals, and occasionally I'll look for it on the Internet. I may even pick up the phone and dial some company's toll-free number if I'm really desperate.

News on current world events comes to me through a variety of sources. My cable TV subscription includes *CNN Headline News. The Denver Post* newspaper is delivered to my door each weekend. When I haven't had time to read the paper or turn on the tube, I look at my PointCast news ticker, log on to My Yahoo!, or check out Business Wire while I am online. I'm *that* hungry for news plus I just want to verify that aliens from another galaxy haven't landed or that Pikes Peak isn't going to erupt any minute. When I'm on vacation, I turn on the TV in my hotel room. If I'm commuting from Colorado Springs to Denver or on a weekend camping trip, I turn on the car radio. Believe it or not, sometimes I actually ask another human being what's new. That's exactly how I found out U.S. President Ronald Reagan had been shot in 1981. At breakfast one morning, I asked someone staying in my London bed-and-breakfast if he'd seen the paper. I gathered my news that morning by word of mouth. I would bet that I am not unique in using a variety of resources, both traditional and new media, to collect news and information. I weigh these separately gathered facts whenever I have to make a decision or form an opinion.

Humans Are Driven by Routine

In the twentieth century, particularly in its final decades, we advanced tremendously in the technological arena. In spite of it all, we're still just creatures driven by habit. Most people use what's convenient and/or what they're accustomed to, and I wouldn't be surprised, if they continue to do so for quite some time. Hence the term *early adopter*. Not everyone is an early adopter. You could be making a big customer-service mistake if you choose to eliminate a certain type of media from your marketing program in favor of a hot new one.

Unfortunately, the attitude of some companies, and the ad agencies that represent them, smacks of elitism when it comes to discussing how they'll approach Internet marketing. While consulting for a well-known Denver-based advertising agency, I was amazed by remarks regarding which customers were worthy of the company's time. Here were people discussing strategies for pitching several of their big accounts, as well as several well-coveted prospects, on the advantages of creating an Internet marketing presence. First, we discussed how the agency would approach its own Internet presence. After all, how can you convince someone to join the club when you're not yet a member?

When the topic of the agency's site design was covered, I suggested that an option be included to allow customers, regardless of their connection speed or browser, to choose a low-tech version of the site. The agency's graphic artists had already decided their Web site was going to be graphically intense, using the latest HTML extensions, long before this meeting. In defense of this view, someone commented, "Look, if these people haven't got a high-speed connection with Netscape, a multimedia setup, and experience surfing the Web, then we don't even want to talk to them." So there. In other words, they only wanted to bother with people who had the same taste in hardware and software. Or worse, they only wanted clients who were technologically savvy enough that they didn't even need to hire this agency. *Oops!* If you really needed this agency's help, you were out of luck.

Your Internet marketing presence is obviously going to reach a lot of online people. As in traditional media, you will not be able to control who eventually sees your message and who doesn't. This is not an undercover CIA operation, you know. So, as you decide how to approach your Internet content and presentation, keep the hidden market in mind. You wouldn't assume that all worthwhile customers are created equal. Don't assume that all worthwhile customers who just happen to be on the Internet are created equal, either.

If It's Not Broken, Don't Fix It . . . Okay, Maybe Just a Little

Before you start making plans to reduce your marketing costs by thousands of dollars by eliminating a part of your program that is a proven sales generator, take an aspirin. If your direct-mail campaign is working, don't trade it for the Internet. If your TV campaign is working, don't trade it for the Internet. If your print advertising campaign is working . . . you get the idea.

When do you use the Internet? Use the Internet to help *enhance* those programs that are already working. If you notice a shift in how customers are gathering your literature and how they are contacting you, then it's time to regroup—but not before. If your marketing programs are *not* working, find out why not. Don't make the same mistakes online. Bad marketing is bad marketing, regardless of the media.

Be Responsible in Your Media Choices

Now, about that thought that you'll be able to cut down on print and literature distribution costs once you go online: Maybe you will, maybe you won't. I've talked to several companies who have claimed that the Internet saved them money in reprinting literature. I've also talked to several companies who have claimed that the demand for their literature is greater now that they have the international reach afforded by the Internet. I'm not going to guarantee what will happen to you one way or the other.

Here's the truth about literature and whether you should eliminate or reduce it. As a customer, if you make it difficult for me to get the help or information I need, I'm going to find an easier way and probably another company. You may end up being eliminated on major contracts you don't even know about. Your potential customer will complain to 10 buddies or business colleagues that you've stopped printing and distributing data sheets. If a customer walks into your trade show booth and asks for a piece of literature and you hand out your Web address, the person might get around to looking you up after the show and, then again, maybe not. He or she doesn't need to spend another hour of valuable time hunting down your online sales literature. All the customer wants is to pick up one crummy data sheet to read on the airplane.

Before you accuse me of being myopic, let me clarify my position. The reduction of printed literature may or may not happen anytime soon. You may be lucky enough to realize a cost savings on your printed literature immediately. You may not. The market has been talking about the paperless office since the days of the first optical disk drive, and we're still killing plenty of trees a decade and a half later. However, if your goals must include lower literature distribution costs, be conservative in your estimate of how fast you will realize this savings.

I'm not saying that all budget dollars should stay the same and you should just invest more money to cover the Internet program. For many companies, that would mean instantaneous death to their dreams of an Internet marketing program. The money has to come from somewhere. Unless your company is very supportive or you are very lucky, the money will sometimes come from other marketing programs. Just be responsible about where you cut corners before you launch that prestigious Web page.

Strategy 2: Use E-mail Strategically.

Want to find customers on the Internet? E-mail is the first place to look. Most likely, your customers on the Internet have already used e-mail to send a message. And why not? E-mail is the easiest to use and the easiest to understand. Free e-mail services abound, many without Web access. The number of people who recognize that Mary-Mary@quite-contrary.com is an electronic mail address exceeds the number of people who recognize that http://www.quite-contrary.com is a Web page address. I still meet people who don't understand the difference between the two, and how that relates to the Internet as a whole . . . but that's another story altogether.

Very few communication vehicles allow you the flexibility and ease of response that e-mail does, especially when no one's there to take your call. Sure, you can always leave a voice mail or fax a note. Who isn't sick of telephone tag and voice mailboxes? E-mail helps you build customer relationships quickly and allows you ample space to explain your needs. There is a definite sense of closure when you send an e-mail message that answers someone's questions quote by quote.

Another nice thing about electronic mail is the ease with which you can communicate with one, two, three, or multitudes of people at once. Besides being convenient, e-mail is even more powerful than the telephone, due to its potentially unlimited reach and low cost. E-mail can service customers, build one-on-one relationships, distribute newsletters, and automatically respond whenever a human is unavailable. Of course, the potential for abuse is just as great as its advantages.

If you have a customer's e-mail address you have his or her attention. Use it judiciously and respect its value. E-mail is the ultimate customer-relationship tool. Once you uncover your customers' e-mail addresses and where they hang out online, you're halfway to uncovering your competitor's customers. Newsgroups and lists are e-mail-driven. You can search these archives by a keyword that suits your area of interest and immediately find out where the good discussions are being held. Be careful. Strategic use of e-mail doesn't mean gathering up lists of addresses to add to your "shotgun" e-mail archives. It includes participating in these discussions in a useful and helpful manner. Yes, it takes time. Lots of people don't want to take the time. That's where they alienate potential customers. And that's where their competitors do a better job of online marketing.

Make a Million Dollars Overnight!

By now, you've probably come across advertisements that promise you the ability to reach millions of prospects on the Internet for little or no cost. These ads sell e-mail address lists. Online marketers who promote the use of these lists claim that they are *providing a service*. They claim that intelligent people *welcome* updates on information of interest to them. Okay. I'm intelligent. You're intelligent. I'll buy that. But who decides what is interesting? I do. Marketers do, too. As a result, too many ads for solar-powered nose-hair clippers, professional dog-walking services, and swampland investment opportunities have ended up in my in-box, only to be met with a quick delete. My nose is fine, I don't own a dog, and I like living in the mountains, thank you.

How happy do you think your customers would be if you launched a telemarketing campaign that interrupted their work flow with annoying phone calls on a regular basis? How long do you think your customers would tolerate your continued waste of their office supplies (i.e., facsimile paper) while you tie up their incoming fax line with ads for your discounted products? While marketers who use the shotgun approach may reap *some* benefits from this type of advertising, the long-term effect is that they've created a reputation for reckless and inconsiderate marketing.

I've seen the results of many of these campaigns, and I have yet to believe that most people welcome unsolicited e-mail. With a dial-up modem connection and a hundred worthless e-mail messages a day, I'm getting a lot of laundry done while my mail downloads. Before you decide to spend money purchasing someone else's bulk e-mail address list, think about whether there is a better, more professional way to approach your marketing.

If you choose to contact your customers via e-mail, do so with caution, incorporating business ethics and professional courtesy. If someone has contacted you, you know he or she is already interested in your company. This is the time to ask that person if he or she would like to receive regular news through either e-mail or another method. Think about offering customers the opportunity to receive e-mail, just as credit card companies do when they include a mail-removal form in your monthly statement. You might even consider drafting a policy for e-mail communications with customers. Spell out what types of e-mail messages are sent and how often. Determine up front how you will respond to requests for information. Make sure that there is a mechanism in place for removing and/or flagging a customer's e-mail address when asked to stop. If marketers don't take on this responsibility, you can be sure that legislators eventually will.

Strategy 3: Cross-Pollinate

Advertise that you're advertising. Few people will know you're on the Internet unless you tell them. Recognize that the Internet can be used in many different ways and not just online. You'll see very quickly how your marketing use of the Internet can and should be made visible. Your customers should be able to notice that you are marketing on the Internet whether they're sitting in front of their computers looking at a Web page or in the bathroom reading a favorite magazine. Think I'm joking? We talk about television programs even when we're not viewing the tube, don't we? The same holds true for the Internet. The Internet can become very visible when it is integrated properly into your preexisting traditional marketing projects.

A good way to get in this frame of mind is to sit down with a list of all of your marketing communications activities. Take out a blank sheet of paper (or open up a word-processing file, if you prefer). Start listing every possible use for every possible marketing element as it relates to the Internet. Do you print an 800 number on your direct mailers? Include your Web address right next to it. Do you tell your customers about upcoming trade shows? Mention your e-mail address. By advertising your online presence in this manner, you have the potential to increase your visibility a hundredfold, and you will have stretched your marketing budget as well. You create added credibility by announcing your online presence in other media. If you're having trouble thinking in this manner, don't fret. We have lots of help for you later on in this book. Once you start making some efforts to incorporate your e-mail address and your URL (uniform resource locator) into all your traditional marketing communications media, it will become second nature.

Product buyers don't have time to hunt around. Put your e-mail and Web page address on your brochures, in cover letters, and in your advertisements. Instruct sales and customer service to routinely promote your Internet addresses. Go out of your way to include traditional contact information online, as well. You can't assume you know every customer's comfort or technical level, or even his or her personal preferences. The Internet is a wonderful tool that has the potential of taking customers all the way through the sales process, from first inquiry to order processing. Guess what? It doesn't always happen that way. At some point during the sales process, customers will want to pick up the phone and talk to a human being. Maybe they'll even want to cue an RFP (request for proposal) already on their hard drive and fax it from their machine to yours. Perhaps they'll like to drop in for a demo, if you happen to be in the same city. The point is, not everyone will take advantage of that nifty order-entry system you've installed at your Web site . . . nor should they be forced to.

Strategy 4: Provide Extra Value

Create a reason for customers to visit you online. With thousands of computers already connected and commercial use of the Internet growing at unparalleled rates every month, you must stand out to get noticed. If you can find something that doesn't exist anywhere else online, you've got it made. If you can find something that exists elsewhere, but can add your own unique and original spin to it, you've also got it made. There are lots of sites that fall short in this department in that they simply offer the basics. There's nothing wrong with that. Somebody has to supply the essentials. If you can go beyond that, you're providing extra value and attracting more visitors. If you can continue to offer something extra on a regular basis, you will continue to attract return visitors and new ones, long after the initial excitement about your Web site has diminished.

Try running a contest along with your other marketing programs. Offer an incentive, such as a customized service or giveaway, for customers who register online. Pay your customers to provide word-of-mouse referrals to their friends and colleagues. Consider offering something not available anywhere else, such as an online calculator for determining costs or making decisions. Consider a product drawing to give away to qualified, registered visitors. This is the same reasoning you apply when you prepare a trade show exhibit and it certainly applies here as well. How do you get people to your booth? Put on a show, do something creative, catchy, or wild, or offer a great demo or tutorial. How do you get them to your Web site and how do you get them back? Yes, you have the idea!

Strategy 5: Analyze Content and Use

Think about how your customers react to your marketing literature or programs. Do they ask for additional materials, or do you supply them with everything at once? Decide whether you want to prequalify Web visitors or e-mail inquiries every step of the way. Companies sometimes take the tiered approach to distributing sales literature. They might choose to supply the essentials to initial contacts. Information gatherers or researchers would receive more detailed information. Finally, the most extensive collateral would be given to those who are truly in the buying mode. You can create tiers of online content as well. For example, you can create an area on your Web for free access by anyone, and provide even more data for those who register as legitimate buyers.

The Use of Your Literature Varies Greatly

Think about how your customers react to information that they gather. Think about how they use that information and the next step they take before they decide to buy your product or services. Use that thinking to create your flow of information on the Internet.

Think about how customers use your marketing literature and what the shelf life is for each piece that they take with them. Do you remember how you approached the development of your product literature? Did you decide to produce it in a three-hole-punched format because you knew that most buyers in your industry liked to file it in a binder? Did you decide to reproduce bulleted versions of individual product benefits on a wallet-size card for the new sales staff to carry? Did you leave plenty of white space or borders in the layout because you knew that your customers liked to have room to jot notes in the margins? If you did these or similar things, then you know what I'm talking about.

The Decision Process Varies as Well

When customers contact you online, what types of questions do they ask? Wouldn't those frequently asked questions be useful if put on your Web site? If you can identify a pattern, any pattern, of use, then you can decide how to approach your content, graphics, formatting, and layout for the Internet. In fact, if you can program your site to recognize those patterns and deliver pages in a personalized manner, that's even better.

Too many times, decisions to supply information on the Internet are made without considering the user's needs. The Web site is designed in a vacuum, or worse, it detracts from other marketing material that has demonstrated success.

Determine how to supply content in a way that is logical, making sure that it complements or enhances your current efforts. Take into account your customer's work flow, decision-making process, and even purchasing time frame. With this strategic data in mind, you can determine the best way to present your material on the Internet.

Strategy 6: Repurpose Materials

Do you want to speed up your Internet launch? Use shortcuts. *Repurposing* is an old multimedia term that means to take content from one media and reuse it on another. Repurpose or reuse the content from existing materials and revise it for the Internet. Your current library of literature may be perfectly acceptable for Web purposes with some alterations.

Scenario 1. Do you keep getting the same routine requests and supplying the same answers? Excerpt text from your sales brochures and/or news releases in brief informational chunks that answer first-tier questions. These boilerplates can reside on your hard drive (if you use an off-line mail reader) or in your online files directory. Paste the documents into your response and *voilà!* You've just saved yourself hours of repetitive customer-service activities. You can also put this information in a mailbot file with a unique e-mail address for automatic retrieval.

Scenario 2. Take a look at your data sheets and brochures. Open the accompanying file on your computer. Strip out the fluffy ad copy, expand on the facts, and reformat accordingly. Now you've just started creating materials that will work in your online document library or Web page.

Let's not get too carried away with this idea of repurposing for the Internet, though. I'm not advising you to re-create your entire literature library on the Web and leave it at that. Of course, during the revision process, you don't eliminate key selling points or your personality from Internet copywriting, either. Enthusiasm for your product will win out over empty and unsupported claims any day.

Some customers will be more than glad to find your news release or company brochure in full-text version on the Web. They'll grab it and forward it to someone else with their own comments, and you'll be glad you went to the trouble of uploading this information. On the other hand, you will have lots of people who expect to find something entirely different when they get to your coveted spot on the Web. And these people are not to be ignored.

Strategy 7: Design with Online in Mind

Repurposing works fine for some portions of your online content, but you'll also need to create new materials specifically for online use. Remember, the Internet shouldn't be an online mirror of your off-line activities. It is acceptable to duplicate certain activities online, as I've mentioned previously, but creativity in capitalizing on the unique features of the Internet should be your ultimate goal.

Ads in cyberspace have a different touch and feel than traditional advertising. Ads on the Internet don't resemble print ads, and users access them differently. Print design elements, such as fancy die-cut shapes, varnishes, pop-ups, and holograms don't translate to online, at least not today. Neither do double-page ads. Sure, you can scroll back and forth in current browsers to view an extra-wide page, but you lose the impact you may have had with an identical print ad. That's why it's important to investigate the special features of the online world and take advantage of them. These features may include e-commerce enable banner ads or special scripts.

To help you become familiar with how online layouts differ, I've included a preliminary comparison chart (Figure 1.1). This chart is not all-inclusive, but it will help you think in terms of the uniqueness of the Internet, along with its similarities. As you can see, on the Internet a marketer must deal with text-based multidocument links, computer-monitor width and height considerations, and graphics and file-size decisions. Not only must you become aware of online aesthetics, but also you must modify your document publishing accordingly.

If creating a Web presence is another one of your many job responsibilities, don't be tempted to learn Hypertext Markup Language (HTML) yourself

Print	Online
Fancy die cuts	Transparent GIF banners, tiled background textures
Double-page print ads	Web pages with frames, computer-monitor limits
Fractional consecutive page ads	Ad banners on unordered and multiple Web pages
Preferred advertising positions	Rotating ad banners at the top/bottom of pages
Catalog order forms	Online forms, HTML–to–e-mail functions
Beginning table of contents, appendixes	Hyperlinks, Java remote windows, search engines
Four-color printing process	Hardware, software, graphics, and HTML limits
Metallic colors and varnishes	Display variances that change or distort
Corporate typefaces	Browser font limitations, viewer display preferences

Figure 1.1   Print versus online design elements.

unless you truly have the time to do it right. Hire a graphic artist and/or programmer with documented experience in designing for multimedia applications, or more specifically, for the Web.

I'm not discounting all the wonderful tools that can help make HTML programming painless. There are some great programs on the market today that have helped make it easier for many people who don't have the time to decipher HTML code. Of course, assuming an HTML editor is going to create great Web pages is like assuming that a graphics program is going to create great art. Sometimes the amount of hours spent developing a layout and graphics for the Web is directly proportional to the appeal and effectiveness of the end result. In other words, if you don't have the time, don't waste your time. Hire a professional. Don't experiment on your image and budget with on-the-job training.

Strategy 8: Plan Frequent Revisions

Computers can deceive you because online files are invisible. As you sit at your computer typing away, you may realize that there are tons of files on the network or on your hard drive that you haven't looked at in months. Gee, the filenames are pretty cryptic. Do you ever wonder if you need to do anything with them? You can fall into the trap of forgetting that your Internet files need updating as well.

Your online materials should be the first set of literature updated. Remember, it's a selling point to tell your customers that the "latest information is always online." Some sites, such as online newspapers, are updated daily. That's usually not a problem because they often have created programs that automate the process. It's the other Web sites and mailbot replies that worry me. If your site is one that grows and grows over a period of time, you may not get around to reviewing and revising those older pages.

In every single online file, include a comment on the date and person who last revised it. Do this with your boilerplate ASCII documents, the files in your FTP site, and your Web pages. If you keep a "golden copy" of each of your brochures for marking changes before the next print run, you already know what I'm going to tell you. Keep a master checklist of all your online documents. Make sure you note the filename, a brief description of contents, and the date each document was uploaded or revised. If at all possible, keep "golden copies" of these documents printed out and filed in a master notebook in a central location for noting changes or errors. Make sure you make those changes on a regular basis and remember to actually upload those changed files to your Internet server. This will help prevent your site from winning an Internet ghost award as an abandoned site.

Strategy 9: Manage for the Long Term

Don't launch a Web site with the idea that you'll "try it out for a while and see if it works." Unfortunately, some of you are wincing now. Your manager says, "Let's go on the Internet and see if we make any money. If we don't see a substantial difference in our sales over the next three months then we'll try something else." If you are working with someone who tells you this, here's some ammunition.

It could be that e-mail was the vehicle your hidden market needed to contact you. If you disconnect your e-mail, it's like telling the world you've gone out of business. You wouldn't disconnect your telephone and expect to keep your doors open, would you? If you aren't in it for the long haul, you won't succeed during the short haul, either. Take your Internet opportunity seriously. Creating and maintaining an Internet presence takes dedication, time, ingenuity, time, resources, and time. Take and assign responsibility for your Internet program and proactively upgrade as your needs grow.

Also, if you can't put your Internet documents on a machine that's running around the clock, then consider using your access provider's machine. The Internet is a 24-hour mall. Your Web site becomes sorely conspicuous if it's closed when the customer is ready to shop.

Strategy 10: Set Reasonable Goals

In spite of what some people would have you believe, this is not a get-rich-quick scheme. Your sales are not going to skyrocket overnight. Decide what you want your Internet presence to accomplish and plan how to achieve those goals. Measure results in reasonable terms, such as enhancing customer service, offering 24-hour access, or decreasing software distribution and packaging costs. Don't let external factors pressure you into believing that the Internet will help you attain something that wasn't possible for your service or product anyway. Be conservative, be fair, and be patient with your expectations.

The Internet has the potential to become equal to or greater than any other element in your marketing mix. By incorporating the preceding strategies into your thinking, you are prepared to begin tackling your online presence. By the time you finish this book, you will have improved your chances of creating the most effective Internet presence possible for your company.

CHAPTER 2

Preparing the Business Overview and Executive Summary

Success is proof that we're getting there.
Carole Guevin, Chief Imagineering Officer, Soulmedia Studio

Business overviews and executive summaries are typical parts of most marketing plans, and for good reason. This section of the marketing plan, whether focusing on traditional, new media, or a combination, reveals the purpose for developing and launching any new marketing program. Business overviews often provide a synopsis of a company's background, outlining both current business activities and future plans. This marketing plan component is often presented in a format that appeals to upper management and boards of directors. The business overview and executive summary serves to establish a base for your marketing program's current existence, setting the stage for its future survival.

Do You Really Need a Business Overview?

Not all Internet marketing plans begin this way. In some cases, you may find that creating this portion of your plan appears to "reinvent the wheel." Several factors affect your need to include this section in your plan, such as your speed in changing direction to meet marketplace needs, the frequency with which you revise your company's business goals, or your current stage in crafting a new or revising an existing Internet marketing plan.

Do you fully understand your place in the Internet market? You may be clear about how the Internet fits or will fit into the big picture. If so, the cre-

---

CASE STUDY: SOULMEDIA STUDIO

As CIO (Chief Imagineering Officer) for collaborative consulting firm Soulmedia Studio, Carole Guevin knows that some typical portions of traditional marketing plans either don't apply or can be obsolete. The Canadian new media firm is positioning itself as "pioneers in virtual business community building," with services that include both marketing consultation and Web design. Their bilingual Web site is graphically intense, demonstrating a dedication to cutting-edge development.

"The business overview I've skipped, since (in) the past three and a half years, it has evolved constantly," says Guevin. The Quebec-headquartered company "is starting to grow. We don't want to rewrite (the business overview)," she added."

---

ation of a business overview may be nothing more than an exercise in educating others about why you should shift some of your marketing focus to the online world.

Whether the business overview section of your plan applies to your individual needs or not, this chapter will help you understand better how your particular company's Internet marketing approach may be influenced by your company's philosophy, history, goals, and objectives.

After reading this chapter, you will draft the introductory section of your Internet marketing plan. Some of the steps in this chapter may seem unnecessary at first, until you see how you might leverage your work and content from this chapter in your various Internet marketing activities. Throughout this book, this chapter included, you'll find case studies of real world companies. After analyzing these examples and completing the exercises in this chapter, you'll be able to create each section of the plan on your own.

Section One: Business Overview and Executive Summary

Any data that reinforces your decision to market on the Internet helps support your Internet marketing program plans. Section One of your Internet marketing plan may include any combination of the following:

- Internet marketing plan introduction
- Company overview
- Products and/or services overview

- Market or industry definition
- Partnerships, mergers, and acquisitions outlook
- A summary of the risks associated with relying solely on traditional marketing activities

Getting the Most out of This Chapter

The activities in this chapter include reviewing and comparing examples of how companies have created executive overviews, whether they are used for corporate brochures, marketing plans, or Web pages. During this process, you will notice that some companies are very long-winded when introducing themselves, while others barely provide any insight at all. Some companies are conservative in their approach, presenting their company history in a very formal tone. Still others are relaxed, injecting humor at every opportunity.

Reusing This Section of Your Internet Marketing Plan

In Chapter 1, I mentioned repurposing materials or content selectively in order to get the most mileage out of your marketing activities. Here's what I mean. Portions of the content created for this section of the Internet marketing plan can be repurposed in one or more of the ways outlined in Figure 2.1.

Company Overview

Do you know where you've been? If not, how will you know where you're going? This variation on the old cliché applies neatly to the concept of reviewing your company's formation and activities. Nowhere else than in a written marketing plan is it more important to understand your company's history. In this section of your marketing plan, you will also provide a brief description of your company, tying it in with your purpose in creating online visibility.

Most of the basic information can come from a company background document, such as a brochure. If you don't have a company background, this will be your opportunity to create an outline for one that can always be used for traditional marketing purposes later.

Some Activities You Can Do Now

1. Go to your favorite Internet search engine or directory site. Many search engines and directories configure or alias additional URLs (uniform resource locators) to indicate a searching subdomain, such as http://

Traditional	Internet
Opening statement of written marketing plan	Opening statement of written marketing plan
Company background brochure or history statement from annual report	Company background or history Web page, as in "about.html"
On-hold message for main telephone switchboard, customer service or other extensions	E-mail autoresponder with basic information about current activities, as in replies returned from "info@wolfBayne.com"
Boilerplate contact information, such as mailing address, telephone and facsimile numbers, found on all company and product literature	Boilerplate company signature block, customizable by individual employees and departments, used for all outgoing e-mail messages sent by company personnel with Internet access
Company slogans, signature phrases, and taglines used in billboard advertisements, trade show signage, and print magazine ads	Company slogans, signature phrases, and taglines used in advertising banners, sponsored discussion list headers, and email signature blocks
Editor's notes included at the end of company news releases	Search engine and Web directory notes included in Web site announcements and postings

Figure 2.1 Selective repurposing: recommended ways to reuse your plan's Business Overview.

search.hotbot.com, http://search.netscape.com, http://search.yahoo.com, and even http://search.mania.com.au. A creature of surfing habit, I've created a link for the Yahoo! Search page in the Personal Toolbar Folder of my copy of Netscape Communicator. I've never broken my conditioned response to starting Web searches this way for one very simple reason—if I don't get enough results from an initial search at Yahoo!, I click on the search partner links found at the bottom of the results page. Both Yahoo! and the Netscape Open Directory send my keywords and phrases with me to the next site without forcing me to retype my search parameters. You'll see how this works in a moment.

2. Once you've browsed to your favorite search page, look for links such as "About *this company*," "Business Overview," "Company overview," "Company background," "Company profile," or "Welcome," Click on "About AltaVista" at the bottom of AltaVista pages, "About Wired Digital" found above the copyright statement on HotBot pages, and "Company Information" found at the bottom of Yahoo! pages. To research other types of companies, enter keyword phrases into the corresponding search field. Use quotation marks to designate phrases, narrowing down the number of search results, or enter keywords individually to garner the

most surfing choices. A recent search at Northern Light, on the phrase "Business Overview" (complete with quote marks), found 7,151 items.

3. Read the corporate overviews at a variety of company sites. If it's not immediately obvious where these pages are located, look for the corporate profile sections or online pressrooms of selected company Web sites. You'll find examples of company descriptions at several news distribution and stock market sites. Check out the "Company Specific News" link at Businesswire (www.businesswire.com) to locate electronic media kits and corporate profiles. Read press kits from trade shows and conferences at the Virtual Press Office (www.virtualpressoffice.com). Search by company name or keyword to locate background information on public companies at Hoover's Online (www.hoovers.com). Look for technology news releases and media advisories each weekday at Internet Wire (www.internetwire.com). Click on PRNewswire's (www.prnewswire .com) link to "Company News On-Call" to view company news by name. Look for brief company boilerplate paragraphs at the end of news releases. Finally, I've included excerpts from sample company overviews later in this chapter.

What Is the Name of Your Company?

Of course, you know your own company name. The question is . . . does everyone else? You may have been prudent in referring correctly to your company over the years, but everyone else has not been. Whether people are referring to your company correctly in print and especially online is part of your image management or public relations program. Whether you have the time, resources, energy, or inclination to correct everyone doesn't really matter here.

Why Is Your Name So Important?

My purpose in having you pay attention to your company's identity at this point in your Internet marketing plan formation is simple. Company and product confusion does occur on the Internet. In many cases, due to the global nature of the Internet, confusion occurs more frequently than in traditional marketing. If your company name contains a common word, you can be sure that someone in another part of the world can stake a claim to your preferred domain name, and possibly create confusion about company ownership, headquarters, divisions, and trademarks.

Take the case of Westwind Computing of Seattle, Washington. Fortunately, it owns the coveted domain names of westwind.com and westwind.net. Other competitors for the same domain name weren't so lucky in the race to register, creating a flurry of domain name pretenders across the Web. Westwind Old

West Artifacts & Collectibles, located in Cedar Crest, New Mexico, became awestwind.com on the Web. Denver-based Westwind Studios Corporation, before its recent name change to Westwind Media.com, had to register the domain name of wstudios.net. Westwind Air Bearings Ltd. in Dorset, United Kingdom, had to settle for the bulky online moniker of westwind-airbearings .com. Similarly, the West-Wind Academy of Massage Therapy, located in Phoenix, Arizona, owns westwindmassageacademy.com.

For companies, this problem can significantly impact sales. Imagine a customer mistakenly sending e-mail to manufacturer.org when the intended recipient was manufacturer.com. Be aware of this phenomenon, and keep alert for potential problems and opportunities from the very beginning. You'd be amazed at the image issues you'll uncover online once you start experimenting with how your company and products are referenced.

Identifying your company's complete name and any variation thereof will help you when it's time to brainstorm about registering an Internet domain name, later in this book. Start thinking now about all the different possibilities, keeping in mind what customers and reporters have called your organization. For example, Federal Express knew its customer base had already nicknamed it "FedEx." The company was able to capitalize on this market identification by changing its logo to match that image and easily publicizing its registered domain name of fedex.com.

You may wish to keep your list of company name variations handy if you decide to put together a trademark page for your Web site. McDonald's has a very extensive trademark page, and if you ever have any doubts as to how much stock the company puts in its corporate identity, just drop by and check it out. For starters, McDonald's main home page is located at www .mcdonalds.com/. For a quick lesson in extensive variations on the name game, check out www.mcdonalds.com/legal (Site Terms and Conditions).

A Rose by Any Other Name . . .

Here are some examples of organizations that have more than one name by which they are or have been known. These are variations that have been both spoken and written, in print and online. Notice that some companies are lucky enough to deal with only a few variations on their moniker, while others are not as fortunate. The most extreme case that follows is the result of multiple name changes and acquisitions of the company over the last decade or so. By the way, not all of the name variations listed are accepted and/or used by the companies involved. Sometimes a company continues to be referenced by an obsolete name for years after it has changed its identification. In many cases, it can be the customer or industry press that decides how the company is referenced, whether the company likes it or not. Of course, this problem is nothing that a good branding campaign can't repair . . . but not necessarily overnight.

Array Microsystems, Inc. Also referred to as Array Micro. A quick search of Network Solutions' Whois interface, www.networksolutions.com/cgi-bin/whois/whois, demonstrates that the domain name of array.com was secured early in the Web presence game (record created on May 8, 1991), thus reducing but not totally eliminating Web name confusion for this high-tech manufacturer. The InterNIC Registration Services database found no registration match for arraymicro.com or arraymicrosystems.com. My one-word search for "array" produced more than 50 records. Had Array Micro-systems dragged its heels in registering its easy-to-remember one-word domain, other technology-based companies, such as Array Instruments (arrayinstruments.com), Array Solutions (arraysolutions.com), Array Soft-ware, Inc. (arraysoftware.com), and Array Systems (arraysystems.com), might have secured this easy-to-brand domain instead.

Westwind Media.com, Inc. Current domain name is westwindmedia.com. Before 1999, the company was known as Westwind Studios Corporation (wstudios.net). Various business units included Westwind Educational Broadcasting, Westwind Studios, and the Westwind Broadcast Network. Employees and business partners verbally abbreviate the company's name, referring to it as Westwind. Hearing it for the first time, individuals often confuse the company name with similar ones in the broadcast industry, such as Westwood Studios of Las Vegas, Nevada (westwoodstudios.com), and the more prominent Westwood One Radio Networks (westwoodone.com and westwoodonenews.com). Westwind Media is involved in radio production and syndication, but oddly enough, the domain westwindradio.com was not registered to their company, as researched in the Whois.net database.

Business Marketing Association. Also referred to as BMA since 1993, formerly the Business/Professional Advertising Association or B/PAA (1973), formerly the Association of Industrial Advertisers (1959), formerly the National Industrial Advertising Association (1922), sometimes nicknamed the Business Marketing Club. It chose to register the domain name marketing.org because bma.org was registered to the London-based British Medical Association. The domain name businessmarketing.org is registered to Kansas City-based ad agency NKH&W, Inc. Hardly a coincidence, since BMA's current Web site, located at marketing.org, was designed by NKH&W.

Discovery Zone Fun Centers. Also referred to as Discovery Zone, DZ (per television commercials), and the Zone. While performing a simple search at search.yahoo.com with the keywords "*Discovery Zone Fun Centers*" found an unaffiliated music site called "Discovery Zone," located at discoverzone.co.uk. A repeated search with the keyword commands of "+Discovery +Zone +children" (the plus sign indicates required words in the search) produced additional unaffiliated sites, but no official Discovery Zone children's site. *Discovery Zone Fun Centers* does *not* own the registered domain name of discoveryzone.com, which belongs to California-based Woodward and Associates nor does DZ own the registered domain name of dz.com, which belongs to Oklahoma-based ProDomains. Another domain name preference, zone.com, is registered by Microsoft Corporation.

Federal Express Corporation. Also referred to as FedEx, Federal Express; may be used as a verb, as in "I'll FedEx this package to you." Registered domain names include fedex.com, fedex.net, fedex.org, and 1-800-go-fedex.com (with half a dozen registered domain variants as well). What more can be said about a multinational corporation whose Web site is bookmarked by thousands of company shipping departments throughout the world?

JCPenney Company, Inc. Also referred to as J.C. Penney and Penney's. Besides the obvious registered domain name of jcpenney.com, the company has registered several domain name variations, such as jcpenney.net, jcpenney.org, jcpenneyinc.com, myjcpenney.com, and shopjcpenney.com. Domain registrations also include various divisions and brands, including Arizona Jean Company (www.arizonajeanco.com, which currently denies access to interested visitors) and Hunt Club (www.huntclub.com, whose three-line home page contains a link to www.jcpenney.com/). Knowing full well that misspellings due occur, the company has also taken the precaution of registering jcpenny.com, jcpenny.net and myjcpenny.com. Other company divisions with online domain protection include jcpenneylifeinsurance.com, jcpenneycredit.com, and jcpenneydrug.com.

Plasmon LMS. Due to numerous acquisitions and mergers throughout the years, this optical and tape mass data storage hardware manufacturer has been referred to as Philips LMS, LMS International, LMS, LMSI, LMSIC, Laser Magnetic Storage International Company, Laser Magnetic Storage International, Laser Magnetic Storage, and even Laser Magnetics. In 1984, it was known as Optical Storage International, and sometimes OSI. Its registered domain name is lms.com.

United States Holocaust Memorial Museum. Also referred to as USHMM, the Holocaust Museum, the Holocaust Memorial Museum, and the U.S. Holocaust Museum. Its registered domain name is ushmm.org. Oddly enough, the domain name of holocaust.org is registered to Montreal, Quebec-based Net Promotions. Don't ask!

Why You'll Find This Information Helpful

Here's a summary of why you should pay attention to your company's name, especially when it comes to promoting your presence on the Internet. By experimenting with variations on your company name, you can do the following:

- Find your company more quickly in online search engines
- Find editorial coverage through a clipping service vendor
- Find identity conflicts with existing companies worldwide
- Find conflicting and misleading registered domain names
- Find a better way to list your company in print and online in order to gain prominence
- Brainstorm about possible domain names based on your company name or products
- Brainstorm about corporate images you wish to create or enhance
- Brainstorm about possible negative connotations in other languages

How Long Has Your Company Been in Existence?

Why would anybody care how long your company has been in business? In traditional marketing terms, it speaks to your company's longevity. Older companies can claim that they are more likely to be around tomorrow if customers need to return a product or buy more parts. Comparatively, in the Internet universe, six months is a long time. Internet service providers (ISPs) that have been in existence for only six months can boast a strong and growing customer base. The difference is that these types of companies emphasize their customer service and product features far more than they do their age. Take a look at the top two browser-software companies: Netscape and Microsoft. Do you think anybody cares right now how long either has been in business when it comes to choosing a favorite browser?

Somewhere along the line you will want to have this historical data on hand, but don't waste energy on compiling a detailed timeline for your Internet marketing plan. While it's nice to show that you're not just some fly-by-night company, most of the information related to company dates is of limited importance for Internet marketing purposes. Of course, including dates in your Internet marketing plan helps put things into perspective by reminding management and others of your progress . . . to a degree. You can always refer to the company birthday or founding date as a starting point when you reference how many changes your company has or has not gone through over the years.

One tip: State your company's age by mentioning the year you were established or founded (e.g., established in 1922) rather than the *number* of years (e.g., 25-year-old company). The reason? For traditional marketing literature, you can avoid outdating your material before its shelf life expires. "Twenty-five years in business" is accurate this year, but what about the next? When you create a brochure, you'll be forced to wait until the inventory depletes or the content changes dramatically before you can fix the date on the next print run.

"So what? This is the Internet. I can update it immediately," you scoff. Yeah, but do you really want to? Publish your material correctly the first time and it will be one less minuscule detail for you to overlook and for those relentless, online nitpickers to notice. If you have some hidden psychological agenda that indicates a preference to stating the number of years, then feel free to ignore what I just said.

If you're a brand-new company, you probably won't use very many reference dates when you repurpose selective materials for your Web site. "Established last month" doesn't sound so hot when you're trying to pitch your company's stability. This is a good opportunity to look at other company strengths, such as its leadership, technology, or product line. If you're still convinced that stating your company's age really makes a difference in your ability to sell your company in either traditional or online marketing, then be brief; include it and be done with it.

Why You'll Find This Information Helpful

Why are dates are important to your company and your market? With dates, you can do the following:

- Demonstrate longevity for your company, both for traditional and online marketing purposes
- Provide evidence that you'll be operating in a year from now when buyers need product replacement parts
- Demonstrate to customers, who are uneasy about online shopping, that you are a reputable, established business
- Establish a track record in customer service over a long period of time
- Find companies with a prior claim to (and possible right to register) your preferred domain name

And if your company is a hot, new start-up, you can

- Find ways to position your company as offering cutting-edge service and products
- Compare your company more favorably in relationship to industry dinosaurs

Real-World Examples

Here are some examples of organizations that have publicized an organizational birthday or founding date as part of their image. Sometimes a date is very helpful in establishing credibility, while sometimes its mention leaves you wondering why the company thought it was important.

The following dates and descriptive sentences were gathered from a variety of sources, including Web site backgrounds and search engine descriptions. By the way, these are just examples. The mention of these Web sites here does not necessarily represent an endorsement of any type. I'm merely including them as differing examples of how some organizations use this aspect of their company's history as part of their Internet and traditional marketing presence.

Abbey of Gethsemani. Even religious communities in the United States know the importance of longevity, especially when it comes to promoting a presence on the Internet. Founded in 1848, this Kentucky Trappist Monastery uses its Web site to discuss the History of the Order, inviting you to purchase its cheeses, fruitcakes, and bourbon fudge. Web site address: www.monks.org/.

The American Mathematical Society. This professional mathematical organization was founded in 1888 to further mathematical research and scholarship. AMS's longevity wasn't lost on its own employees or members, either. Yahoo! recommends you visit this site by including the "must see" (eyeglasses graphic) icon in the search results. Web site address: www.ams .org/.

Architectural Association of Ireland. Looking for a group well versed in the basics of engineering and structural dynamics? This organization's longevity might interest you. Founded in 1896, AAI's purpose is "to promote and afford facilities for the study of architecture and the allied sciences and arts, and to provide a medium of friendly communication between members and others interested in the progress of architecture." Web site address: www.archeire.com/aai/.

Free Cuba Foundation (Fundacion Cuba Libre). Smart contributing patrons often investigate the history of nonprofit organizations before forking over huge donations. Founded in 1994, this nonprofit and nonpartisan organization uses its presence on the Web to promote its "work towards the establishment of an independent and democratic Cuba using non-violent means." In case you're wondering, the domain name freecuba.org is registered to Washington, D.C.-based Freedom House. Web site address: www .fiu.edu/~fcf/introd.html.

Madshus AS. If you're concerned about breaking a leg on faulty ski equipment made by newcomers to the field, you'll be glad to know that this nordic and telemark ski manufacturer was founded in 1906, making it the oldest ski factory in the world. Web site address: www.madshus.com/.

Regis College. If you're female, planning to return to school, and surfing for an established educational institution with information on the Web, you might look into this Catholic women's college located in Weston, Massachusetts. Founded in 1927. Web site address: www.regiscollege.edu/.

What Type of Business Is Your Company Engaged In?

Use this section of your Internet marketing plan to identify areas of your company's products and services that would do well online for whatever reason. Take a good long look at your product and service line and its relationship to Internet marketing. You'll soon uncover some good opportunities on which to capitalize. This is where you get down to business and tell what you do for a living. This is the tip of the iceberg when it comes to deciding whether you should be online.

During conference and seminar presentations, audience members often ask me whether a particular company should market on the Internet. I once believed that not every company would benefit from being online, but over the past few years I've changed my tune. Every business and individual can reap the benefits of achieving added credibility in local and global communities by launching an online presence. And these days, it's practically impossible to find a business or industry that doesn't have at least some type of online competition. Remember, business movers and shakers don't sit by idly while someone else in their industry sets the pace by etching out a market on the Web.

Companies such as Leiser Painting & Decorating Co. (see Figure 2.2) know that the Web is an easy way to reach commercial and industrial customers who are online. Located at www.leiserpainting.com, Leiser knows that its business benefits through publishing a description of its services on the Web.

If you're still looking for justification to launch an online presence, you'll be glad to know that industry associations are usually the first to establish a Web site and can provide you with contacts in your field. If you were looking for links to members' Web sites, an association site would be a good place to browse.

The Fairfax, Virginia-based Painting & Decorating Contractors Association, located at www.pdca.org/, uses the Web to promote its certification program, information on industry standards, an upcoming convention and trade show, awards and contests, and its involvement in legislative activities.

Writing This Section of the Plan

While you're writing this section, avoid superlatives, such as "the greatest company on earth," "foremost in its field," and "an industry leader." If your company is all these things, everybody in your company knows it anyway. If they don't, and it's true, you should be able to demonstrate it rather quickly without puffery. Statistics are useful, as are sales figures and references to good product reviews.

Now you may be thinking, "Hey, but this is an Internet marketing plan. I

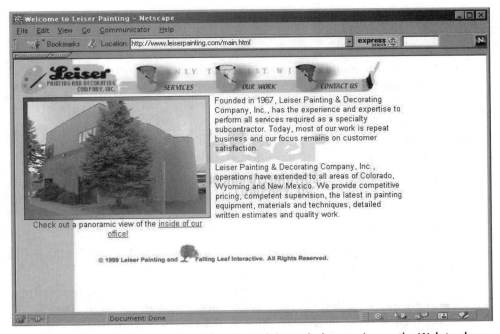

Figure 2.2   Leiser Painting & Decorating (www.leiserpainting.com) uses the Web to show-case samples of its work.

know I'm going to reuse some of this stuff and sweeten it during implementation, but management is going to read the real stuff first! They like superlatives." Okay, I'll grant you that. Management *is* going to read it first. Show them respect and give it to them straight. Remember that you have to live with the final Internet marketing plan document. Save your personality and clever prose for online. If management chooses not to approve your plan because you took my advice, you've got bigger problems than a simple style issue.

Real-World Examples

Here are some examples of organizational descriptions and how they were translated into various documents and/or keywords (as used for Web page coding and directory registration). Keep these applications in mind as you decide how to leverage the work on your Internet marketing plan for other marketing activities.

Most of these examples are from the final implementation, as seen on the companies' Web sites and press releases. See if you can tell the difference between the sweetened text (the advertising or publicity slant) and the facts (basic information that you'll start with for your Internet marketing plan).

REBECCA'S MOM LEOTARDS HOME PAGE (WEB SITE ADDRESS: WWW.LEOTARD.COM)

News Release. Web Launch: Rebecca's Mom, the leading supplier of gymnastic workout leotards in Southern California, has gone online. Gymnasts throughout the world will now be able to purchase this high-quality product through the Internet. The initial group of leotards available is from the company's popular line of classic velvet leotards.

Tagline, Motto, or Slogan. Home Page: The finest workout leotards from Southern California. Don't you deserve a new leotard today?

ALT Text. According to searchenginewatch.com, AltaVista, Infoseek, and Lycos all index ALT tags. At press time, this site did not capitalize on this opportunity to include keywords or descriptions in the HTML code that sources its company graphics.

META Tag Description. Premier site for velvet & hologram leotards for children & young adults.

META Tag Keywords. Leotard, leotards, dance, gymnastics, cheerleading, ice skate, ice skating, velvet, hologram, frosted, tie dye, iridescent, scrunchies, Rebecca's Mom, sports, activewear, sportswear, children, acrobatics, acro, tumbling, trampoline, rhythmic, ballet, modern dance.

Sample Web Site Section. Rebecca's Mom FAQ: Rebecca's Mom is a leotard design and manufacturing company, started by Candy Dengrove in 1993. Candy's daughter is named Rebecca and she is a level 9 gymnast at Gymnastics Olympica in Van Nuys, California.

4WORK (WEB SITE ADDRESS: WWW.4WORK.COM)

News Release. Located at www.4work.com, the innovative new site allows job seekers to type a skill-based keyword into the site's search engine. The 4WORK database is then checked for any job posting (by state) that uses the keyword. Employers create their ads based on keywords job applicants would likely use in their searches. The database finds potential matches, then notifies the job applicant of each opportunity.

Tagline, Motto, or Slogan. Home Page Banner: Looking for work? You've already found it!

ALT Text. Home Page Banner: jobs, work, employment, careers, volunteer.

META Tag Description. Lists job opportunities across the US and classified by a variety of keywords. 4WORK is free to job seekers. Updated daily.

META Tag Keywords. Jobs, work, employment, careers, volunteer.

Sample Web Site Section. Frequently Asked Questions (FAQs): Why should I choose 4WORK of all the employment or career sites on the web? What? You need more reasons? Not hard to please, are you? In a nutshell: We are one of the top services on the web. Job Alert! is the only personal job search agent of its kind on the web. It only takes 5 minutes to register with Job Alert! and less time than that to conduct a search. We accommodate every person and every type of job under the sun, moon, and stars.

INSIGHT (WEB SITE ADDRESS: WWW.INSIGHT.COM)

News Release. Insight is a leading direct marketer of computers, hardware, and software, offering a broad line of more than 100,001 brand-name products primarily to businesses in the United States, Canada, the United Kingdom, and Germany. Products are sold by a staff of customer-dedicated account executives through outbound telesales and via the Internet. Insight's net sales for the 12 months ended December 31, 1998, were more than $1 billion.

Tagline, Motto, or Slogan. Home Page Banner: Your discount source for computers, hardware, and software.

ALT Text. Home Page Graphic: Welcome to Insight.com.

META Tag Description. Insight—America's discount source for computers, hardware, and software.

META Tag Keywords. Insight, home, computer, hardware, software, discount, games, hard drive, modem, memory, network, printer, CD-ROM, floppy, SCSI, EIDE, IDE, monitor, mouse, keyboard, multimedia, power protection, Internet, video, audio.

Sample Web Site Section. Company Information: Insight is a global direct marketer of name-brand computers, hardware, and software, offering a broad line of more than 100,001 brand-name products sold at discount prices to business, education, government, and electronic customers throughout the United States, Canada, the United Kingdom, and Germany. We use a knowledgeable sales force, targeted marketing, and streamlined distribution, together with an advanced proprietary information system to achieve customer loyalty and strong profitable growth.

SCANTRON CORPORATION (WEB SITE ADDRESS: WWW.SCANTRON.COM)

News Release. Founded in 1972, Scantron Corporation, a wholly owned subsidiary of Atlanta-based John Harland Company (NYSE: JH), is a leading provider of software, services, and systems for the collection, management, and interpretation of data. Related lines of business include: Scantron Scanning division, a provider of scannable forms; OMR software and scanners; Scantron Service division, a provider of maintenance and installation services for scanners, personal computers, and network systems; and Scantron Technologies, a provider of enterprise data collection systems, survey services, and educational software products.

Tagline, Motto, or Slogan. Provides creative solutions for information management in business, education, government, and health care. (Web site description as cataloged by Yahoo!.)

ALT Text. Home Page Graphic: ALT tags are usually visible to the Internet user who hovers or pauses the mouse over a graphic. ALT tags at this site only duplicate a filename, as in ParSystm.gif or WB01342_.gif.

META Tag Description. Scantron Corporation is a leading provider of survey services, utility and application software, automated data entry products, scannable documents. . . . (Note: This description was found indirectly through a phrase search for "Scantron Corporation" on AltaVista, a directory that incorporates META tags into its indexing features. A random search of HTML source code at the Scantron site did not uncover data for this HTML tag.)

META Tag Keywords. Scantron, Scanner, ParSCORE, ParSURVEY, Pulse-Survey, Data Entry, scanning, data collection, testing, survey, Application Software, ScanMark, Education, ScanBook, Par, ParSYSTEM, optical mark readers, OMR, computers, peripherals, software, forms, computers, peripherals, software, forms design, printing, distribution, installation, repair, client-server, bar-code, market research, opinion, John Harland, PulseSurvey, ScanSurvey, ParScore, ParTest, ParGrade.

Sample Web Site Section. Home Page: Scantron Corporation is a worldwide provider of assessment tools, survey solutions, data management systems, and a nationwide leader in support services to education, business, and government institutions.

Product and Market Definition: Understanding Your Place in the Internet Market

Ask yourself if an online market exists for your products and services. Keep in mind, however, that the lack of an existing Web community for your products is not an indication of whether you belong there. You could have been lucky enough to have found an untapped opportunity on which to capitalize, in which case, now's the time to act and establish a new community of your own.

The definition of your products and services, along with online factors related to them, will be briefly included in your Internet marketing plan. Let's begin by gathering some basic information now. If you already know that your products are being marketed online, then you're ahead of the game. If not, you'll need to do some preliminary online research, such as searching for the following:

- Companies that are similar to yours
- Products that are similar to yours
- Services that are similar to yours
- Online communities that are similar to your off-line market

One key to successful Internet marketing lies in your ability to translate what you do in the physical world to what you plan to do online. Your online presence may merely be an extension of your "bricks and mortar" or real-world business, or your online presence may be an entirely different animal. If your business has been established for a while, you know exactly what makes your customers stop by or telephone. On the Internet, you may have to rediscover what attracts those same customers and where those customers congregate.

An Honest Evaluation: Do You Belong Online?

A great way to determine if the Internet is ready for your company is to start hunting around for applicable online communities. For example, a search of the Mining Company Web site (www.miningco.com) uncovers hundreds of pages dedicated to hobbies. Related content includes newsletters, bulletin boards, and chat sessions, all consisting of information-hungry users interested in finding out more about a favorite pastime.

Internet-savvy advertisers have found that placing ads or sponsorship-related links in similar niche portals is a great way to reach interested buyers. If you're a business that serves the home market, sites such as the Mining Company and HGTV (www.hgtv.com) will help you get that much closer to finding out if your customer is online.

Some Activities You Can Do Now

- Select a search index or directory.
- Enter keywords (such as food, health, youth) or key phrases (such plastic surgery, music education, figure skating) for your company, products, services, and industry.
- Search for the company names of your competitors, too.
- Click on any links to niche portal sites. These are those consolidated collections of content or links to related online resources. Go to these sites to find information on similar companies.
- Take copious notes and make browser bookmarks for your Internet marketing plan.

Why You'll Find This Information Helpful

Here's a summary of how you'll be able to use keywords in your marketing program. With keywords, you can do the following:

- Select categories for product and company listings in industry publications and directories
- Insert keyword META tags into your Web documents, so search engines and Webcrawlers can index your site more easily
- Use keyword descriptions for registering with manually compiled Internet directories
- Use keyword searches for finding your competitors in these same search indexes and directories
- Use keyword searches for sites that would be good prospects for swapping reciprocal links

Why Are Some Companies Online?

Some quintessentially bad examples (or good, depending on your viewpoint) of why companies fail in their marketing efforts can be found on the Internet. By searching in any of a dozen directories, you can find companies that not only don't know why they are online, they don't even know why they are in business.

I often pay attention to television programs and commercials that display their Web site addresses or URLs. The other night, I noticed that the majority of car commercials shown during prime time were of local car dealers. Most of these car dealers displayed a Web page address boldly on the screen while a talking head told the viewer how many cars the dealer *had* to sell by "sundown tonight." I've always wondered why some auto dealers feel it is important to brag about how many cars they have to sell to meet their quotas. I'm much more impressed with low prices, quality products, personable customer service, and selection.

Some of these car dealers had no real reason to be online. I expected descriptions of the special services they offered to their online and off-line customers. I expected a map of the nearest car lot. I expected searchable color photographs of used and new car inventory. What I found were ads—pages and pages of ads. I wanted to know what I could hope to gain by shopping online, or even in person, at any particular car dealer. There was no reason for me to ever visit some of these sites again, which is unfortunate, considering I was in the market for a car.

Despite the failings of a few select Web sites, as a whole, the automobile industry is aggressively and successfully pursuing electronic commerce. Compared to a half dozen years ago, the content, design, and interactive features of both car manufacturer and local dealerships' Web sites have greatly improved. For example, John Elway AutoNation USA (www.elwayautonation.com) maintained my interest well past those first crucial minutes of Web browsing. I could search for either a new or used car by make, read about service center guarantees, and locate a store through either a quick link or a map. Another Colorado-based car dealer, Phil Long Autonet (www.phillong.com), allows me to apply for credit online or search for online parts specials. Before I forked over the money on my latest motor vehicle, I researched car values and pricing at Kelley Blue Book (www.kbb.com) and obtained a complete vehicle history at CarFax (www.carfax.com, see Figure 2.3). And these automobile industry examples of improved customer service and support are just the tip of the iceberg.

Until you can identify why you should promote your services and products online, and what customers will gain from your Internet presence, your site will be nothing more than a very pale imitation of your traditional advertising and public relations campaigns.

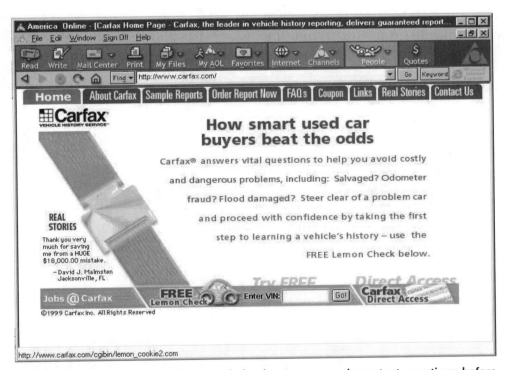

Figure 2.3 CarFax (www.carfax.com) helps buyers answer important questions before they purchase.

How to Complete the Worksheets

The accompanying media for this book includes worksheets for drafting this section of your plan. Following, I've included instructions for all worksheet sections.

For sections best illustrated by examples, I've cited content and comments from real-world Web sites and spokespeople. For additional examples of content, review company examples found earlier in this chapter.

In preparing your plan, don't duplicate your efforts. Read the following examples and you will discover that content from one section of a worksheet is often addressed by answers in a different section.

Materials Checklist

In preparation for writing the first section of your plan, gather all the off-line and online research material you've identified. (See Figure 2.4.)

- Check off each item as you locate it.
- Additional research material should be selected to support your draft of this section of your plan.
- In the blank lines listed at the end of the checklist, note any additional material you may have used to prepare this plan section, including the Web page titles of any new types of sites not covered by this checklist.

☐ Prior year marketing plan and schedules
☐ Annual report
☐ Clipping-service order
☐ Corporate brochure
☐ Corporate identity manuals
☐ Corporate news releases
☐ Customer newsletters
☐ Direct-mail pieces
☐ Executive profiles
☐ Stationery and business cards
☐ Editorial-clipping files
☐ Product literature: catalogs, data books, data sheets
☐ Miscellaneous literature on your company and products
☐ Literature title

Completed by: _____ Date:_____

Figure 2.4 Materials checklist: preparing to write your Internet marketing plan.

Drafting the Business Overview

Figure 2.5 shows the first section of the Internet marketing plan.

What Is the Name of Your Company?

- Mention variations on your company name, as illustrated by examples found earlier in this chapter.
- List all parent companies, divisions, business units, and so on.
- Use this information to determine needed strategies for dealing with online identity conflicts.
- Use this information to brainstorm about new domain name registration opportunities.

Are There Any Significant Company Dates or Events?

Include those dates relevant to your company and its marketing programs. If you believe your founding date is a competitive advantage, include it as well.

Examples

1. Scantron Corporation describes itself as "Founded in 1972" and "a wholly owned subsidiary of Atlanta-based John Harland Company."
2. BURST! Media was founded in the fall of 1995 and sold its first ad in June 1996.
3. According to its Web site, the Citizen's Council on Health Care (cchc-mn.org) was incorporated by the state of Minnesota on August 10, 1998.

What Type of Business Is Your Company Engaged In?

This is your market and industry definition.

- Describe your position or place in both the real world and on the Internet.
- Outline your target market.
- If possible, summarize your company sales figures and ranking within your industry.

What is the name of your company?

_____

_____

_____

_____

Are there any significant company dates or events to consider as you formulate your future plans?

Date(s)	Event or Milestone
__/__/__	Company Founded
__/__/__	
__/__/__	
__/__/__	
__/__/__	

What type of business is your company engaged in?

_____

_____

_____

_____

_____

_____

What are your company's business charter and/or philosophy?

_____

_____

_____

_____

_____

Which future business developments could affect your Internet marketing programs?

_____

_____

_____

_____

Figure 2.5 Drafting the business overview and executive summary.

What are your company products and services?

_____

_____

_____

_____

_____

_____

_____

How would you describe your company, products and services using brief keywords and/or phrases?

Company, Product or Service Name	Keywords or Phrases

Who is your competition?

_____

_____

_____

_____

_____

_____

_____

Figure 2.5   *(Continued)*

What are your competitive advantages?

Product Name	Strengths	Weakness

Why you are writing an Internet marketing plan?

_____

_____

_____

_____

_____

_____

Write the first draft of your Business Overview and Executive Summary.

_____

_____

_____

_____

_____

_____

_____

_____

_____

_____

_____

_____

Completed by: _____ Date: _____

Figure 2.5 *(Continued)*

Examples

1. Brian Alpert, manager of Internet Marketing for Telogy Networks, defines his company's target market as "engineers, product managers, executives of networking equipment manufacturing concerns; others interested in learning about using embedded software to transmit voice and fax over the Internet."

2. The Learning Company is "the leading provider of online genealogy content," according to Charles S. Merrin, senior director and business unit manager, Genealogy Online.

3. Jarvis Coffin, CEO, writes that BURST! is an "advertising sales representative for a network of web sites." BURST! is contracted by World Wide Web sites to act as their intermediary with advertisers and advertising agencies.

4. "We are an e-commerce company selling DVD products," clarifies Susan Daniher, vice president of marketing for DVD EXPRESS.

5. Scantron characterizes its company as "a leading provider of software, services and systems for the collection, management and interpretation of data."

6. Bruce Clay views his positioning statement as "one of the top Web site business consultants (in the world) with a focus on promotion."

7. The World of Fishing is "one of the most popular destination sites for those interested in fishing," writes Larry Thompson, co-owner of fishing world.com. Due to its quality and uniqueness, Thompson has identified his Web presence as "a desirable site for the location of advertisers content."

What Is Your Company's Business Charter or Philosophy?

- Mention company goals, objectives, or philosophies, which may already be outlined in a preexisting traditional media marketing plan.

- Analyze how your Internet marketing presence will support your business goals.

Examples

1. The Learning Company's goals include being "the premier provider of online genealogy resources."

2. The World of Fishing is a true Web community with "a symbiotic relationship between our visitors, our advertisers and us as content publishers. All of our advertisers' material is hosted on the World of Fishing and

their content becomes part of our content. There are no links that sends our visitors—our advertisers' customers—away from this community. From the time this site was established, it was designed as the destination site for anglers."

3. In drafting an Internet marketing plan, Bruce Clay recommends that marketers "promise nothing, exceed expectations, help others make money, and smile all the way to the bank." By joining in on the right ideas, playing an important role, and managing the vision, the payoffs to online businesses are "beyond your wildest dreams." He suggests approaching an Internet marketing presence "like a venture capitalist."

Which Future Business Developments Could Affect Your Internet Marketing Programs?

- Comment on future business deals.
- Include summaries of any forthcoming products, mergers, acquisitions, joint ventures, and strategic alliances.
- Include insights in how these may affect or be affected by your Internet marketing activities.

What Are Your Company Products and Services?

This is an overview of your products and/or services, rather than a detailed product catalog. You may wish to include the overall and significant key features, advantages, and benefits of your product and service lines.

Examples

1. Through its proprietary software, BURST! Media delivers, monitors, and controls the advertising on its affiliated Web sites.
2. Scantron Corporation is a leading provider of survey services; utility and application software; automated data entry products; scannable documents; and computer, peripheral, and network maintenance.

How Would You Describe Briefly Your Company, Products, and Services?

- Review all company products and services.
- List keywords and key phrases for your company, products, and services.
- Summarize your market and industry in a few short phrases.

- Include taglines, mottos, or slogans that may be proprietary to your company.
- Review the examples found earlier in this chapter for how this information is incorporated into a company's public relations and Web presence.

Examples

COMPANY, PRODUCT, OR SERVICE NAME	KEYWORDS OR PHRASES
BURST! Media	Advertising sales network, Internet marketing
DVD EXPRESS, Inc.	DVD products, entertainment
Hobby Markets Online	High-end collectibles, collecting, auction, hobbies
The Learning Company	Genealogy, family, software, hobbies
Scantron Corporation	Software, services, systems, data management, data collection
Bruce Clay	Internet marketing, consulting, promotion
Telogy Networks, Inc.	Embedded software, networking, Internet FAX

Who Is Your Competition?

- Include both serious and up-and-coming competitors in your industry.
- Research both online and off-line companies.
- Include the year each was founded and explore how you will position your company comparatively.

Examples

1. BURST! Media noted similar Internet advertising companies such as DoubleClick and 24/7.
2. Yahoo!'s agreements with broadcast.com and spinner.com makes Lycos Radio Network a competitor.
3. According to articles in industry publications, auction site FairMarket competes with FastParts Trading Exchange.
4. Barnesandnoble.com counts Amazon.com as its direct online competitor in the online retail book market.

What Are Your Competitive Advantages?

- Summarize significant key features of your forthcoming or preexisting product offerings.

- Complete the same exercise for your company and its divisions.
- Provide a similar evaluation of your Web site.
- List the significant strengths and weaknesses of your products and services.
- Brainstorm about ways in which your Web site will support the strengths of your company, its products, and/or services.

Examples

1. Jeffrey Eisen, director of marketing for Hobby Markets Online, defines his site's strengths by summarizing it as an "Internet auction site for premier, high-end collectibles," setting it apart from other more general auction sites or those with more common, lower-cost collectibles.

2. BURST! is one of the largest and fastest growing advertising sales representative firms on the Internet with over 2,500 Web sites in its network. Currently, BURST! serves over 10 million banner impressions a day (300+ million per month), reaching 22 percent of all Internet users (Media Metrix, January 1999).

3. If these real-world examples aren't working for you, here is an example from an imaginary company called Totally Peripheral:

PRODUCT NAME	STRENGTHS	WEAKNESS
ColorShift 3000 Laser Printer	Unlimited 300-year service agreement on all parts and labor	Programming glitch causes paper jams whenever nearby telephones ring.
Lazy Daisy 2000	Unsurpassed low prices and a lifetime supply of free ribbons	Market peak reached years ago. Users no longer buying these types of products.
PenJam Plus	The only portable infrared pen on the market for the Palm Pilot	Using the device across the room from the Palm Pilot's location makes it impossible to see the screen while writing.

Why Are You Writing an Internet Marketing Plan?

This is your Internet marketing charter. Briefly explain your reasons for drafting this document.

- Review all worksheet answers in relationship to your proposed plan.
- Compare the strategies and tactics of other industry players to your immediate and future goals.

- Express your reasons for marketing online in terms of market opportunities, competitive concerns, and business goals.

- Evaluate advantages and disadvantages, opportunities and risks to establishing an Internet marketing presence for your company.

- Evaluate the risks for your company of relying solely on traditional marketing activities.

- If you are not yet convinced of your company's fit for Internet marketing, complete this section later. At this point, you may not be able to express this aspect of your plan eloquently until you've done more research and book exercises.

Examples

1. "Our business (is) Web site promotion, so it was mandatory," says Bruce Clay, owner of Bruce Clay LLC, a California-based commercial company located at www.bruceclay.com. Clay says he entered the Internet space because of these opportunities:

   - Few others could keep up with technology, so it would be a black art for a while.

   - Complexity discourages clients from wanting to do it themselves.

   - Content is readily available, but very badly organized.

2. "Our customer base is exclusively online. We needed a Web presence to communicate with them," observed Jarvis Coffin, CEO for BURST! Media.

3. "We do not see a great deal of direct-marketing click-and-buy (given the expensive and complex nature of our software)," says Brian Alpert of Telogy. "Yet we don't underestimate the value of being seen in the same space as other industry leaders."

4. Catalog company Harry and David (*www.harryanddavid.com/*) saw its top reasons for creating a written Internet marketing plan as the following:

   - Evaluating the potential of the Internet as well as the costs required

   - Identifying Internet strategies that would leverage the existing core competencies of their organization

   - Providing their organization with a workable guideline to focus attention on this emerging channel

5. BURST! Media defined its top three advantages to joining the Internet community as the following:

   - A new, largely virgin market of Web site publishers with a need for outside sales and marketing expertise

- A need among advertising buyers for single-point accountability for advertising purchases

- With regard to the preceding two advantages, no business model risk—ad sales representation is a proven business model in every other media industry

6. The Learning Company "entered (the Internet space) 3.5 years ago. At the time, there were really no risks (for the software developer)," says Merrin. As the company increased its investment in "infrastructure and resources, we needed to ensure that we maintained a profitable position," he continued.

7. According to Jeffrey Eisen, director of marketing for Hobby Markets, his company's reasons for creating an Internet marketing plan were to

- Create strategic direction for marketing efforts

- Create a cohesive vision that everyone can understand and buy into

- Set objectives, strategies, and tactics for the marketing team—which support the achievement of forecasted member acquisition and sales

Write the First Draft of Your Business Overview and Executive Summary

When compiled, the business overview and executive summary for BURST! Media's Internet marketing plan might read as follows:

Example

BURST! is one of the largest and fastest growing advertising sales representative firms on the Internet with over 2,500 Web sites in its network. As an advertising sales representative, BURST! is contracted by World Wide Web sites to act as their intermediary with advertisers and advertising agencies. BURST! sells advertising on its 2,500 affiliated Web sites in exchange for a percentage of the gross revenue.

Through its proprietary software, BURST! delivers, monitors, and controls the advertising on its affiliated Web sites. A typical advertisement consists of a banner ad at the top, bottom, or side of a Web page that allows a viewer to click through to the advertiser's home page. Currently, BURST! serves over 10 million banner impressions a day (300+ million per month), reaching 22 percent of all Internet users (Media Metrix, January 1999). BURST! was founded in the fall of 1995 and sold its first ad in June of 1996.

CHAPTER 3

Analyzing Internet Market Statistics

Hard numbers can be powerful motivators.
Joe Copley, Copley Internet Systems, in a March 29, 1999,
post to the I-Sales Discussion List

Most typical marketing plans quote applicable market statistics; therefore, I've included a chapter in this book on selecting that data. Market statistics are important because they outline, in general and in detail, what the market is all about. Statistics can make or break your company's decision to participate. They are a barometer of your involvement in the fast-paced world of Internet commerce. This chapter will help you understand how Internet market statistics vary considerably. Reviewing applicable and reliable statistics will help determine if you are considering marketing on the Internet for the right or wrong reasons.

In Chapter 2, Preparing the Business Overview and Executive Summary, you wrote section one of your Internet marketing plan. You reviewed your company history, your products, or your services. You also decided whether to continue developing an Internet marketing plan.

In Chapter 3, Analyzing Internet Market Statistics, you're going to write section two of your Internet marketing plan. This is where you tell everyone how your particular company, which you've previously defined, fits into the Internet marketing picture. You will use Internet demographics, both general and industry-specific, to support your plans to create an Internet marketing presence.

The activities in this chapter just might be the icing on the cake when it comes to negotiating for those coveted Internet marketing dollars. You may wish to read this chapter first, before you consider writing a plan at all. Yeah, I know. Now I tell you. Of course, if the facts you gather while completing this chapter don't sway or delay you, then Chapter 3 is appropriately placed.

Section Two: Analyzing Internet Market Statistics

Your Internet marketing plan is best supported by including data that reinforces your decision to market online. Section two of your Internet marketing plan may include any combination of the following:

- References to general Internet studies
- References to market or industry-specific studies
- A summary of how market reports advocate Internet marketing for your company

Getting the Most out of This Chapter

The activities in this chapter include examining the different types of Internet statistics being generated by market research firms and consultants. During this process, you will take notes on data that is useful for your company to include in its Internet marketing plan.

You'll notice that some market reports provide general information with little analysis, while others are very detailed in their approach. Some reports contain descriptions of their report methodology, while others would have you believe that all data should be taken at face value. Still others are detailed in their reporting methods, but their methodology may be flawed.

Do You Really Need Internet Statistics?

The single most important decision you'll make regarding your Internet marketing presence will be whether you *even have* an Internet marketing presence. For your company, your industry, or your products, Internet marketing may already be a foregone conclusion. For example, if you work for a computer or electronics manufacturer, most of the companies in your industry are on the Internet already. High-technology marketers were early Internet adopters; therefore, market data on this industry's use of the Internet is fairly plentiful. If you're working in an industry that's familiar with Internet marketing, you can probably skip over parts of this chapter and just use the checklists. You have all the justification you need. Just start jotting down what you already know about the Internet and your market. After you've massaged the information into typical marketing plan prose, you can call it section two of your Internet marketing plan. However, if you're still trying to prove that the Internet is "the place to be," please keep reading.

Active versus Passive Internet Marketing

After finishing this chapter, you may decide there isn't any point in getting involved in e-commerce or even launching a Web presence. You could look at the market trends or the Internet demographics and decide that you have no business spending money in creating an online presence . . . at least for the next several months. If you do, then "so long." You'll no doubt shelve this book and come back three months from now to try again. At least I hope you return to reevaluate.

You should never totally "write off" the Internet's potential as a marketing vehicle. You can be sure that your competitor is already here, rounding up as many online opportunities as time and resources allow. Anticipate that the Internet will become the perfect marketing choice for your company as early as next week. If you think the online marketing decision is completely determined, controlled, and played out by you, you'll reconsider when I tell you that your company is online already. You just don't know it. Sans a conscious decision to manage an online marketing presence, you're a *passive* Internet marketer, whether you like it or not.

I'll explain. There are two distinct and complementary approaches to a company's Internet marketing activities. I've defined them as *active* and *passive*. One type of Internet marketing won't survive very well without the other.

Active Internet marketing involves the proactive execution of an ongoing program that creates and maintains an online image, for whatever end. *Passive Internet marketing* includes activities that aren't necessarily visible. For example, if you're strictly a passive Internet marketer, your company has no Web site. You have no definable Internet marketing budget. You don't publicize your e-mail address. Maybe you don't even *want* to publicize your e-mail address.

For the sake of those marketers whose companies are not active in creating visibility on the Internet, but who still consider themselves Internet marketers, I'll expand the *passive* category. Under passive Internet marketing, I'll include keeping up with the information that's out there, as in the phrase "lurker marketing." Maybe your company uses the Internet to perform market research and track editorial coverage for public relations purposes. You're just not publishing or distributing any information of your own online.

You may be convinced that your market isn't big enough to warrant active Internet marketing, and you're convinced it never will be. You're still not off the hook. If you don't handle your Internet marketing presence for your company, someone else just might. Even if you never put up a Web site or answer someone's e-mail inquiry, you'd be courting disaster if you didn't use the Internet to track news and opinion. Do you know what everyone is saying about you, your industry, and your closest competitor? Whether you know it or not, somewhere, someplace on the Internet, your company has been referenced.

For this reason, I'd like to include *reactive* Internet marketing in the passive category. If you don't have a Web page or any kind of original content initiated by your company, you still have an Internet marketing presence, just not a very big or controllable one. You might suddenly find your company listed somewhere as one of the "all-time worst product manufacturers in the history of the world" just because someone felt like it on a Friday afternoon. At this point, you'll probably track down the culprit and ask for some type of retraction, correction, or chance to air your point of view. You're used to doing that . . . after all, you probably called the editor of that trade magazine to amend the incorrect data that appeared in a recent article. If this ever happens to you—for instance, you find something online about your company that makes you cringe—I hope you'll *reactively* evolve into an *active* Internet marketer so it never happens again.

We'll discuss how you can continually monitor online information in future chapters. For now, we want to concentrate on determining whether there's enough evidence to support your case that a viable Internet market exists or can be developed for your products or services.

Gathering and Applying Data

Now you have to do your homework, which means going to these Web sites, reading industry reports, and contacting people to uncover the most up-to-date and applicable trends. In some cases, you will need to spend some of your marketing budget for specialized reports in order to unearth the most valuable data.

What Type of Information Do You Need?

The type of Internet statistics you'll need to support your quest for a decent budget will vary. There is no boilerplate requirement of supporting data across companies and industries, just as there's no boilerplate set of studies and surveys. Locating and analyzing applicable data depends on your online marketing goals.

A word of advice: Due to the increasingly fast pace of the Internet, the resources listed in this chapter may already be out of date. New data and research firms are emerging daily. The reports of well-known and established providers of market statistics will continue to be questioned and reassessed.

It's too easy to take a piece of old information and rely on it to justify your choice to marketing on the Internet. I'm only going to tell you this once: use current research. It's the only way to be sure that current market situations apply to you.

In the interests of increasing the longevity of this chapter, I'm going to reference the *types* of reports that are being generated now and how to use them in your marketing plan. You probably still have that old article on Internet demographics sitting in your file cabinet that you're hoping to use. If you want to hammer out a quick-and-dirty marketing plan and don't want to spend any additional time and money, that's certainly your choice. Now that I've hammered it into your head about the pitfalls of using stale data and I've nagged you about staying current, let's get started.

Fun with Internet Statistics

No other marketing media has generated as much hype as the Internet. Take a look at some of the different numbers on Internet growth. If you're like me, you're already excited about the possibilities for your company and the future of Internet marketing. Just to keep from getting in hot water, here's a disclaimer. I don't endorse any of the Internet research companies or reports mentioned in this chapter. Nor do I impugn any of them. By the time I warn you that company A doesn't know the difference between the Internet and a fishing net, they'll have issued a startling new report that no one dares challenge . . . at least for another three months anyhow.

How applicable are general Internet demographics to your unique situation? Don't assume anything until you see the qualifying description for each report. Look at the facts and how they were gathered; determine who has the best data for your situation; and ask for references in your industry.

"Come on!" you protest. "Who has the best reports now?" I can't tell you that either, mainly because Internet marketing statistics are so subjective and the numbers change so often. However, I will be glad to comment very briefly on information-gathering methodology.

It's most useful to find a research company that surveys individuals both online and off. Telephone calls and mail surveys are not obsolete just because you have a convenient e-mail account and a few thousand e-mail addresses in your database. Any research company that limits itself to surveying only individuals who are willing to answer a question by e-mail risks eliminating data about a major portion of its market. Trying to reach only online users? Well, just because someone has e-mail doesn't mean that e-mail is the most effective way to get answers. Some people are more receptive to a human voice on the telephone than to one more e-mail survey in the in-box.

Misusing Numbers and Other Mistakes

It's amazing how well people have learned to falsify facts or devise digital data in the pursuit of business excellence, reminding me of Darrell Huff's 1954 classic book *How to Lie With Statistics*. Mind you, I'm not recommending that you read this book for unethical reasons but I do wonder if certain unnamed suppliers of marketing statistics haven't done so already. Beyond recognizing that you could easily be trapped in someone else's Web of deceit, consider that you are your own worst enemy when it comes to justifying your online presence.

Everyone would like to discover incredible proof of a pot of gold at the end of the e-commerce rainbow. This desire colors our judgment when compiling data for an Internet marketing plan. Out-of-context statistics are often waved patriotically in the quest for a new or bigger Web site. Examples of misused statistics are demonstrated daily by analyst and marketing firms issuing news releases about an all-knowing, all-powerful "industry projection."

For example, following is a list of applicable news release headlines found online. I've brainstormed about some possible misinterpretations or false conclusions that could result should online marketers take company announcements at face value. After you read each headline, ask the associated questions I've posed. The truth behind the headlines can be obtained by further research, often found at the appropriate company's Web site.

Whenever you select Internet data, don't just embrace superficial information in a hasty effort to support your marketing activities. Ask discriminating questions about any new report that outlines trends, demographics, or survey conclusions. Brainstorm for yourself how headlines and selectively quoted statistics could mislead you, as well as other members of your company's Internet marketing team.

Selected Headlines on Internet Trends

"Access From Foreign Domains Approaching Half of All Internet Traffic" (InternetWire, June 10, 1999). Questions that need to be answered: *What is the breakdown of country-by-country access for Internet traffic? Are these English-speaking nations? How many unique visitors were accounted for?*

"Forrester Technographics Study Finds That Brands Don't Matter to Young Consumers On-Line" (Business Wire, June 24, 1999). Questions that need to be answered: *Why do big name youth-oriented brands, such as Coca-Cola, spend money on television advertising to promote a Web presence? When did young consumers become less brand-conscious? Are off-line branding efforts unnecessary when marketing to certain age groups? Can online branding efforts succeed without the support of off-line branding?*

"InfoBeads Study Shows 55% of U.S. Internet PCs Involved in E-Commerce" (Business Wire, June 14, 1999). Questions that need to be answered: *Are 45 per-*

cent of Internet PCs used to research products, for example, "window shop," as opposed to actually buying something? What was the sample size and demographics of the survey participant pool?

"Instant Call (SM) Buttons Increase Online Sales of Travel Service by Over 30%" (Internet News Bureau, February 18, 1999). Questions that need to be answered: *What is the name of the firm that conducted the survey on this product? Were only customers surveyed? Does corroborating data by an independent company, such as an analyst firm, exist to support this claim?*

"More Than A Million New High-Tech Jobs Added To U.S. Economy In Mid-1990s" (InternetWire, June 2, 1999). Questions that need to be answered: *How many U.S. high-tech workers were employed in previous years? What types of jobs were cataloged as high-tech? Was this report conducted through or by a government agency or a job search firm?*

"INTECO Confirms Number of Online Shoppers Up 250 Percent" (PRNewswire, January 25, 1999). Questions that need to be answered: *How many buyers are online now compared to a year ago? What percentage of total Internet users is found to have purchased on the Web?*

"Ernst & Young Study Finds State and Local Tax Revenues Minimally Impacted by the Internet" (Business Wire via COMTEXT, story filed on June 21, 1999). Questions that need to be answered: *How much tax money was collected via traditional sales channels? What are government estimates for lost tax revenue due to untaxed Internet transactions?*

Some Activities You Can Do Now

1. Go to your favorite Internet search engine or directory. Enter one, two, or three of the following keywords: Internet or online, marketing statistics, research, demographics, geographics, analysis, trends, projections, forecasts, facts, reports, studies, and/or surveys. I started with Northern Light at www.nlsearch.com for this exercise. I entered the keywords *Internet* and *trends*.

2. Sift through your results to find statistics related to the World Wide Web or Internet and start reading. My search produced 25 separate hyperlinks on the initial results page. Additional results were filed in categories, seen as file folders on the left side of the browser window. During my sort through the many hits, I found several Microsoft PowerPoint presentations converted to HTML, archived by presenters from different conferences. Don't discount these slides, should you find them during a search, since they often demonstrate how other business professionals analyze and present similar Internet marketing data. Review slides for inspiration on how to illustrate the statistics you include in your marketing plan.

3. Search for news releases announcing current studies. Again, I looked to Northern Light for assistance. I clicked on a top-of-the-page link to "simple search" then on to another area offering current news. Remembering one of the news release headlines found earlier, I entered the word *study*, selected the last two weeks, sorted the results by relevance, and limited news coverage to "Computing & Internet." My search for current news produced 84 items.

Entire reputations of Internet industry gurus have been made and built on a willingness to prognosticate. My favorite misused Internet projection or estimate is referenced at the Anamorph site: "There are 27,000 Web sites, and this number is doubling every 53 days."

Right now, take a doughnut break and browse over to the Internet Irresponsible Internet Statistics Generator (Figure 3.1) located at Anamorph, www .anamorph.com/docs/stats/stats.html. Play around with this page by using the Web Statistics Generator to make an irresponsible prediction based on the preceding doubling prediction. Select a date in the drop-down menu and click on the button. Now see if you can't find supporting data elsewhere verifying that these were valid statistics on the date in question. Although the statistical generator stopped making predictions a while back, as demonstrated by its historical choice of dates, it is still interesting to analyze how overblown predictions about Internet growth might have affected the rise and fall of various Internet companies.

The creator of the calculator, Robert Orenstein, is applauded for his foresight in providing this tool to the Internet community, especially at a time when Internet marketing budgets were needlessly sucked dry due to misinformation. He wrote, "Keep in mind that it is impossible for Web growth to

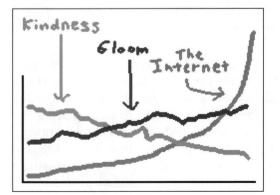

Figure 3.1 Irresponsible Internet statistics.

Copyright © 1995 by Robert Orenstein, Anamorph (*www.anamorph.com*).

continue at this rate." Sun Microsystems Distinguished Engineer Dr. Jakob Nielsen arrived at the original doubling estimate. Nielsen stopped believing in the 53-day estimate early in the e-commerce game. He wrote an explanation of how he came up with it, how his statement has been misused, and how and why it permeated the industry. His column titled "Kill the 53-Day Meme" can be found on the Web at the Sun Microsystems site, www.sun.com:80/950901/columns/alertbox/index.html. Nielsen wrote, "Of course, growth rates this fast cannot continue indefinitely." His explanation is worth reading even after all the Internet history that's archived to date. It'll remind you that many "too good to be true" Internet statistics should always be taken with a grain of salt.

Who Cares How Many Web Sites There Are?

What do the number of Web pages or sites have to do with supporting the theory that Internet marketing is a viable option for your company? I just don't get this fascination with how big the Web has become. Companies have always published hoards of useless data in an effort to get noticed. Why are Web pages any different?

Using the number of existing Web sites as a pivotal justification point in your Internet marketing plan is like claiming the number of pages in your product catalog is directly proportional to size of your customer base. Since most Web pages are self-promotional, I think the number of Web sites is only an indication of how much time professional users have to create more useless reading.

Showing a growth in Web pages *could* point to some kind of trend. You could claim that the number of Web pages demonstrates an increase in Internet activity and use, which you could extrapolate to mean market acceptance. Does that mean your market or someone else's? Basically, the number of Web pages by itself doesn't demonstrate anything tangible from a marketer's point of view without additional qualifying data. If you don't agree, then tell me why the Internet is touted as the great online town hall, the biggest family picture album, or a great place to hang out with friends. What is the business value of someone's personal collection of scanned images of actor Don Johnson?

By the way, I'm a big help in adding personal Web pages and sites to the Internet for my friends and family. My miniature dent in somebody's Internet survey statistics doesn't have anything to do with any company's sales except the Internet service provider's.

Some Internet statistics are useful. Some are not. And some need a little bit more dissection to be useful. Now that you're ready to review these numbers with a more down-to-earth attitude, I'm ready to give them to you.

Estimates of Users by Age

"92 million people over the age of 16 are using the Internet," according to a Nielsen Media Research/CommerceNet study. News release dated June 18, 1999. (*Source:* Business Wire, www.businesswire.com)

"The median age of the Net user . . . is now 38 years old. (*Source:* eStats, www.emarketer.com/estats/demo age.html)

"26.2% of Net users are age 26–30," according to the results of a Web-based Internet survey conducted by Survey.net. Results posted at Web site on July 15, 1999. (*Source:* Survey.Net, www.survey.net/inet1r.html)

Rarely do two different research firms report their statistics similarly. Sometimes it's difficult to find market segment reports that even measure and convey the same information. Market research firms are always looking for that unique angle with which to survey Internet users, thereby positioning themselves as having discovered some uncharted territory. (By the way, e-mail me if you'd like to be included in a survey on the habits of over-30 career women with gifted elementary school-age daughters who use the Internet to keep in touch with relatives on the East Coast. Granted, it'll be a niche segment of the population, but the results will no doubt spawn new online applications uniquely targeted to our needs, making a fortune for some Internet start-up.)

Until you read the body copy, rather than just the headlines, you're comparing apples to oranges. Are the numbers in one report representative of a subset of another company's report? How does the number of Internet hosts translate into the number of Internet users? Or does it translate at all? How do these different reports complement or contradict each other?

The second thing you'll notice is that not everyone agrees exactly how many users are on the Internet. Let me correct that: Not everyone agrees on *approximately* how many users are on the Internet. As demonstrated by a chart at the CyberAtlas site, cyberatlas.internet.com/, estimates of the number of U.S. Internet users varies greatly, from a low of 5.8 million to a high of 35 million (Figure 3.2). Why is that so?

It's nearly impossible to know how many people inside an organization have e-mail addresses that are assigned by a specific domain name. A research firm is not going to find that out by counting how many unique names it uncovers in newsgroups. Companies that own multiple domain names account for some of the confusion, as do ghost accounts. I'm referring to those accounts, such as info@wolfBayne.com, that aren't really created for a specific employee, but rather for a particular function or department, such as customer service or public relations. Just as an example, I have several dozen user names for each of my domain names. Some of these are used to trigger autoresponders on my server, so I don't have to manually reply to every message. That

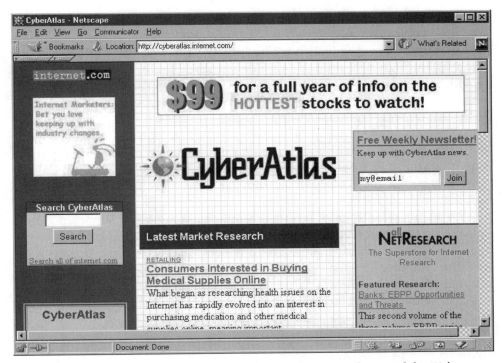

Figure 3.2 CyberAtlas has pointers to the latest market research around the Web.

means that I get a dozen or so of the same piece of junk e-mail every day and someone somewhere thinks they're counting bodies.

System administrators and company managers could probably provide us with an idea of how many real human beings in their organizations have e-mail addresses, if they could find the time to help us out. Then there's the daunting task of contacting the thousands of small businesses around the world and surveying *their* distribution of account names versus domain names versus real employees. When market researchers make these survey telephone calls, sometimes they get an accurate answer, sometimes a best guess, and sometimes they just get disconnected. Sometimes the researcher has had enough on a Friday afternoon and just wants to go home. Such is life for those hardworking research folks. That's why you keep hearing references to "statistical samples." Simply put, it's humanly impossible to survey everybody . . . so there's a whole lotta guessin' goin' on.

Finally, assuming that everybody cooperated with the Internet surveyors and gave them all the information they needed, you'd still be in a bind trying to estimate how many unique users are actually online. Many people in an organization have e-mail addresses but never use them. Does that make them potential online customers for your company or not?

Now about those duplicate e-mail addresses. I have several Internet access accounts, through a combination of independent ISPs and commercial service providers because of the type of work I do. Lots of people have more than one e-mail account: one at home, one at the office, and maybe one at school. How do these surveys account for that?

Unlike magazine subscription mailing lists where you can weed out many of the duplicates, the Internet has no central mechanism for identifying duplicate individuals. At least not currently. Is Mary Mara from Sausalito, California, the same person as Mary Mara from Syracuse, New York? Only Mary and her mother know for sure.

With such a wide span of reported numbers, many being superseded on a daily basis by whomever can get the most attention, it doesn't hurt to dig deeper in your quest for meaningful answers. That's why you'll need more than the "number of online users" or the "number of hosts" to support your Internet marketing program. Now that I've said all that, I'll warn you. You'll still hear some Internet surveyors boast that they can estimate the size of the Internet. Well, I'm still reserving judgment.

Growth of the Internet

"The number of Internet users in the U.S. and Canada grew by 20 million over the past year, according to a new Nielsen Media Research/CommerceNet study." News release dated June 18, 1999. (*Source:* Business Wire, www.business wire.com.)

This measurement of Internet growth has more credibility than the "53-day meme" mentioned earlier. Admirably enough, CommerceNet qualified its statement by declaring that these calculations represent "respondents." The company doesn't try to add to the hype by inflating the significance of its report in the overall scheme of things. As you review the examples you find during your preparation of this section of the plan, keep this in mind.

The number of survey respondents is an important factor in determining whether the research firm did a good and thorough job or just went through the motions. Percentages of respondents surveyed are even better. If you know that your market consists of 40,000 professionals, and the research firm has obtained completed surveys from 2,000, you know that it has compiled a report based on 5 percent of your target market. If a certain publication has 35,000 subscribers, and the publishing company has obtained completed surveys from one-twelfth of its entire subscriber base, that gives you something more to go on as well. It's worth asking more questions so you can better interpret the research company's findings.

How Are Growth Statistics Useful?

Showing growth can affect your decision to select a particular media, such as the Internet. If no one in your industry is placing ads on the radio, for example, you're going to look much harder at this choice for your marketing mix. If you regularly review the media kits of trade or business publications during your media planning, then you know the value of showing growth. Publications that can demonstrate additional advertising-page placements can show the media buyer that some type of positive industry activity is occurring to warrant ad placements. You can bet that my nephew Michael isn't skewing these growth statistics unintentionally by placing ads in *Electronic Engineering Times* just to impress his high school friends. Not so with his Web page placement on the Internet.

Print publishers also use growth information to demonstrate that their publication garners more ad pages than the nearest competitor. As a marketer in the computer and electronics industry, I repeatedly heard from competing sales managers about how *EDN* magazine measured up to *Electronic Design.* Editorial content, accuracy in reporting, and the reputations of managing editors and reporters were key factors in determining an engineer's choice of one publication over another. "Okay, Okay," I'd agree, "You have my attention." For decades, print publications have done an excellent job of showing everyone where the activity lies in their markets. They can easily demonstrate where media buyers are putting their dollars and why.

In similar fashion, Internet market researchers mention how many business Web sites exist as proof of the growing Internet business market. Internet service providers, as a subset of the entire Internet service market, also quote how many business Web sites reside on their servers. It's a nice positioning statement for attracting more customers.

These Internet growth statistics have some bearing on the growth of Internet marketing, some bearing on the increase in ISP service quality, and some bearing on the development of new technologies and software. General Internet growth statistics, while useful in setting the stage for your plans, are only part of the picture.

If you're going to place an advertisement based on a print publisher's growth statistics, do it because there also exists evidence that you're reaching your target market with that particular publication. Therefore, if you're going to develop a Web site because of Internet growth statistics, do it because the statistics you're using show more growth of Internet users in your market than in the Internet in general.

Revisiting the CommerceNet quote, think about the increasing number of respondents who had access to the Internet. If I'm marketing my products to automobile enthusiasts, the number of wilderness hikers who have access to the Internet doesn't impress me very much . . . unless I can show some correlation between the two. In order for this report to be useful to me, I'm going to have to ask more questions . . . and so will you. Is your product a mainstream, consumer-based product with a diverse customer base? I would say that these general Internet statistics are going to be a lot more useful to you than to the company selling high-end vacation getaway packages to white-collar professionals in upper income brackets.

International Reach

Studies on the international reach of the Internet bring us to the question of whether the Internet is truly an international medium. For any business that wants to expand its market beyond domestic shores and position itself to compete with multinational corporations and their worldwide sales offices, the answer is a resounding yes. The Internet is, can be, and often should be used as an international medium.

What if the international aspects of marketing on the Internet are not as enticing to your company as the national, regional, or even local marketing aspects? Should you consider the Internet if you're not an international company? Again, the answer is yes.

It's a marketing fact of life that local companies bow to the market reach of the regional companies, regional companies to the national ones, and the national to the international. The smaller businesses are and always will be dwarfed in the shadow of the IBMs and the Microsofts of the world. (That is, of course, until the smaller companies *become* the next IBM or Microsoft.) These are powerful, very successful companies. They have big budgets. They have big staffs. They have lots of money. Maybe you don't. Maybe you're a start-up company. If you're not a start-up, maybe your company is manageable in light of your current business goals. Maybe that's just fine . . . for now.

You're thinking about using the Internet to develop local business and you have no intention of dealing with international prospects any time soon. Is that wise? Yeah, why not? Buyers are on the Internet in your hometown. Localization is a great online strategy. Why wouldn't you offer local customers the convenience of reviewing your product catalog while ignoring buyers in Israel? Your HTML META tags let you define geographical limits. If someone in another country finds you anyhow, you can make it clear at your Web site how you define your market geographically. If you get those international inquiries anyway, then build some goodwill by creating a referral network. Who's to say that you won't be able to justify a business expansion if the inquiries become lucrative?

Internet Users by Gender

Statistics that segment by gender can be useful if your product is targeted to a male or female audience. If a well-researched study reveals that there are now more female Internet users on the Internet than ever before, this information can be used to support a reassessment of the marketing mix and a reallocation of advertising dollars. Recently published studies have pointed to this type of trend. As a result, companies who have traditionally courted the female market through television and magazines are now courting the female market through the addition of online services and the Internet.

How Do These Numbers Apply?

As you can see, Internet statistics come in every shape and size and there's going to be a set of figures that fit you. You can justify your Internet marketing plan based on a variety of data, not just one source. Figure 3.3 shows a sampling of the different types of Internet surveys being published today and some suggestions for applying them.

Survey Type	Possible Applications
Overall estimate of worldwide users, host	Starting to justify an Internet marketing program
Growth of Internet use within your industry	Determining expanding market opportunities
Average age of selected users	Marketing to youth, middle-age, and elderly users
Internet users by gender	Marketing products to women versus men
User profiles by education, job titles, and income	Targeting specific online users and industries
Internet business usage trends	Formulating marketing communications strategies
Breakdown of Domain name registrations	Demonstrating an increase in industry users
Impact of the Internet on other media	Supporting the reallocation of marketing dollars
Purchasing behavior and revenue	Proving growth patterns in online commerce
Computer and Internet proficiency among users	Evaluating Internet development options
Browser, platform, and connection speeds	Deciding Web design and navigational issues

Figure 3.3 Applying Internet statistics.

The number of industry research firms is growing. In addition, there are several consulting firms which conduct their own market research for use by selected clients (Figure 3.4). Occasionally one of them will publish the data to get your attention. Aside from these firms, professional associations are very useful in locating market-specific statistics. Here are just a few such organizations.

Organizations and Associations

Many marketing and industry specific associations offer their members reports, white papers, and research papers on trends in new media for a nominal charge. If you are not a member of a particular organization, you may still be able to purchase some of its reports.

- American Marketing Association, www.ama.org
- Business Marketing Association, www.marketing.org (Figure 3.5)
- International Association of Business Communicators, www.iabc.com/
- Public Relations Society of America, www.prsa.org

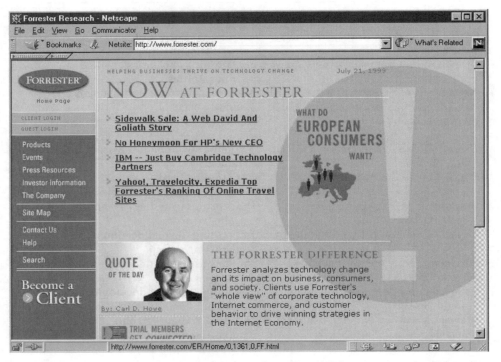

Figure 3.4 Forrester analyzes market trends and publishes reports to aid online marketers.

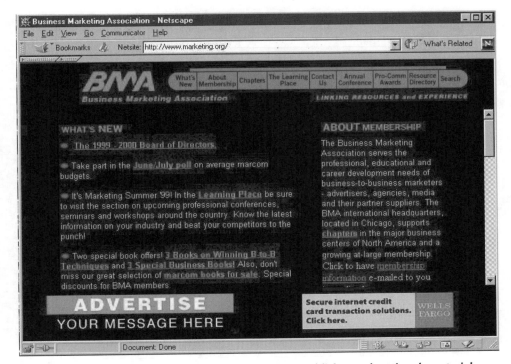

Figure 3.5 The Business Marketing Association publishes educational materials on different aspects of marketing effectively.

The *Encyclopedia of Associations* (Detroit: Gale Research Company) is a multivolume reference set that may be found in the reference department of public, academic, or corporate libraries. It contains national, international, regional, state, and local associations of the United States, including trade and professional associations. The encyclopedia is also published on CD-ROM for easy searching.

Trade Magazine Publishing Companies

Trade publishers offer their advertisers surveys, benchmark reports, and studies on trends in new media and marketing. Completing the forms in this chapter will help you evaluate and apply statistics offered by such companies. A good place to start is www.mediafinder.com. Start searching by keywords for your industry and you'll soon notice a pattern of which companies publish in which market sector.

In summary, once you know where to look for useful statistics to support your marketing program, evaluate each of these resources accordingly (Figure 3.6).

Complete an evaluation form for each report you are interested in using in your Internet marketing plan.

Title of report: _____

Cost of report: $

Organization(s): _____

Contact information for additional questions:

    Person: _____

    Address: _____

    _____

    Telephone: _____

    E-mail: _____ FAX: _____

    Web address: _____

Applicability

This report is (check one):

❑ General to Internet marketing

❑ Industry-specific or contains sections that are industry-specific

❑ Both general and industry-specific information is included

❑ Other. Please specify: _____

Figure 3.6 Evaluating Internet statistics.

Describe the focus of this report. (Include the goals and objectives of this study.)

_____

_____

_____

_____

_____

_____

Briefly list sections of this report that may be applicable to your Internet marketing plan.

_____

_____

_____

_____

_____

Report Dates

When was the survey conducted?

　　　Start (month, year): _____

　　　End (month, year): _____

When was the final report issued? _____

Has this report been updated? If so, when? _____

Is this the most current report available? _____

When will this report be updated? _____

Figure 3.6 *(Continued)*

Respondents

Is the report segmented by job titles or industry? _____

What percentage of respondents are included in your target market? _____

Credibility

This report contains an explanation of its methods for:

❑ Selecting respondents
❑ Distributing surveys
❑ Gathering data
❑ Analyzing data
❑ Other. Please specify: _____

This organization is (check all that apply):

❑ Association (business, trade, industry). If trade or industry, explain:

_____

❑ Commercial online service
❑ Conference, trade show, or seminar organizer
❑ Consulting firm or independent consultant
❑ Educational institution
❑ Industry analyst or market research firm
❑ Internet service provider
❑ Publishing company (business and trade magazines, newspapers, books)
❑ Other. Please specify: _____

Was this survey conducted by my company or an affiliated company?

_____

Figure 3.6   *(Continued)*

Was this report commissioned by another company? If so, by whom?

_____

How many years has this organization been conducting surveys? _____

If this is a new organization, please include any additional information to support its ability to properly conduct this survey. (Name notable staff members, parent companies, etc.)

_____

_____

_____

_____

_____

_____

Name other companies who are currently using data from this report.

_____

_____

_____

_____

Circle the companies listed above that are in your industry.

Describe the reputation of this organization. (Include information from its promotional literature, opinions of sales representatives, editorial opinion, colleagues' and executives' opinions, sales report, and your own assessment.)

_____

_____

_____

_____

_____

_____

Figure 3.6 *(Continued)*

Circle comments listed above that were gathered from the company's promotional literature or sales representatives.

List other similar reports by this organization. (Include dates of issue.)

_____

_____

_____

List any negative comments about this particular report that you may have heard.

_____

_____

_____

Respondents

Estimate of possible respondents in market surveyed: _____

Number of initial contacts made: _____

Number of respondents (included in results): _____

Compute percentage of market actually surveyed: _____

Information Gathering

How were users contacted and interviewed for this survey? Check all that apply.

❑ E-mail
❑ Web site form
❑ Telephone
❑ Fax
❑ Surface mail

Figure 3.6 *(Continued)*

❑ In person (trade show survey, door-to-door, etc.)

❑ Other. Please specify: _____

How were questions asked?

❑ Open-ended (user supplied answers without prompting)

❑ Multiple choice (pick one: *A, B, C*)

❑ *Yes, No,* and *No answer*

❑ Rating scale (points, from 1 to 10, high-low, relevant versus nonrelevant)

❑ Combination of the above

❑ Other. Please specify: _____

Report Findings

Is this report easy to understand? _____

Are unfamiliar terms explained? _____

Are summaries brief and to the point? _____

Can portions of this report be easily used to support your Internet marketing plan? _____

Is any additional interpretation needed in order for this report to be useful? If so, explain:

_____

_____

_____

Your Overall Assessment

Circle one number on each scale.

This report is free of bias or slant.
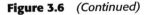
        Low   **1**   **2**   **3**   **4**   **5**   **6**   **7**   **8**   **9**   **10**   High

Figure 3.6 *(Continued)*

This report is free of information that is ambiguous or contradictory.
Low   **1**   **2**   **3**   **4**   **5**   **6**   **7**   **8**   **9**   **10**   High

This report is thorough in its findings for its specific purposes.
Low   **1**   **2**   **3**   **4**   **5**   **6**   **7**   **8**   **9**   **10**   High

This report is relevant to my Internet marketing plan.
Low   **1**   **2**   **3**   **4**   **5**   **6**   **7**   **8**   **9**   **10**   High

This report is reasonably priced or fits within my budget parameters.
Low   **1**   **2**   **3**   **4**   **5**   **6**   **7**   **8**   **9**   **10**   High

Total score: _____ (out of a possible 50 points)

Completed by: _____ Date: _____

Figure 3.6   *(Continued)*

CHAPTER 4

Formulating Marketing Communications Strategies

As we realized the importance of becoming an information provider, it became clear that we needed a different kind of strategy to market ourselves.
Channing Dawson, Senior Vice President of New Media
for Home & Garden Television

This chapter defines the schemes and approaches to developing and managing your Internet marketing presence. Your success in online marketing hinges are your ability to understand where you are going and how to get there, which is why I often refer to this portion of the plan as "the destination." Think about this chapter as preparing for your mission to market online. What are you going to pack for the trip? What tools will you use to get there? Once you understand your company's objectives in marketing on the Internet, you can begin devising strategies and tactics for achieving them.

In Chapter 3, Analyzing Internet Market Statistics, you wrote section two of your plan. You reviewed the different types of Internet marketing numbers being tallied today and discovered how to use them best to support your plan. You uncovered some problems with Internet marketing statistics and became familiar with what to look for. You also educated everyone, including vice presidents, managers, and coworkers, about how your company ranks in the Internet marketing world based on current market trends and studies.

In Chapter 4, Formulating Marketing Communications Strategies, you will complete section three of your Internet marketing plan, creating another foundation for your online marketing blueprint. Here, you'll review how recent developments in the strategies of some online companies have made it impossible to sit idly by. You will take a look back at your company charter, defined earlier, to resolve how you can best tackle marketing and sales challenges to compete online effectively.

Section Three: Formulating Marketing Communications Strategies

Including data that reinforces your decision to market on the Internet best supports your Internet marketing plan. Section three of your Internet marketing plan may include any combination of the following:

- Marketing plan objectives and goals
- Specific strategies for achieving them
- A summary of how the use of the Internet will strengthen your overall marketing goals
- A list of competitor's shortcomings and how your company can meet these market needs
- A list of potential Web site with whom your company can partner to achieve its online goals

Getting the Most out of This Chapter

This chapter contains activities for reviewing and comparing examples of other companies' strategic case studies as well as a general overview of how market changes may be affecting your online strategy. While reading this chapter, make note of applicable objectives and strategies for your company, and highlight those useless tactics that it is advisable for your company to avoid. In addition, think about ways you can find untapped opportunities, which are windows of opportunity for your company to shine through.

Some companies are very determined to win and win big with their Internet marketing. Some companies are conservative in their approach, waiting for proof every step of the way before they proceed with another phase. Still others are satisfied with simply "being there," as though they are no longer conspicuous by their absence. Finally, some companies, realistic about their own limitations, will find a way to build a bigger Internet presence than initial funds or resources can afford.

Tapping into Strategic Alliances

Strategic alliances used to be the best kept secret of corporations. Today, everybody's doing it. The first proof of the influence of such alliances is still visible on the Internet today—the "reciprocal link." One Webmaster e-mails another Webmaster asking for an exchange of links to each other's site. Reciprocal links mirror the saying, "I'll scratch your back and you scratch mine." Granted, reciprocal links are a very elementary approach to developing online strategic alliances. Regardless, asking for a return link became an online habit as more sites posted endless pages of interesting links.

The strategy behind this widespread phenomenon is very simple—site owners want to provide as much value-added content to their online visitors as possible. In the process, Web site owners want to attract as much attention to their own work as possible. Creating original content is a laborious and expensive process. By selectively providing quality links to other related sites, you provide a nice visitor bonus that's supposed to cost you little in time and energy. And visitors appreciate your efforts in guiding them to additional online information.

Reciprocal links are free and can be fairly easy to manage, as long as you recognize their limits. Keep in mind: Too many reciprocal links are cumbersome to maintain, especially with the daily emergence and revisions of thousands of sites throughout the Web. Endless pages of threadbare links, sans site reviews or descriptions, don't provide much in the way of needed site content. Finally, outside links are a poor strategy for maintaining your own site's "stickiness." After all your dedicated work in aggregating off-site resources, you could accidentally encourage visitors to surf elsewhere before investigating your full offerings. That's why any linking strategy should be reviewed with care. Guide your Webmaster to be more selective when deciding which useful URLs to highlight from your site, and how to highlight them.

What Does It Take to Create a Strategic Alliance?

Real strategic alliances take more work that a few lines of HTML hastily inserted into an often-forgotten and neglected page. An untold amount of negotiating and reciprocal nurturing is required for strategic alliances to succeed. It's well worth the effort, because forming a strategic alliance with the right partner can make or break your entry into a competitive area. Not all Internet marketers are up to the task; nonetheless, these online business relationships are growing at an amazing rate. How popular are they? On any given day of the week, dozens of announcements hit the various news wires, trumpeting the decisions of two or more companies to leverage each other's strengths. Throughout the Internet you'll discover the PR (public relations) handiwork of a different company coordinator of online relationships, senior vice president of Internet strategy, or manager of corporate alliances.

After analyzing dozens of news releases announcing partnerships and relationships between established and emerging Internet players, I noticed a distinct pattern. Pretty much, everyone has the same goals in mind—they even sound familiar, along the lines of "Everything I Learned About Internet Marketing, I Learned in Kindergarten." You'll read plenty of online evidence that everyone is playing around the digital neighborhood in pretty much the same way.

What they said: Our company today announces a partnership with their company.

What they meant: We are going to share our toys, our friends, our rooms, and/or our allowance.

What they said: This alliance allows our customers to do business on the Internet more easily.

What they meant: It's more fun to ride our friend's bike when we can move the seat to fit our legs.

What they said: Our jointly packaged e-commerce solutions are being offered to businesses worldwide.

What they meant: We want everybody in the neighborhood to like us so we make lots of new friends.

What they said: Our company will provide marketing expertise and creative direction, while their company will provide programming development and technical project management.

What they meant: We're not really good at this. We'd like somebody else to do it and maybe teach us. We're going to need some help and we promise to teach them what we know, too.

What they said: We're pleased to welcome this company into our partnership program.

What they meant: He's my best buddy . . . this week.

With my childhood analogies, am I guilty of trivializing business relationships? You bet, but no more so than many online businesses who naively undertake this strategic opportunity for gaining online prominence. It's this childlike innocence of business relationships that has taken the word *strategic* out of the phrase "strategic alliance." Many online alliances are for PR purposes only, nothing more, causing many Web sites to resemble a trophy case of icons, logos, banners, and links to other sites.

Managing and Nurturing a Business Relationship

Notice how many e-mails end up in your in-box containing content resembling an afterthought? These are usually from someone who thought finding an online partner involved searching for a few dozen superficial prospects, sending off e-mails, and waiting for the results. After several half-hearted efforts, the Web surfer finally gets a bite. The two involved companies continue conversations until either someone agrees in principle that a relationship is established on some point or the principals involved both get busy with more important projects. If both companies finally agree on a relationship, they trade whatever it is they have to trade. They even give each other links and buttons on each other's Web sites, maybe a sponsorship message or two on a conference program, but nothing of any depth ever develops beyond the initial trade.

If you're pursuing a strategic relationship, you hope you'll get increased traffic from the visibility and piggyback off the other company's online and off-line marketing presence. They hope you'll continue to promote them in your various contacts with customers, too. Three months down the road, nothing more has been done besides the initial flirting and an occasional date. One day, a new Web designer comes on board at their company headquarters. He asks about the logo on the home page and whether it's okay to reposition it for layout purposes. The new Internet marketing manager looks at it and can't remember why it's there, or when was the last time he even heard from you. Boom. Your logo gets taken off their site. Soon, your site referral logs indicate that you're no longer getting any hits from the other site. You check out their home page and discover your link is now gone. You hammer out a nasty e-mail wondering why they failed to live up to their end of the bargain, or worse, you never contact the other company at all. Ties are severed and the relationship is over.

Unlike links, whose placement position is often negotiated on the reciprocating site, real strategic alliances are much more complicated. In order to succeed, you must find the best way to trade strengths with someone, a requirement that's hardly met by simply issuing a news release. Strategic alliances are meant to be a win-win situation built on sharing business sense and talent, rather than fulfilling a mutual desire for self-promotion. If you're not doing at least one of the basics, you don't have a strategic alliance, no matter what the trade papers say.

The basic components of strategic alliances include the following:

- Sharing people
- Sharing expenses
- Sharing resources and tools
- Sharing knowledge

If you're the owner of a small business, hoping to connect with a larger company, you're in luck. Different-sized companies can and often do play together in cyberspace. In today's online environment, some contributions are valued more highly than others are. It's impossible to calculate an exact price tag for

THE WORD IS *COOPERATION*

Strategic alliances should be undertaken with care and should be nurtured to continue. Assuming you can learn to do it right, why should you pursue such a relationship? No one business can afford to do everything it would like. Most everyone, with the possible exception of a few unnamed Web monoliths, must make painful decisions regarding how to spend a marketing budget—whether limited by either financial resources or simply talent. Strategic affiliations with other companies are a great solution to your marketing limitations, allowing you to test the waters before you commit to anything permanent within your business.

every possible business contribution. Some companies have special abilities that even the biggest companies can't emulate. That's why bigger companies are always buying up the smaller ones. The key is that each participant has something tangible to trade in the way of time, money, and space, and of course, bodies. The perceived value of each of these elements is always up for interpretation.

Some online alliances are fairly straightforward. Some are very complicated, upping the ante with regard to the expense of creating an association. One thing is certain—companies who can manage real strategic alliances know how to leverage business relationships expertly. Bottom line: In the online world, as in the real world, well-drafted and executed strategic alliances separate the e-men and e-women from the e-boys and e-girls.

Best Practices of Companies with Alliances

As you decide what you want your strategic alliance with another company to accomplish, think of any future potential relationship as an opportunity to get into the Internet game quicker and better than you could have on your own. For example, imagine that you're a shareware or independent software developer, who is also the owner of a small company reliant on a small talent pool. You devote most of your talents to product creation, but you also sense that you lack the ability to grab market share. You know that hot products often attract imitators. If you drag your heels, you can't build enough market momentum. If you delay, someone will eat your lunch. If you're interested in staying with the business for a while, a good strategic cooperative marketing alliance will help you build your customer base. Finally, the development of a strategic sales alliance will afford you the opportunity to go where no one (in your company) has gone before. Through strategic alliances, you can experience new business activities. You can achieve success in new areas. By leveraging these advantageous relationships, you can grow your business in a manageable way, deciding when and whether to hire additional people, buy outside services, or lease more computer equipment.

How'd They Do That?

Remember the old business proverb about time, information, and power?

Time. No strategic relationship is complete without a time frame. How soon do you want results? If you're a software developer, you're accustomed to working with milestones. The success of the Internet has greatly accelerated your goals in getting a product to market. As you form your strategic alliance, evaluate the individual milestones on any given aspect of this joint project. What does your gut tell you and what can you verify with market statistics? Assume that the market will move faster than you can accommodate it.

Information. Taking an honest look at your business and technical strengths will tell you what you can and cannot accomplish on your own. Your potential partner will want to know. In the joint news release I referenced on Concentric and MySoftware, each company has a boilerplate positioning statement that defines its place in the online world. Perhaps yours will be modeled after the business overview and executive summary statement you wrote for your Internet marketing plan.

CONCENTRIC AND MYSOFTWARE

On Tuesday, July 6, 1999, Concentric Network Corporation and MySoftware Company jointly issued a news release to announce a newly created partnership. Largely a co-branding effort, their alliance is designed to provide Web hosting, direct marketing, and leads management solutions.

What did each of the parties bring to the equation? According to PR Newswire who distributed this announcement, "Concentric Network Corp. [is] a leader in value-added IP network services" while "MySoftware Company [is] a leader in Internet direct marketing services and software." By getting together, these two organizations can better help "small- and medium-sized companies" to "grow their business(es)." MySoftware benefits by being able to co-brand technology services to its customers. Concentric can offer its customers new marketing tools. Together, the two companies complement each other by offering small businesses a more complete solution for their online marketing and sales needs. Both companies were good at building their businesses, but together they are even better, allowing them both to dig deeper into the market.

But the relationship doesn't stop there. Both MySoftware and Concentric executives are expected to expand their alliance to "forge new initiatives serving small- and medium-sized businesses."

Power. When seeking a potential partner to assist you with your online marketing, you have to be able to market yourself well to *it*. If you can't convince your partner that you have the right stuff, how will you convince the market, even with a partner? Future investors want to know how you're holding up your end of the bargain. And nothing's more irritating than being accused of riding someone else's coattails, in politics, entertainment, or even on the Internet. To put this in biological, or even Star Trek terms, in business partnerships, you want a *symbiotic consociate* not a *leech.* Finally, just because you can lasso a coveted partner on the digital range doesn't mean you'll be able to ride it over the mountains, or that anyone will care if you do. Ask yourself, "Will this partner help me get where I want to go and will people be excited to meet me when I arrive?"

Internet Wire

At its Web site, Internet Wire publishes its "Strategic Partnerships Classification Guide" which defines different ways to do business with this growing online news service company. Choices consist of the following:

Distribution partnerships. Linking to Internet Wire services such as Internet Wire Headlines, Internet Wire ExpertNet, Daily Debuts from your site.

Content partnerships. You would like Internet Wire to distribute and/or link to your content/site.

Technology partnerships. You have a technology that would enhance the Internet Wire service.

E-commerce. Partnering with Internet Wire for e-commerce.

If you decide to pitch Internet Wire with a strategic relationship, you need to provide it in as clear terms as possible. Define what's in it for them. Due to the popularity of its service, it gets too many requests for partnering to really undertake them all. Like most Internet companies, it wants to know what you can offer in the way of demonstrated site content, valuable content, or innovative technology, to name a few areas of possible contributions. It warns visitors to this section of its site that any information submitted "shall be considered non-confidential," protecting the company from the claims of scam artists who wish to take advantage of Internet Wire's good nature in considering a request.

Some Activities You Can Do Now

Evaluate what talents or resources you lack to meet your online goals. Take a look at your business goals and make a short list of three top needs that aren't being fulfilled right now.

1. Look around for potential partners who have tackled this aspect of an online presence or who, at the very least, demonstrate finesse in approaching it. For example, if you are inept at handling sales order fulfillment, you might want to look around for someone who has this aspect of e-commerce down pat.

2. Evaluate what your potential partner is lacking. Do you have something to trade in return? Query the company customer service department about services that aren't readily apparent. Maybe there's an opportunity for you here.

3. For initial inquires with potential partners, draft your proposal in simple terms—one page or less is a great idea. Don't provide too much detail. If your partner isn't interested, you can reuse this information in a different pitch, but don't give too much away. It's a competitive world out there. When you reuse this content in your written Internet marketing plan, you can expand on the cogent details there.

4. Don't put everything in an e-mail, but rather suggest a time to talk. For this project, you need the personal touch. Get ready to schedule a telephone call to introduce yourself, hoping to plan an in-person meeting at an upcoming trade show or conference.

Understanding Objectives, Strategies, and Tactics

If strategic alliances are not your cup of tea, that is, you intend to go it alone for now, then you might want to look at devising your own online strategy. But how does one tell the difference between objectives, strategies, and tactics? Many marketers are baffled by these terms, mistakenly using them as synonyms. Assume that you want to take a business trip. You may know where you're heading, but you may not know how to get there. For example, every week you drive back and forth between Denver and Colorado Springs, which means you have to make some choices:

- Drive an automobile
- Ride in a chartered or scheduled bus
- Take a commercial or private airplane
- Walk or hitchhike

Now suppose you decide to drive an automobile. Your objective or goal is to get to Denver and your tactic is to drive a car. Your objective might include arriving by a certain time to meet someone. You now have a *revised* objective (get to Denver by nine o'clock to meet someone) and a tactic (with your car).

You still don't have a strategy. You need a strategy or you won't make it by your designated time. You also need additional information.

If you honor the speed limit on Interstate 25, it'll take you about an hour and a half to drive from Colorado Springs to your destination in Denver, unless you get caught in rush hour traffic. Perhaps you need to take into account the traffic flow and possible road construction around the time you plan to travel. Starting at seven o'clock, rush hour will slow you down in most major cities, especially during the week. If you don't leave early and drive at least the posted speed limit, you will not arrive in Denver by nine o'clock. You don't want to speed, because that would be dangerous and illegal, to say the least. You will also want to consider unforeseen circumstances such as running out of gas or having a mechanical failure. Here's how it all fits together.

OBJECTIVES:

- Get to Denver.
- Meet a business colleague.
- Make it there by nine o'clock.

STRATEGIES:

- Arrive in Denver with time to spare.
- Avoid rush hour traffic.
- Avoid the road construction near the city of Castle Rock.
- Circumvent the roadblocks.
- Avoid getting stopped by the highway patrol.

TACTICS:

- Make sure your car is fueled and serviced before leaving.
- Bring a map for alternate routes.
- Bring your AAA auto club card and your digital phone for emergencies.
- Leave early.
- Start your car and drive toward Denver.
- Take Highway 87 rather than Interstate 25 to avoid the construction.
- Drive the speed limit.

What is an objective? A goal you would like to accomplish with your Internet marketing plan.

What is a strategy? An approach to achieving your Internet marketing goals.

What are tactics? Actions you will take during your Internet marketing program implementation.

Traditional Marketing Principles Revised

Now that you can distinguish objectives from strategies, let's look at how different strategies are formulated. Many marketers create strategies based on tried-and-true principles of marketing. These principles are those that they have learned throughout the years, either by formal education or by on-the-job training.

There are some unique characteristics of the Internet that make it appear somewhat confusing to use. The uniqueness is the area that we'll focus on, and we'll see what the Internet marketer can do to ignore the reasoning that occurs as a result.

Revisiting Old Marketers' Tales

Marketers who haven't yet grasped the power of the Internet cling to a few alleged "principles of traditional marketing." As a result, some so-called principles of *Internet* marketing have emerged over the past few years and continue to haunt Internet marketers. These old marketers' tales have these things in common:

- They are based on defective logic.
- They are subject to individual interpretation, often being manipulated to make a point.

By these varied definitions of "marketing common sense," many companies go full speed ahead with their Internet marketing plans, however ill-conceived. Let's review a few false marketing principles that have been given new life and possibly immortality on the Internet.

Principle 1: If You Have Money, You Can Do Anything

Does this mean that big companies will always have success when marketing on the Internet? All you have to do is look at how some well-known giants of Web and traditional marketing are struggling to keep up with customer demand. Once in a while an entrepreneur comes online that is so creative, the bigger enterprises just have to buy him or her out to stay on top.

How about a contrasting marketing principle? On the Internet, insightful Web design or good customer service has no typical dollar amount.

There are no absolute answers to succeeding in the online world. Companies can create a great and exciting Web site with practically no budget at all. Large-budgeted Web sites often fall on their faces, due to some ridiculous oversights. Success in the online world depends on how well the Internet marketing team develops and executes an Internet marketing plan, how well they continue to evaluate, elect and manage staff and outside vendors, and how well they meet or beat original marketing goals. I'd like to revise this old marketers' tale as follows: "If you take the time to plan your Internet marketing program, you will be *more inclined* to succeed, regardless of your budget." My revision won't be quoted on the evening news as a clever sound byte, but it doesn't have to be. You get the idea.

Principle 2: Any Web Site Is Better than None at All

Oh, phooey. Do you really believe this? Remember all the trade shows your company went to at the last minute or for half-baked reasons? Lots of good those sales leads did you. The show was a sloppy fit and despite your best efforts at burning the midnight oil to make it work, you fell short somehow. Your company wasn't ready, your product wasn't ready, or your staff wasn't ready. End of discussion. Now take this example and apply it to any Web site you've ever seen that looked like it was perpetually under construction. Yuck.

Every time I write a review of someone's poorly conceived Web site, I ask myself, "What *were* they thinking? Is it possible that someone gave them bad advice or did they come up with this all on their own?" I'm not talking about sites that are modest because of limited resources. I'm talking about sites that are either impossible to navigate without creating visitor frustration or are missing chunks of crucial information.

Principle 3: All Internet Marketing Activities Must Generate Sales

What if you are still battling about encroachment issues with manufacturers, distributors, and resellers? In this case, your Web site might be better positioned as a public relations vehicle for selected products, rather than an e-commerce one.

Some very successful sites on the Internet are the result of a well-managed PR campaign. These sites don't take sales. They provide information. They promote goodwill. They build readership. They provide a free service. But somehow, these sites impress you because they present an image worthy of your business.

That isn't to say that you can't measure the impact of your PR-oriented Web site on your marketing program. Marketing measurement is a worthwhile endeavor for evaluating the overall effectiveness of your programs, including those on the Internet. You should definitely measure impact, even if you can't measure sales. A well-managed marketing department can install a measurement system that evaluates different aspects of PR activities and recommends future plans of action. Most of the time, however, analysis and summaries are subjective. Public relations is not an exact science. An exact dollar calculation of the impact of image on income is impossible.

Forget about PR for a moment. Image is one thing; sales are another. If you want to prove your Web site generates sales, you are going to have to track where your leads are coming from. If your Web site is set up to accept orders online, and your customers feel comfortable that your secure server is configured to protect their credit card entries and process those orders, then your objectives to generate sales should work. If your Web site does not accept online orders—that is to say, orders are taken by some other method—you will have to install a procedure for determining where those unidentified leads came from. In the majority of companies, zero processes are in place to track how leads turn into sales, which means some hapless souls think they have godlike intuition in determining their next business moves.

PR approaches and measurement doctrines aside, marketing on the Internet *can* result in increased sales for your company. If your management dictates increased sales as an objective for your Internet marketing plan, then you have your objectives already laid out for you. However, many companies choose not to devise strategies based on generating money from a Web presence. A sales-generating Internet presence is no more valid than a presence designed around a public relations, news, or educational model. It's just different. Depending on your market niche, it can be perfectly acceptable to establish an Internet marketing program for the sole purpose of building a reputation or enhancing an established one. It is also perfectly acceptable to change objectives once your Internet marketing program is launched, measured, and evaluated.

Principle 4: Your Major Internet Marketing Objective Is to Copy Your Competitor's Web Site

Imitation is the sincerest form of flattery, right? Well, that's one way to look at it. In fact, every major portal must be secretly applauding its competitors because that's what everyone is doing—imitating each other. There are still so many uncharted areas to discover. Why does everyone have to be all things to all people? This trend in offering online users the same menu of services over and over again sounds like the covenants in a homeowners' association contract:

- Everybody has to have a brown aluminum door on the back porch.

- No one is allowed to put garbage out the night before it's picked up.

- Homeowners may not park more than two automobiles per unit in the common parking area.

These types of rules are useful if you're concerned about maintaining high property values for Mr. and Mrs. Cate and their neighbors. The reasoning on which they are based has no real application in Internet marketing. Have you noticed the trends in Web services?

All over the Web I can get free e-mail, free Internet faxing, free instant messaging, free Web hosting, free lists, free counters, free this and free that. It's getting to the point that I can't tell one so-called portal from another.

You could certainly include the basic Web tools in your offerings, but don't stop there. As long as you know your market, your products, and your industry, don't be afraid to come up with your own way of meeting your customer's needs. Your most successful Internet marketing activities may be those invented while you were sitting around with your colleagues mocking your competitor's programs. We've all come up with some crazy but exciting ideas when we were "just kidding."

There are and will continue to be new ideas for attracting online customers. For example, everyone wants to get customers' attention long before they log onto the Internet. Once they've logged on, you've lost them because they already have a destination in mind. So how do you get them to think about your site before they enter their passwords? One way is to create an application that adheres to a preexisting desktop application such as a browser. By sharing desktop space with an application that's used off-line, you're more likely to be on the visitors' brains when they jump online. Be quick, though. This coveted desktop real estate won't be available for long.

Principle 5: If You Know What You're Looking for, You Can Find It Yourself on the Internet

It is very inefficient to surf on the Net. Search engines never produce the results you're looking for, so you're constantly forced to refine your search, only to eliminate the very sites you wanted to find. Unless you have experience in locating useful market information on the Net, don't hinge your Internet marketing program on what you can dig up in a few short hours. Get some help. You'll be a lot happier if you ask colleagues for referrals to their favorite sites. If you need some data with meat, you may have to pay online search fees to your local information broker to pull up what you need more quickly. Meanwhile, take a class in searching the Internet more efficiently.

Principle 6: Computing Services Should Be Your Primary Contact for All Internet Development Efforts

Please tell me that nobody believes this anymore. A long, long time ago, before the arrival of Internet marketing, this was true. Marketers had to bargain for timely hardware configuration, database development, and even e-mail access to support their day-to-day marketing functions. Therefore, along this same line of thinking, many companies categorized Internet marketing as a technical development effort.

Notice that this old marketers' tale says "primary" contact. Everyone in your company has a stake in the success of your Internet marketing efforts, some more than others. Computing services, the data center, or whatever you call them in your company, are an important part of your Internet marketing team. Regardless, don't relinquish your authority in this area if your company is serious about online marketing.

The authorities on marketing should be marketers, with input from the technical side. The authorities on Internet access should be computer professionals, with input from the marketing side. There is so much overlap between responsibilities in an Internet marketing program that no one department or person should be the primary anything. Except, of course, for the Internet marketing team manager. With any luck, and with a savvy ability to navigate company politics and personalities, it just might be you.

As a team manager, you will direct traffic, and not just the Web kind. Your team will assess what you need done, if it's even possible, how long it will take, and so on. All of the plans, goals, hopes, and dreams for your Internet marketing program must be analyzed in the context of *reality*. You will enlist the aid of the computing services staff in helping your dreams come true. You will tap their knowledge base in hopes of discovering capabilities you didn't even know existed. You will convince them of the importance of meeting marketing milestones and reward them for their involvement. You will respect their opinions. They, in turn, will respect yours.

The success of any marketing effort, whether it involves traditional or new media, lies in the marketer's ability to work from a team approach. If you're a small company, you're not exempt. If you want to launch your Internet presence anytime in the next year and you want it to be an effective one, enlist the aid of at least one other resource besides yourself to put it all together.

Principle 7: Internet Marketing Obtains Faster Results than Traditional Marketing

One of the Internet's biggest selling points has been that it is much faster and easier than traditional means of communicating. Any salesperson who's stood for 12 hours or more on the trade show floor, gulping down breath mints and stretching his or her legs, will have a bone to pick with that reasoning. Let's just say that the speed of Internet communications is relative.

Internet communications are so relatively fast that every newly promoted marketing manager is bragging about how quickly he or she has made contact with the customer base. Everyone is excited about how much easier it is to answer inquiries. Companies are distributing more and more product information on the Internet as time goes by. All this low-cost literature distribution must be a good thing. Eventually, it will result in increased sales.

Some companies are very customer-service-oriented in that they will go out of their way to provide customers with non-Internet options for receiving their product information. Meanwhile, some companies have already lost track of the impact and subsequent value of these other traditional forms of communication. Evidence of the fact that the business world's fascination with new media has gone full circle appears in an increased used of traditional media by Internet-only concerns.

Remember: not everyone is online and you still have to communicate with off-line customers to convince them you're a great reason to get online. When it comes right down to forking over the cash, it doesn't matter if you have your entire catalog up on the Internet. It doesn't matter because several of your customers are not surfing the Internet and won't anytime soon. Yet they still manage to do a good job of reviewing purchases for their companies and families and continue to be satisfied. They read consumer and trade magazines, go to local malls or trade shows to say hello to that tired sales associate or booth staffer, and talk at length to their neighbors and colleagues. The *speed* of Internet communications has no influence whatsoever on these people's buying habits. Now let's look at your customers who *are* on the Internet and discuss why the Internet *still* doesn't obtain faster results than traditional marketing.

While the Internet *can* expedite the *information-gathering* process, it *does not* always expedite the *decision-making* process. Even if the majority of your customers are on the Internet, you still have to deal with other nontechnical matters—human nature, company politics, budgeting issues, and various issues out of your immediate control impact the way in which you communicate with your market.

Most large companies have a decision-making process in place that involves employees, purchasing agents, cost comparisons, and sometimes an approved vendor list. By providing information to these companies in a timely manner, which may or may not include your company's Internet marketing activities, you are helping that process along. Once you have done your job and stated your case, the rest is up to the buyers. You may not gain any points at all by claiming that they got your information quickly at your Web site.

Most families do research, which includes price and features comparisons, when considering the purchase of a big-ticket item. Your company can continue to help sales along by contacting customers and prospects the way they wish to be contacted. You provide product demonstrations and an incentive to come into the local store. Your executives and technical personnel give speeches and lectures at local association meetings. Your sales force meets customers for lunch. Your customer-service department follows up with telephone calls within a few hours. Your Internet faxing service distributes those technical bulletins in a timely fashion. Internet marketing programs some-times come in first, second, or even third in the race to build company sales.

There *are* companies that are reaping the benefits of improved communica-tions through use of the Internet. In some cases, these online marketing efforts produce very measurable results. Internet marketing is very tangible to these companies, as evidenced by their increase in direct online sales. As you know by now, all Internet marketing programs are not alike. Therefore, whether your Internet marketing program produces faster results compared to other, more traditional media is relative. Results in your market are primarily a func-tion of how your company, your industry, and your product are purchased.

Principle 8: Internet Marketing Should, Can, and Will Replace Traditional Marketing Media

Don't get me started. I hope that's not going to happen anytime soon. I enjoy slouching on the couch watching TV commercials and so does my family. We consider them a main form of entertainment at our house because most of them are so funny or cool, and it's nice to sit back and just watch. I want to lay back with a pillow behind my head while in bed and casually watch what's on the screen. I don't want to sit for another moment at my desk in a stiff chair clicking away at screens.

Computers don't meet every human need. Thank goodness. Customer ser-vice isn't the same on the Internet. I can't easily tell the tone of the e-mail reply I received from the customer service department of a well-known Web site. After my third e-mail inquiry into how to change my forwarding address at its site, I'm not sure I want to know.

I cringe when I hear about a company with plans to either bring or force *all* their customers online. Yet I don't want to appear shortsighted. I'll admit that stranger things have happened with technology in a few short years.

Will Internet marketing replace traditional marketing? Radio didn't replace newspapers. TV didn't replace radio. Although, in my house, the computer has *displaced* some of the hours we used to spend with TV, but not all. My daughter and I still cuddle up for a few minutes before bedtime and watch our favorite TV show from underneath the covers. You make the call.

Principle 9: Successful Internet Marketing Requires All Internet Tools, Technologies, and Techniques

I don't think so. Whatever happened to selecting or even offering a tool because it meets a particular need, not just because everyone else has it? Using every Internet gadget or gizmo mainly to prove to the world that you're expertly "wired" is like adding hyperlinks to every other word on a Web page to prove you can do it. As with every other marketing vehicle you'll use, select Internet marketing tools, technologies, and techniques because they are *each* a good and proper fit. That goes for all the free Internet goodies you plan to offer your customer as downloads from your site, too.

Deciding to merge even one Internet tool into your Internet marketing program involves deciding its applicability to the following:

- How your company views its overall Internet marketing objectives and image
- How your product and services are sold and distributed
- How your other marketing programs work together
- How much knowledge and the types of skills your marketing staff possesses
- How much time you want to sleep between midnight and 6:00 A.M.

There are plenty of Web sites that are uncluttered, well designed, and useful to online customers without incorporating a lot of fuss. There are several great tools on the Internet worth using that will make your life easier, and you should consider offering these to your customers from your Web site. There are also plenty of examples of companies that actively use or offer only two or three Internet tools and *still* manage to have an effective Internet marketing presence.

I'm an early adopter so I like to try new things. I dump them when they fail to meet my expectations or immediate functional needs. I have e-mail, instant message, and so on. But each time I visit a new site, it has a different spin on the same type of tool, rather than something new. I don't have to evaluate how many different lines of text I can crowd into my five-line signature block. Remember: Being all things to all people is a difficult Internet marketing strategy to manage. My advice: Keep it simple.

Principle 10: Traditional Marketing Principles Apply to Internet Marketing

There are many lessons to be learned from companies BI (Before Internet). I wouldn't totally discount what lessons you've garnered before then. There *are* traditional marketing principles that can be applied to the Internet. What are they? Let's take a look at a few and evaluate what works online.

"I wish our company could do better at sales, but the competition has beaten us to the punch. Now the only reason they have a big share of the market is because they got there first." How many times have you heard those comments? In traditional marketing, getting a product to market first can be an important step in gain-

ing a major share of the market. Getting there first can mean many other things as well. Just because you can't be the first in your market doesn't mean you can't be the first at creating something unique. This canon also applies to Internet marketing. The Internet offers all kinds of opportunities for "getting there first" because new technologies and approaches to using them are invented every day.

Marketing principle 1. Being first and being unique are equally important. On the Internet, as in the off-line marketing world, ample opportunities exist for you to declare your own niche, regardless of the competition.

"It's very frustrating to do business with them. I'd like to take my money elsewhere, but they're the only ones who sell what I need. They don't have to care." The Internet is growing everyday, with new business entrepreneurs who are great at management, great at attracting financing, but lousy on the creative side. That's why so many people continue to "build a better mousetrap," that is, build on someone else's success. If you're the first one in your market to build a mousetrap, understand that someone will come along to try and top your feat. Understand that if someone in your market built the mousetrap first, you will always find something about *that* mousetrap to gripe about, and in doing so, will have uncovered an open opportunity to top *that* feat. When a company remains the only player in its field for a long time, it can get a swelled head and treat customers with less respect. Sometimes the only thing distinguishing new players from established competition is top-notch customer service and care.

Marketing principle 2. Establish a reputation for good service. On the Internet, as in the off-line marketing world, plenty of opportunities exist for you to lose your customers, especially if you let success go to your head.

"I've liked their products in the past, but this one just isn't as good. I think their biggest problem is that they're in over their heads." There are so many different ways to expand a product line or service offering. It's fulfilling to find ways to extend a market reach. Of course, some ideas are more feasible than others. The most obvious and most successful augmentation of a company's business lies in what it already markets. The company doesn't have to learn a new trade. The sales force is better able to pitch the new products. The technical service department finds it easier to lend support. The customer expects this from you. The customer *wants* this from you. Take advantage of it.

Marketing principle 3. Master the obvious first, then master it again. On the Internet, as in the off-line marketing world, plenty of opportunities exist for you to maintain and improve your current market position by marketing what you already know.

"I agree that there's a need for this product, but it has so many problems. I'd rather wait until the next release than deal with installing it now." Have you ever installed a new software product and wished you hadn't? I look at my computer every day and wonder why a certain piece of software ever made it to market, let

alone to my office. Eventually, I'll get around to uninstalling it, since I can't stand to use it anymore. I've heard that the latest version has all of the features the first one didn't have, and it runs better. It has some new features I never even thought of. At this point, my budget is shot and I'm not in the mood to set up the software again. Maybe later, just not now.

Internet marketers are under a lot of pressure. Marketers in general are under a lot of pressure. The competition is fierce out there. The market appears to be moving very fast, hastened by the excitement of the Internet. In high-technology companies, it's a fact of life that products will constantly be released before their time. Management has a vision. Engineers have a mission. Sales has a quota. Marketers have a Rolaids.

Marketing principle 4. Know when to put on the brakes. On the Internet, as in the off-line marketing world, plenty of opportunities exist for you to rush to market, often before you are ready.

"Well, they used to be a leader in the market, but now they're history. I guess they couldn't or wouldn't adapt." When my daughter was very little, she was very, very active. Occasionally, she would wriggle out of my arms to get down and then bolt out into the street, without a care in the world. She'd often find herself in the middle of the road staring at the front grill of a car that was screeching to a halt. She didn't know how to respond. Rather than get out of the way, she stood paralyzed, much like a deer caught in the path of bright headlights. Believe me, my heart almost stopped a few times as I sprinted to pull her to safety. Being a parent is not easy. For that matter, neither is being a marketer. As with most growing children, my daughter finally adapted by paying attention to the traffic flow, but not before I taught her a little song: "Stop, look, and listen before you cross the street. Use your eyes, use your ears, then use your feet."

In the business world, customers are very, very demanding. Occasionally, your customers will appear to bolt out and purchase your competitor's product without stopping to look at yours. Sometimes they find themselves with a product that doesn't meet their needs. Many times, however, the purchase was a good decision and you have lost a sale, for whatever reason. Your company doesn't know how to respond. Your company doesn't even know why the customer bought the other product. Rather than finding a way to adapt, you stand paralyzed, much like a deer caught in the path of bright headlights. Your mother or father doesn't come to rescue you, so you get run over. In other words, pay attention to your market. Stop and assess your current position. Look at the market. Listen to your customer. Use the facts. Use your instincts. Use your head.

Marketing principle 5. Pay attention to your market and learn to adapt appropriately. On the Internet, as in the off-line marketing world, there exist plenty of opportunities for you to suffer setbacks by not recognizing the trends.

Now, if some aspects of these marketing principles appear to contradict each other, you're absolutely right. Marketing is not an exact science. The art in applying traditional marketing tenets to Internet marketing resides in your ability to balance them carefully when formulating your objectives and strategies. That's where we'll go next.

Tackling Trends, Risks, and Opportunities in E-Commerce

Certain misconceptions continue to exist regarding the rise and fall of entire industries as they relate to the Internet. Let's explore the example of the U.S. Postal Service versus Federal Express.

When FedEx was founded a few decades ago, consumers and industry analysts thought this was the beginning of the end for the U.S. Postal Service. Overnight delivery services simply inspired the post office to offer competitive services but at a substantially reduced price. By and large, the average consumer still continues to value price when it comes out of the personal wallet.

For another example, look at maps. Consumers can stop by a local gas station and pick up a map for a dollar or two, but can get free access to maps posted on the Web. Consumers haven't stopped buying maps. It's still easier for your carpooling companions to unfold a map while riding in the car, rather than hunch over a portable computer balanced uncomfortably on the lap.

Let's take this cost versus service debate one step further. When Web marketers try to determine how to make a Web site presence pay off, they often debate whether to provide Web services using a "free versus fee" comparison. This comparison has different meanings for the business or professional Internet user. For the Internet marketer, advertising placement opportunities mean free access or products can draw more eyeballs. For the consumer, there may be no charge for all or a portion of Web access or product use.

Web Pricing and Payoff Structures

A Web site may choose to offer a product or service free off-line and free online. The following variations on that theme do not resemble any particular company nor should these examples be interpreted to mean that all companies in a particular market niche follow or should follow these patterns.

Giveaway sales literature. Free off-line, free online but sometimes requiring site registration

Shareware distribution. Freely distributed both on- and off-line, but offering varying degrees of functionality or time limits on evaluative use

Banking services. Selected services are free off-line, such as asking a teller to check an account balance, fee or free online with registered Web access

Research services for trademark verification. Fee off-line, fee online

Brokerage houses. Fee off-line, smaller fee online

Daily newspapers. Small fee off-line, free on-line with selected content fee-based

How you choose to price your Web content or product access depends on your individual business goals and market research. Many Internet marketers, concerned about how the Internet will impact traditional pricing and business strategies, are tackling the online world with the same enthusiasm and skills needed to survive in the real world. For example, when establishing their initial Web presence they use many of the same marketing techniques online as they do with traditional media.

For branding, these Web sites prominently display their logo for an established brand, thereby creating a Web site that is a consolidated product to showcase their off-line activities. While their online Web site may not have the same look and feel as their more traditional corporate identity, they quickly learn that branding is an essential element, regardless of the company's position. However, be aware that online branding value can vary among different demographic groups.

For customer service activities, online marketers learn how to take advantage of the unique qualities of the Web, creating a customer-driven experience by offering a technological choice to the visitor (e.g., frames or no frames). Personalized or customizable pages, shopping baskets, and savable shopping lists are becoming the norm for assisting the customer in placing the online order.

In the area of advertising sales, off-line print publishers offer online customers the same opportunity to place an advertisement, perhaps offering a discount to print advertisers. Demonstrating that there's little to no erosion in their off-line sales channel, they routinely combine off-line advertising opportunities with complementary online products. In essence, their Web sites become conduits for regional publications, such as a city edition of the widely distributed classified advertising newspaper, The Thrifty Nickel. Thriftynickel.com is positioned to accept ads online for an established off-line product.

Riding the Internet Wave: Adjusting to Sales Challenges

A classic example of how the Internet was used to restructure a company's sales channels is demonstrated by Egghead.com, now a discount e-retailer of computers, software, and related products. Egghead was previously known as solely a "bricks and mortar" business. Operating since 1984, this company decided to revamp its entire business sales model to take advantage of e-commerce, strategically, before it was too late. A publicly held company, Egghead transformed into an Internet-only retailer in 1998.

Did e-commerce erode Egghead's traditional sales channel or would it soon do so? Egghead made the right moves by eliminating its physical world presence and repositioning itself as an e-commerce vendor. Prior to Egghead's change from real-world marketing to digital-world marketing, its stock valuation was mediocre. By comparing Egghead's past prices with the year of transition, any user of Web-based stock market data can easily see that Egghead executives are making waves in a very competitive space.

How Do You Price Your Products?

Beyond the elementary level of Web site revenue and payoff concerns, there are even more strategies worth addressing. How do you price your products?

Are you accustomed to the status quo of applying fixed prices to selected products, such as groceries? Do you expect customers to continue participating in a shopping experience that includes not only accepting such price stickers, but also paying without question? In a typical retail situation, the customer fills up the shopping basket and checks out. With the possible exception of advertised specials, clipped coupons, and damaged goods, rarely does the consumer challenge the fixed pricing model.

Typically, a company will advertise via traditional media (on the radio, on the TV, or in the local newspaper) and promote products for a significantly reduced price. This advertising and sales technique attracts both first-time and loyal shoppers. The term *loss leader* has also been used to refer to free products with a purchase or two for the price of one. The retailer either loses money or barely breaks even on such products, but needs to offer them in an effort to attract customers. Businesses bank on such customer incentives. In the real world, rarely will a customer drive across town to buy just one inexpensive item and nothing else. You might drive across town to shop at Albertson's or Safeway because one of these grocery chains offers your favorite frozen entree at 25 percent off, but you'll stay to buy your entire list of weekly groceries because it's convenient. Some businesses hope you'll stay because you feel guilty for getting such a steal and you'll be willing to pay market price or more on other products just to make up for it. But not for long.

Online Bidding Games

If your business is dependent on fixed pricing, you'll discover that negotiating is second nature to experienced Web shoppers. Auction houses and bidding services threaten traditional pricing and margins models as well. Web sites such as eBay, zdnetauctions.com, and the auction subdomains of major portals (auctions.yahoo.com and auctions.excite.com) and retailers (auctions.amazon .com), have taken hold recently. These dynamic twenty-first-century business models create concern for businesses accustomed to two things: (1) predicting sales volumes and (2) determining future inventory. Many of the online auction services accept bids starting at more than 40 percent off the manufacturer's suggested retail price. This includes even big-ticket items, such as home theater systems and vacations.

The travel industry is also taking a hit in its traditional pricing models, which has been changed drastically by such companies as Priceline.com. Surplus goods, often disposed of in off-line government auctions or in Army surplus retail stores, are now made available online through such sites as Auctions.com. On June 17, 1999, Sales OnLine Direct announced that a 1951 New York Yankees road jersey, worn by the late Joe DiMaggio, was among the list of sports paraphernalia to be auctioned online. On June 18, 1999, AOL announced its plans to sponsor a week-long celebrity sports auction on behalf of the Special Olympics.

Comparison Shopping Tools

Sales activities are experiencing a shakeout in the online world as well, as consumers are offered more choices than ever before plus an easier way to research those choices. Now, thanks to technology, free online tools offer one-click shopping to the online consumer. Remember the express mail industry I mentioned earlier? There is even a free service that compares prices of the various shipping companies so consumers can save money on sending those overnight parcels—it's called SmartShip.com.

In November 1998, Compare.Net launched its holiday shopping guide that showcases comparison shopping for brand-name retailers including Macys and Sears. LifeShopper.com is a service that empowers the customer with free tools for obtaining competitive quotes, offering consumers an opportunity to save up to 70 percent on term life insurance. EnergyMarketplace.com provides businesses with Internet-based comparison shopping for utility companies including San Diego Gas & Electric, Southern California Edison, and Pacific Gas & Electric.

This trend in online comparison shopping hasn't gone unnoticed. Industry leaders, concerned about competing with variable pricing models, are gobbling up comparison shopping sites in the same manner they've gobbled up other lucrative ventures. For example, Junglee is now a part of the Amazon.com family, under the subdomain of Shop the Web.

For online shoppers who are loyal to Internet directories such as Yahoo.com, this search engine and major portal site offers comparison shopping as well. Its customer-driven features, such as the ability to view products placed in an online shopping basket and the status of an order, speed the purchase process along. Prominent Web features highlight selected vendors, point out seasonal gift giving and specialty merchandise offers, and help drive sales. Finally, Yahoo! offers customers the choice to shop the stores at Yahoo! as well as other stores throughout the Web.

But some critics of portal-based comparison-shopping tools feel that such sites are cheating, because they have a vested interest in promoting their own sites. Critics claim they don't really offer a true picture of comparable products available on the Web. Another comparison-shopping site called Clickthebutton (see Figure 4.1) intends to challenge this alleged conflict of interest and offers consumers a true choice as an independent provider of a new comparison-shopping tool. At ClicktheButton.com, a customer is treated to an interactive demo of a book shopping and comparison engine. The sample search results provide the customer with Webwide comparison shopping for the same title.

The entire pricing structure of products and services is affected by world-wide access to the Internet. The real impact of e-commerce is seen in price stickers that don't stick anymore. When MySimon.com announced its Pocket-Shopper, a downloadable price comparison application for a palm top computer, everything retailers held near and dear changed. No longer can retailers afford to rationalize that the Internet will stay in its corner of the world. Eventually, we'll see more and more customers walking into nearby stores comparing prices in real time for exact products found through a wireless link to the Internet. Yes, the risks associated with maintaining the status quo in product pricing means you're subject to technologically advanced customer scrutiny through price comparison. Those risks are real and exist today.

VENDOR	PRICE	SALES TAX	ITEM
Amazon.com	$104.25	WA	Order
Barnes & Noble	$79.00	NY, NJ, VA & Canada	Order
BooksAMillion	$62.55	AL	Order
BooksAMillion Millionaire's Club	$56.30	AL	Order
Borders	$82.00	MI and TN	Order
BuyBooks	$93.82	N/A	Order

Figure 4.1   In this online Web-based demonstration, Clickthebutton finds the lowest price for a selected book sold by a variety of online booksellers.

Protecting Sales Territories

Beyond price comparisons, the distribution of sales territories have already been affected by the global nature of the Internet. For example, some manufacturers in the footwear industry fear price erosion based on Internet comparison shopping. Currently, select footwear manufacturers are responding by restricting retail outlets from advertising prices for certain shoes on their store-related Web sites.

As industries struggle with the issues of manufacturers' relationships with product distributors, sales reps, and retailers, Internet businesses are finding ways to eliminate the supply chain middleman. This isn't a new phenomenon, as demonstrated in past years by product drop shipments found in the mail-order environment. Eliminating the middleman, as in a retail sales environment or a sales distributor situation, is an activity that both big and small businesses on the Internet are definitely pursuing.

The last, big, driving force in the change in sales distribution channels is the obsolete and now, inexcusable, delays associated with product delivery, delays that severely contradict the Internet's "fast-food" approach to information and product acquisition. For an example, review the hot area of online brokerages. For the average investor, the inability to reach a traditional online brokerage, in an effort to save a plummeting financial portfolio, is now unacceptable. Investors have logged on to Internet brokerages and taken control. According to a news release by CyberCorp, Philip Berber, its founder and CEO, says that the company's new Windows-based application, CyBerX, "will provide real time, direct access execution using an intelligent order routing technology to find the best price for the investor at the exact moment they place their order."

Take a look at the CyBerCorp site (Figure 4.2) to see how it manages its Web presence: CyBerCorp's competitive positioning is enhanced by free software support, training CD-ROMs and online tutorials, and a trading simulator. For quick answers to those customer technical concerns, a backgrounder and FAQ (frequently asked questions) document are within easy reach. CyBerCorp knows how to leverage positive editorial coverage by showcasing it online.

E-Commerce Growth: The Trends

So now that we recognize how sales channels have been affected, how will future trends affect e-commerce over the next five years? Now that we know that the fixed pricing model is under scrutiny, we must be ready and able to adjust our online marketing strategies on the fly, if need be. Any product that is readily available, either online or off-line, is subject to sales channel and distribution challenges over the next couple of years. All of this will continue to be lead by customer-driven empowerment through new technology. For products not as clearly in the line of fire, for example, specialty items, we'll see the electronic commerce opportunities continue to grow and develop.

Figure 4.2 CyBerCorp is an electronic trading technology group that develops high-end, real-time electronic stock trading and execution systems for day traders and active investors.

Now that I may have frightened you about your business future, you may be asking yourself whether small businesses can continue to compete. It seems inconceivable that the "little guys" can succeed in attracting customers if the big guys on the Web are pushing them aside. Have heart. Small business will continue to flourish. Not everyone can compete on price, nor do they want to. Businesses who don't compete on price will find another way to remain in business—perhaps by offering better customer service—faster delivery, extra services, and personalized shopping to instill loyalty. And while I may find it cheaper to purchase a product on the Web, I still believe that the Internet is a poor substitute for a smiling face and a helpful human being. As a social animal, the ability to talk face-to-face with a warm body behind the counter keeps me shopping at my favorite department store whenever I need immediate and friendly product advice. At least once a week, our family drives to the local Borders bookstore in the mall to peruse the shelves. Knowing we get to take the book home with us that night helps us realize that the Web isn't going to replace this family activity any time soon.

Think about the Customer

So now you understand how some e-commerce trends have and will continue to affect your Internet marketing strategies, you need to focus on the critical areas for successfully launching or expanding your online presence. Before you start writing this section of your plan, I have two final ideas on servicing your online customer that will affect how you approach your marketing strategies.

First, Internet marketers must select the right strategies and tactics to build customer relationships and loyalty. For example, if your business niche relies on word-of-mouth marketing, this is where you need to concentrate your efforts. Install Web features that encourage customer referrals or provide unique ways for customers to pass the word easily, such as offering discounts through such sites as GiftCertificates.com. Capitalize on the opportunity to extend sales incentives to frequent shoppers through opt-in e-mail newsletters. This could mean something as simple as offering subscribers-only specials and discounts and bonuses for customer referrals; in essence, providing the customer with a real reason to be loyal to the online brand. Customers like to be treated like royalty. By selecting you from the myriad of Web sites to do business with, online customers are signaling that they want and need your undivided attention.

Second, it is no longer acceptable to continue to publish Web pages that are nothing more than immobile clones of off-line sales literature, nor is it acceptable to believe that users will allow you to dictate the online experience. And for many of us who spent the last five years repurposing our off-line literature for the Web, organizing content the way we saw fit, this is a scary proposition. Customer-driven Web sites and related off-line tools will continue to attract and empower Internet clientele. As an online marketer, you may feel like you're being stripped of traditional control over the sales process by incorporating Web site functions that automate activities. Accept that online users can be categorized by their interest in "doing it my way." Accept that you need to adjust your Web site marketing strategies and your Web development efforts to meet their voracious "back-seat driving" needs.

Establishing an Internet Marketing Vision

In this section, you will brainstorm and begin to formulate your online marketing strategy (Figure 4.3). You will think about the trends in your market, what your competitor is doing, and how your company can respond. You'll also think about your customer's needs that have gone unfulfilled and how you might address them. For this section, it's a good idea to have the following materials ready for reference:

- Your traditional marketing plan, if you have one
- Competitive literature
- An organized bookmarks file of competitors' Web sites

- Industry analyst reports
- Studies and reports from industry associations and organizations
- A stack of trade publications to skim through

Instructions

- ◆ Review your company's traditional marketing plan.
- ◆ Review your competitors' literature for an indication of their objectives.
- ◆ Browse your competitors' Web sites to review their About This Company pages.
- ◆ Review industry analysts reports for statements about market trends and case studies.
- ◆ Review trade publications for features on market trends and case studies. Pay particular attention to quotes and interviews by company officials.
- ◆ Review trade publications for features on companies on the Internet. Pay particular attention to quotes and interviews by company officials.
- ◆ Fill in this form using bullets, brief statements, or a combination of the two.
- ◆ Use the answers to draft the next section of your Internet marketing plan.

Name 10 marketing objectives that your competitors hope to accomplish with their marketing programs.

Competitor's Name   **Marketing-Objective Statement**

In the above list, circle all objectives that match your own, whether for traditional or Internet marketing.

Figure 4.3   Phrasing your marketing communications strategies.

Name 10 objectives that your market in general hopes to accomplish in the next year.

**Area Definition
(marketing, technical, other)**   **Objective Statement**

In the above list, circle all objectives that match your own, whether for traditional or Internet marketing.

Name five opportunities that no one else in your market has explored.

Area Definition   **Marketing Objective**

In the above list, circle all objectives that your company can reasonably tackle, whether for traditional or Internet marketing.

Figure 4.3   *(Continued)*

Check off all the objectives you circled that your company can reasonably achieve this year, whether for traditional or Internet marketing. Now think about how you can modify these objectives to create your own unique image online. Draft a succinct paragraph that explains your company's objectives for its Internet marketing program.

_____

_____

_____

_____

_____

_____

_____

_____

_____

Briefly state your strategies for achieving the above objectives.

_____

_____

_____

_____

_____

_____

_____

_____

Figure 4.3 *(Continued)*

Summarize how the use of the Internet will strengthen your overall marketing goals.

_____

_____

_____

_____

_____

_____

_____

_____

_____

Completed by: _____ Date: _____

Figure 4.3 *(Continued)*

Forming the Internet Marketing Task Force

If you do outsource, pay for performance. Also, hire
experience or be willing to invest in your staff.
Kevin Johansen, CEO of 4WORK, Inc.

This chapter covers several activities involved in selecting and evaluating members of your Internet marketing task force or team. I don't assume you are operating a small, medium, or large company, but I do believe that you will need some degree of help in creating and maintaining your online presence. Regardless of your company's size, there are several options available, from technical support to Web design to online promotion and so on.

In Chapter 3, Analyzing Internet Market Statistics, you examined and investigated Internet demographics, geographics, and so on, using data that was both general and industry-unique to your situation.

In Chapter 5, Forming the Internet Marketing Task Force, you will learn to evaluate the capabilities of your in-house staff as well as a variety of outside service providers, regardless of the task put before them. After evaluation, you will be better equipped to make recommendations on the formation of your Internet marketing task force. This chapter will make up section four of your Internet marketing plan.

Section Four: Forming the Internet Marketing Task Force

Including data that reinforces your decision to market on the Internet best supports your Internet marketing plan. Section five of your Internet marketing plan may include any combination of the following:

- Recommendations on task force leadership
- Suggestions for different staffing options
- Capability statements and bids from outside vendors and service agencies
- Brief job descriptions of required additional staff
- Salary estimates for new hires or internal promotions
- Costs on both outsourcing Web hosting and maintaining it in-house

Getting the Most out of This Chapter

The activities in this chapter include comparing and contrasting one or more options for carrying out your Internet marketing program. Review these options with your colleagues, coworkers, human resources department members, personnel administrator, and/or upper management. There may be some individuals currently employed within your company who have the skills needed to assist you in your program. If you are a small business with a limited budget or even a company that is more inclined to hire and promote from within, consider this: You'll instill loyalty if you offer job skills training to existing personnel.

If you still find that you need to hire new faces or even rent temporary talent, start gathering recommendations on interactive agencies, Web design boutiques, computer consultants, and so forth. Don't forget that the Internet is a great place to locate Web presence providers as well. Use it to review portfolios and obtain apples-to-apples bids via e-mail.

Do We Want to Farm This Out or Not?

Why would you use employees to implement your Internet marketing programs? For too many companies and individuals trying to make an online living, this question is a "no-brainer." There are no funds to hire outside help, so you *have* to do everything in-house. That's where your creativity and business acumen really comes into play. Fortunately, there are tons of free or low-fee based options for businesses without the staff to manage all the details and aspects of an Internet marketing presence. But even large companies should consider keeping *some* Internet marketing projects in-house, especially when internal personnel issues such as career opportunities, existing skill sets, and avoiding the employment "revolving door" are at stake here.

Why would you use outside services to implement your Internet marketing programs? That's truly the $64,000 question: to outsource or not to outsource. It takes a lot of dedication to get an Internet marketing presence off the ground. You need to explore what all these different Internet presence providers can offer.

Before you decide one way or the other whether to outsource, ask yourself these questions.

Self-Evaluation

1. Do you personally have the time to develop Web pages, monitor online discussions and news, and so on?
2. Do you actually like performing Internet marketing activities?
3. Can you manage additional duties without siphoning too many hours from valuable business management time?
4. How does the addition of Internet marketing activities fit in with your current workload, interests, career goals, or skills? Are you overloaded now?
5. How well do you manage your time?

Staff Evaluation

1. Does anyone on your marketing staff or in your company have the time to take on added responsibilities?
2. Have you asked him or her how these activities might fit in with current workload, interests, career goals, or skills?
3. Is there anyone else in another company department who could assist you, even temporarily?
4. How do these activities fit in with his or her current workload, interests, career goals, or skills?
5. How does this employee's supervisor feel about loaning or transferring this employee?

Policy Review

1. What is your company policy for hiring new employees, temporary personnel, or outside vendors?
2. Will delays in hiring delay your launch of a vital aspect of your Internet marketing program?

Information Technology Review

1. Is your computing services department experienced in configuring Web server software?

2. Does it have the time to adequately maintain an in-house Web server, in addition to all its other responsibilities?

3. Does your computing services staff value your Internet presence, enough to make staff available 24 hours a day?

4. How reliable is your computing services department when it comes to system outages?

If you're in charge of proposing whether to hire additional staff and/or outside services, you'll need to know both sides of the argument (see Figure 5.1). We'll presume that you're considering hiring someone or some agency to handle the marketing part of Internet marketing. I'll shoulder the devil's advocate role as we review this issue from both sides of the fence.

Everyone has a different opinion about whether you should assign all or none of your Internet marketing responsibilities to an employee or an outside specialist. Your best choice is to evaluate the options and propose your best plan of action, which is almost always some combination of the two. You may decide that only certain activities should be hired out. Outsourcing is rarely an all-or-nothing proposition.

If you manage a marketing staff, discuss your Internet marketing plan with them in great detail. Offer interested employees the choice to retain some or all implementation activities—*especially* if interest, skills, and time are on your side.

If your marketing department has experienced layoffs recently, this might not be a good time to suggest additional projects. If you're in a hurry to beat your competitor to market, you might stumble as you scramble to get there first. So, here is one important consideration: Employees in other parts of your company may be your best answer (Figure 5.2). Burned-out, long-time staffers often need to change jobs or take on different responsibilities in order to help them refocus. These loyal crewmembers could be your best Internet marketing asset, since who else but current employees understand your company's unique needs?

In Favor of In-House Development	**In Favor of Outsourcing**
On-site employees are easier to manage.	*Outside agencies require less supervision.*

Figure 5.1 In-house versus outsourcing comments we've all heard.

In Favor of In-House Development	In Favor of Outsourcing
Outside agencies cost money.	*Employees have other responsibilities.*
Outside agencies have no respect for budget.	*Employees have no concept of cost overruns.*
The company doesn't have a big budget.	*The agency is willing to negotiate.*
Using current employees will save money.	*Using outside agencies will save time.*
Employee salaries and wages are already a given.	*Agencies use fewer people for the same work.*
Employees already know the company and products.	*Outside agencies already have the skill set.*
The market is full of HTML editing tools.	*A software package doesn't make you a designer.*
Employees can be trained in HTML.	*Novices can make embarrassing mistakes.*
In-house employees are more trustworthy.	*In-house employees never meet deadlines.*
Management wants us to hire and promote within.	*Outside consultants can offer on-site training.*
If anything goes wrong, the agency's to blame.	*If anything goes wrong, the employee's to blame.*
If anything goes wrong, marketing's to blame.	*If anything goes wrong, the agency's to blame.*
Hiring a vendor requires bids and paperwork.	*Using an in-house employee requires staff hours.*
Our last outsourcing project was a disaster.	*You hired the wrong agency or consultant.*
Employees respect the chain of command.	*Agencies know whom to talk to to get things done.*
Temporary personnel services can solve this.	*All the best people are already employed.*
Outsourcing makes the marketing staff obsolete.	*Outsourcing makes the marketing staff look good.*

Figure 5.1 *(Continued)*

Which functions are handled by your marketing communications department? (Check all that apply.)

- ❑ Advertising
- ❑ Co-op programs
- ❑ Public relations
- ❑ Other: _____

- ❑ AV production
- ❑ Corporate identity
- ❑ Sales support
- _____

- ❑ Collateral materials
- ❑ Direct mail
- ❑ Trade shows
- _____

_____   _____   _____

_____   _____   _____

_____   _____   _____

How many hours per week does your average marketing employee work?

_____

How many hours per week can your department devote to Internet marketing activities? _____

Can you devote enough time with current personnel to complete major portions of your Internet marketing program within a reasonable period of time?
❑ Yes ❑ No ❑ Unsure

Has your company or department been downsized lately? ❑ Yes ❑ No

If yes, how has that affected your department's mood, enthusiasm, or workload?

_____

_____

_____

How will employees react to added responsibilities in Internet marketing?

_____

_____

_____

Figure 5.2 Evaluating in-house resources.

Does anyone in your company have any Internet marketing–related skills that you can tap?

❑ Yes ❑ No ❑ Unsure This can be further answered by: _____

_____

If yes, list these company employees.

Employee name   Internet marketing–related skill or activity
_____   _____
_____   _____
_____   _____
_____   _____
_____   _____

Circle all employees above who are in your marketing department.

Check off all Internet marketing–related activity *not* covered by the above employee review.

❑ Audio conversion   ❑ CGI scripting   ❑ Copywriting
❑ Domain name selection   ❑ Forms design   ❑ Graphic design
❑ HTML   ❑ Java scripting   ❑ Literature conversion
❑ Plan development   ❑ Market research   ❑ Promotion
❑ Scanning services   ❑ Server installation   ❑ Site hosting
❑ Staff training   ❑ Video conversion   ❑ VRML
❑ Web design   ❑ Other (list below): _____

_____   _____   _____
_____   _____   _____
_____   _____   _____

Circle all the above functions that can be implemented in-house with the proper training.

Figure 5.2 *(Continued)*

What training or educational options are needed to keep these activities in-house?

Function	Training or education	Provided by	Training cost
_____	_____	_____	_____
_____	_____	_____	_____
_____	_____	_____	_____
_____	_____	_____	_____
_____	_____	_____	_____
_____	_____	_____	_____
_____	_____	_____	_____
_____	_____	_____	_____

Incorporate this additional cost information into your Internet marketing budget.

Completed by: _____ Date: _____

Figure 5.2 *(Continued)*

HIRING STAFF MEMBERS

The Internet has spawned a wealth of new job titles over the years. There are new careers in just about every aspect of creating an online presence—from the Internet Marketing Manager at a major corporation to the New Media Director at a Madison Avenue advertising agency. If you are responsible for hiring, training, and/or managing new staff members, you'll need to define the scope of the individuals' duties within your department. The best way to become familiar with the skills needed to succeed in a fast-paced Internet-driven company is to check out online job postings. At a variety of Internet job sites, I found listings for the following open positions:

- **Director, Internet Computing Strategies**
- **Internet Advertising Sales Manager**
- **Internet Application Specialist**
- **Internet News Researcher**
- **Internet Business Consultant**
- **Internet Marketing Director**
- **Internet Recruiting Specialist**
- **Internet Research Analyst**
- **Internet Sales Specialist**
- **Internet Web Site Developer**

- Manager of Internet Commerce
- Online Media Planner/Buyer
- Online Promotions Manager
- Program Manager, E-Business
- Senior Vice President, Internet Strategies
- Vice President, Internet Marketing
- Web Programmer

Most of these job titles are variations on established corporate themes—perhaps targeted at marketers and technical specialists who've added the Internet to their skills set and senior-level executives who've learned to specialize in new media. Some new and interesting job opportunities appeared as well, obviously directed at potential job candidates who are able to think "out of the box." My accompanying commentary notwithstanding, such unusual career paths demonstrate the Internet's unique impact on our business culture.

Ad Watcher—Internet (Get off that TV couch and start surfing for competitive online campaigns!)

Affiliate Launch Manager (What better way to generate revenue without building an in-house sales force?)

Community Developer (You're tasked with rounding up and catering to those elusive affinity groups.)

Internet Café Worker (One hopes that intoxicated patrons are the exception.)

Internet Evangelist (Be ready and willing to preach to the unconverted few.)

Internet Wizard (A sorcerer's apprentice need not apply.)

InterNut (No, it's not a typo! Sleep is probably a nonrequisite.)

Strategic Internet Marketing Thinker (Finally, a title worthy of an Internet Savant!)

Web Interface Specialist (Just what would this person be handling—people, content, or technology?)

Web Developer Guru (No, a specialist wouldn't do, here. You would have to be more proficient than that.)

Lord Overseer of Portals (Okay, I admit I made that one up. But it could happen!)

For some more fun, visit the page titled "Job Titles Of The Future" at www.fastcompany.com/online/resources/jobtitle.html. Here, you'll see such bleeding-edge job designations as Chief Energizing Officer, Chief Imagination Officer, Content Guy, Director of Bringing in the Cool People, Messaging Champion, Necessary Evil, and VP of Progress.

(Continues)

HIRING STAFF MEMBERS   *(Continued)*

At such sites as CareerBuilder.com, you can find job titles and descriptions for the following tamely titled, sample positions.

Job Title: Web Developer Guru

Location: New York, NY

Job Category: Internet/New Media

Description: Exciting online start up seeks individual with Oracle Certification and at least two years minimum experience in Web site and database development.

Job Title: Community Developer

Location: Dallas, TX

Job Category: Internet/New Media

Responsibilities: Monitor, develop, and participate in defined online communities. Assist in planning and staffing scheduled live events. Respond with personalized replies to incoming subscriber e-mail. Screen all member-submitted content. Gather, analyze, and report on consolidated member data.

Qualifications: Basic understanding of HTML and CGI scripting. At least one year of community experience managing and moderating e-mail discussion lists, bulletin boards, and/or chatrooms. Good writing skills with some sales and or marketing experience helpful. Strong organizational skills and the ability to multitask a big plus. Customer service experience is helpful.

As you can see by these two previous examples, today's fast-paced Internet-driven company doesn't value so-called longevity (whatever that means in Internet terms) as much as it values skills. A few years ago, 10 years or more in marketing could peg you as a veteran in some circles. Today, an Internet veteran is often defined as anyone who was online when the World Wide Web was launched.

Other valued Internet employee assets include initiative and attitude. Having worked in high technology for a while, I also know that Internet start-ups often prefer employees with an ability and willingness to work long, ridiculous hours for a small initial payoff and the promise of a bright future. So much for people who have a life.

With the shortage of available qualified personnel to choose from, you'll have to figure out how to position your company as *the* place to work. And don't forget that these career sites are as much for job seekers as they are for companies with positions to fill. Once you've identified the type of person and skills you need, post your job openings online in a variety of career-oriented areas.

Determining Staff Salaries

Deciding what to pay new employees can be a challenge, especially when you have to compete for qualified candidates with all the new and exciting Internet start-ups that emerge every day. Some typical, but general salaries are listed online at such sites as workingwomen.com.

On ZDNet's SalaryZone at zdnet.com/enterprise/salaryzone, touted as the compensation resource for Internet professionals, you'll get a better idea of what the budget hit will be for Internet marketing talent. For example, a survey of Internet professionals under the category of "online marketers" indicated that the majority of respondents (19 percent) were earning $29,000 to $35,000 USD per year, 11 percent were earning $36,000 to $40,000 USD, and 9 percent were earning $41,000 to $45,000 USD.

If you're the founder of an Internet start-up, salary may be your only concern . . . at least for a while. The survey indicated that 51 percent of respondents received a salary and not much more. Twenty-three percent confided that their stock options, bonuses, and other company benefits amounted to an additional $18,000 to $23,000 above their base salary.

Some Activities You Can Do Now

1. Go to your favorite Internet job or career site. For example, I searched Interscape's database at jobvertise.com, the Monster Board at jobsearch.monster.com, and jobs.internet.com.

2. Using a wide variety of keyword and key phrases, search for job listings similar to positions you plan to fill. At jobs.internet.com, I found a listing under *Job of the Week*, which is how I discovered what one company valued as qualifications for a director of sales candidate. I also searched for Internet-related marketing positions in Colorado Springs. None were available so I registered for a "Personal Search Agent," so the search wasn't a total loss. The site responded with "as matching positions are identified you will be sent an e-mail notification."

3. Create a job description for your potential job candidates based on a combination of Internet skill sets and your own unique needs.

4. Estimate a reasonable salary range for this new position based on industry studies, interviews with colleagues, and/or online job postings.

You won't find exactly what you need online for every new media job in your company, especially if your company is breaking new ground with regard to Internet applications. Still, job-related Web sites are a good start. If you have the inclination, some off-line job resources, such as the *Dictionary of Occupational Titles*, often found in the reference area of your public or academic library, can sometimes be useful in creating succinct job descriptions. The

Complete Searchable DOT is available for purchase from theodora.com/dot_index.html.

Who Will Bake the Bread?

Once you've decided on the bodies you'll need for your Internet marketing venture, you need to assign responsibilities. Use the worksheet on forming an Internet marketing task force (Figure 5.3) to list who will do what, including specific job titles, and so on. Remember, job descriptions in any Internet-driven company are meant to be flexible, so don't get hung up if you don't find the exact person to fill the position you thought you needed.

Evaluating Outside Vendors and Services

Before you begin looking for outside help, be very clear about which services you need. You'll find that prices for services vary greatly. If you are willing to trade some autonomy for price, you can obtain many online services for free.

The Internet marketing task force will be managed by (list in order of authority):

_____

_____

_____

Do you plan to hire additional employees?   ❑ Yes ❑ No

Our company/department will:

Hire (number) _____ of permanent employees

Job title: _____ Salary/wage/hours: _____

Job title: _____ Salary/wage/hours: _____

Job title: _____ Salary/wage/hours: _____

Job title: _____ Salary/wage/hours: _____

(For hourly employees, estimate the total number of hours per week dedicated to Internet marketing.)

Figure 5.3 Forming the Internet marketing task force.

Hire (number) _____ of temporary employees

Job title: _____ Salary/wage/hours: _____

Job title: _____ Salary/wage/hours: _____

Job title: _____ Salary/wage/hours: _____

Job title: _____ Salary/wage/hours: _____

(For hourly employees, estimate the total number of hours per week dedicated to Internet marketing.)

Use current employees only.

List company employees who will be included on the Internet marketing task force. (Include all marketing and technical personnel, as well as those individuals who will join your team from other company departments.)

Name	**Department**	**Internet Marketing Responsibility**
_____	_____	_____
_____	_____	_____
_____	_____	_____
_____	_____	_____
_____	_____	_____
_____	_____	_____

Completed by: _____ Date: _____

Figure 5.3 *(Continued)*

Here is a selected list of common Internet marketing services that are performed either in-house or by outside agencies.

Internet Marketing Services

- Audio conversion
- CGI scripting
- Copywriting
- Domain name selection

- Forms design
- Graphic design
- HTML (Hyper Text Markup Language) programming
- Java scripting
- Literature conversion to HTML
- Marketing plan development
- Online market research
- Online promotion
- Scanning services
- Server installation
- Site hosting
- Site integration
- Staff training
- Video conversion
- VRML (Virtual Reality Markup Language) programming
- Web design

Working with Computing Services

If you are a marketer without much experience in the technical aspects of the Internet, or even computers in general, you may feel somewhat intimidated when it comes to discussing your program with your company's computing services personnel. Perhaps you feel that they really don't understand what you are trying to accomplish. Or you feel that you won't understand them.

I'm not going to guess what type of relationship you have with these technical colleagues, but I do believe that the proper attitude goes a long way in enlisting their support. Perhaps part of this concern is due to an issue of authority. Perhaps company management has decided that computing services will be your primary contact for all Internet marketing development projects.

Here's some advice on working with Internet services, LAN (local area network) support, database development, or other computing services departments. If you treat computing services as the ultimate authority in deciding how to approach your marketing program, then you might as well go into another line of work. On the other hand, if you tell computing services that you want this form, that programming, this capability, and that server, without regard for their expertise, work flow, and other responsibilities, take a number.

If you treat computing services staff members as know-nothing outsiders who just fill your order, then you *will* have a primary contact . . . for failure. And I won't blame them one bit.

So just in case the hair on the back of your neck is standing up at the thought of working with those same people who helped you recover that file last month, here are two tips:

- Don't discount the unlimited amount of knowledge these midnight engineers have amassed over the years.

- Don't let them discount yours.

Evaluating Internet Service and Web Hosting Providers

If you find that in-house computing services personnel are unable, or even unwilling, to meet your needs for Internet marketing, you may have to look elsewhere for technical support. This quest may include evaluating and selecting an Internet service provider (see Figure 5.4).

Several Internet resources can provide you with leads for either Web hosting or Internet provider services. Here's a short list:

- *Boardwatch* Magazine's Directory of Internet Service Providers at boardwatch.internet.com/isp/

  You can search this directory, acquired by Internet.com, by state and telephone area code. It's fairly comprehensive—I was impressed to discover how many new ISPs serviced my city of residence.

- HostReview.com

  At this Web-hosting directory and search engine, you can search for Web hosts according to the features and price you want, retrieving specific information on different providers.

- Web Developers Corner at www.rtcservices.com/wdc/host.htm

  Here you'll find a comparison chart of services for about a dozen providers, including such details as start-up costs, monthly fees, megabytes of storage, traffic restrictions, and additional services.

If you prefer using a consultant in developing your Internet marketing program, here's a short list:

- National Consultant Referrals, Inc. (NCRI) at referrals.com

  Select consultants from the drop-down menu on the home page and click on the go button. This service offers you referrals at no charge, as found in its talent bank of skill descriptions.

Instructions

- ◆ Contact individual service providers and/or your colleagues to complete this form. The more viewpoints the better.
- ◆ Copy this form for each ISP you wish to review.
- ◆ Complete more than one evaluation per ISP and average the results.

Name of Internet service provider _____

Web URL: _____ E-mail address: _____

List the services this Internet service provider offers:

_____ _____ _____ _____
_____ _____ _____ _____
_____ _____ _____ _____
_____ _____ _____ _____
_____ _____ _____ _____
_____ _____ _____ _____

Rate each of the following:

Customer-service responsiveness

          Low   **1**   **2**   **3**   **4**   **5**   **6**   **7**   **8**   **9**   **10**   High

Customer-to-staff ratio

          Low   **1**   **2**   **3**   **4**   **5**   **6**   **7**   **8**   **9**   **10**   High

Downtime and outages

          Low   **1**   **2**   **3**   **4**   **5**   **6**   **7**   **8**   **9**   **10**   High

Experience level

          Low   **1**   **2**   **3**   **4**   **5**   **6**   **7**   **8**   **9**   **10**   High

Figure 5.4 Internet service provider evaluation.

Features and services

       Low   **1** **2** **3** **4** **5** **6** **7** **8** **9** **10** High

Pricing

       Low   **1** **2** **3** **4** **5** **6** **7** **8** **9** **10** High

Speed and connections

       Low   **1** **2** **3** **4** **5** **6** **7** **8** **9** **10** High

Technical support

       Low   **1** **2** **3** **4** **5** **6** **7** **8** **9** **10** High

List hours: _____ A.M. to _____ P.M.

Circle days that you can reach a human by phone:

      Sun. Mon. Tues. Wed. Thurs. Fri. Sat.

Other (specify): _____

       Low   **1** **2** **3** **4** **5** **6** **7** **8** **9** **10** High

Other (specify): _____

       Low   **1** **2** **3** **4** **5** **6** **7** **8** **9** **10** High

Other (specify): _____

       Low   **1** **2** **3** **4** **5** **6** **7** **8** **9** **10** High

Other (specify): _____

       Low   **1** **2** **3** **4** **5** **6** **7** **8** **9** **10** High

Other (specify): _____

       Low   **1** **2** **3** **4** **5** **6** **7** **8** **9** **10** High

Overall quality of this ISP (this answer is an average of the above answers):

       Low   **1** **2** **3** **4** **5** **6** **7** **8** **9** **10** High

Completed by: _____ Date: _____

Figure 5.4 *(Continued)*

THE BUSINESS CARD LITMUS TEST

Every ad agency, PR firm, and marketing consultant in America has hung out a shingle advertising Internet marketing services and expertise. There you sit, not knowing the difference between FTP and STP (one goes in your car). You know you need help, but how do you separate true Internet marketers from Internet expert wanna-bes? Here's a quick and easy way to uncover fakers at your next business social. Fade in to a COMDEX cocktail party. Sounds of happy conventioneers and loud rock music is heard from a nearby hospitality suite.

Tom: We've been advising our clients in how to use the Internet more effectively. I'd be interested in discussing with you how we can meet your business marketing needs.

Kaitlyn: Really? Do you have a business card? [*She takes card and notices the corporate identity confusion.*] I see you have a Web site, but why are you using your AOL address for incoming e-mail? Why don't you use your registered domain name?

Tom: Uh . . . my new cards are being reprinted as we speak.

Kaitlyn: So, you just started doing Internet marketing?

Tom: Oh, no. We've been online for years. But our technical guy hasn't figured out how to forward our incoming mail to our AOL accounts yet.

Kaitlyn: Why are you using AOL? Can't you just pull in your mail with something like Eudora? I mean, the AOL e-mail address doesn't impress me much from a marketing standpoint.

Tom: [*starts sweating*] Well, our employees like the AOL interface.

Kaitlyn: Yeah, but sending e-mail from an AOL account doesn't help your agency's online branding, especially since you're trying to build a reputation as Internet-savvy.

Tom: Most of our established customers are used to that address and we don't want to confuse them.

Kaitlyn: Uh-huh.

Tom: Our ISP doesn't have local dial-up access in the cities where our account executives travel. Most of our people don't have laptops and it's easier to access e-mail remotely this way.

Kaitlyn: Did you know that you could sign up for a Web-based e-mail account that allows you to specify the reply-to address as your own? Some let you pull in e-mail from POP accounts and then back out again when you return to the office.

Tom: [*shaky voice*] We do use Web-based e-mail for our outgoing mail, but I guess I should look into that reply-to thing you're talking about. Well, I'm new to the firm but they've used all the Internet tools. I thought my AOL address would be easier to remember. Here, let me write down my Internet address for you. [*He writes his numeric address @compuserve .com.*]

Kaitlyn: [*tentatively*] Uh, okay, but you're still not using your agency's domain name. So who hosts your actual Web site?

Tom: Well that's really the technical guy's area. I'm into the marketing end of things.

Kaitlyn: How long have you personally had an Internet account?

Tom: Two years.

Kaitlyn: [*raises left eyebrow*] Is there someone else I can talk to about your agency's capabilities in Internet marketing?

Anything less than a couple of years with direct, hands-on, in-depth Internet experience for someone claiming to be an expert in this field is unacceptable. But it doesn't stop there. Some individuals, despite their "longevity" on the Internet, still don't get the simplest of marketing basics. For example, why would you ever want to brand someone else's domain name rather than your own? That's what you do every time you send an e-mail with someone else's domain name in the FROM field.

And when did anyone on the company side ever care about an agency's in-house technical issues, that is, enough to excuse incompetence? Agencies or marketing consultants can either use the Internet effectively or not. If not, how can they possibly convince anyone that they know what they're doing in the marketing realm?

Then there's the issue of which new Internet tools exist now and how to use them more effectively. I once read that the majority of software users only employ a small percentage of available application features. If that's true, using that fact alone would be a great way to unearth just how Internet-savvy a traditional advertising agency has become.

Keep in mind that no one becomes an expert overnight, or even by association. Furthermore, an Internet marketing agency that either doesn't have or doesn't use its own domain name isn't worth the paper its business card is printed on. Period. And any so-called Internet marketing guru, who flaunts a hard-to-remember, multidigit, CompuServe address is too absurd to even acknowledge. Online tools have been a strategic part of marketing research and communications for years. Consequently, online experts have a history of working in this medium long before Internet surfing was in vogue. Ask your agency rep or consultant-to-be how long he or she has been using online tools, what kind, and for what purpose.

(Continues)

THE BUSINESS CARD LITMUS TEST *(Continued)*

Be wary of the Internet access or service provider who's suddenly moonlighting as a marketing specialist. Access providers are mainly in the business of selling Internet connect time, leased lines, and associated services; they are not in the business of providing marketing advice.

Internet marketing agencies and consultants should have a background that includes a balance of Internet and marketing communications experience. Quiz candidates on the differences between using traditional and online media. This critical conversation should reveal a mastery of the Internet, marketing strategies and tactics, and how the two fit together.

In any industry, experts often make their mark by publishing and speaking at industry conferences. Have senior executives from this agency or has this consultant been published in the area of Internet marketing? Look for a byline on a magazine article or book or a listing in an upcoming seminar brochure. Hiring an Internet marketing expert and accompanying help translates to the bottom line: Can you trust this professional to meet your needs in the most efficient way possible?

Updated and based on an original opinion piece by Kim Bayne appearing in *Business Marketing* magazine, Dec. 15, 1994, 79 (12): 9. Reprinted with written permission.

- Consulting Women Web Site at consultingwomen.com

  This is a network of women consultants in the greater Washington, D.C., area who have joined together to offer their skills and expertise. Given that the Internet is a global media and we are all becoming more accustomed to working in a virtual office environment, I would encourage you to explore this site's resources. This site is organized well, segmenting areas of expertise by topic, such as marketing.

- The Expert Marketplace at expert-market.com

  This online database catalogs over 200,000 firms involved in different aspects of consulting. If your Internet marketing project is for less than $50,000, you can get instant free access to the database by completing a brief Web-based form.

Selecting an Internet Marketing Agency

If you've decided that you need a turnkey operation for your Internet program, you may be ready to evaluate an Internet marketing agency (Figure 5.5). There are just a few ground rules to consider:

Instructions

Interview your professional colleagues and the Internet marketing agency's client contacts to complete this form. The more viewpoints the better.

Copy this form for each Internet marketing agency you wish to review.

If you are missing information, contact the agency directly to fill in the gaps. Ask them for additional references.

Complete more than one evaluation per Internet marketing agency and average the results.

This form may also be used to evaluate independent consultants and Web design boutiques.

Internet marketing agency: _____

Contact information: _____

Person being interviewed: _____

What percentage of your company's Internet marketing activities are handled in-house or outsourced?

_____ % in-house   _____ % outsourced

How long have you been working with this Internet marketing agency?

Weeks _____ Months _____ Years _____

Were you the person responsible for selecting this Internet marketing agency?

❑ Yes, by myself.   ❑ Yes, as part of a team.

❑ No, I inherited this agency.   ❑ No, someone else hired them.

How many other Internet marketing agencies did you or your company interview before you hired this one? _____   ❑ None, they were the only one contacted.

Figure 5.5 Evaluating an Internet marketing agency.

How long has this agency been:

In business? _____

On the Internet? _____

Does this agency have its own e-mail address?

❑ Yes, it is: _____   ❑ No

Does this agency have their own Web site?

❑ Yes, it is: _____   ❑ No

What is the mix of technical to marketing expertise at this agency?

_____ % technical background   _____ % marketing background

Would you consider this a good balance?   ❑ Yes   ❑ No

If no, why not? _____

_____

Respondent: Rate these statements on a scale of 1 to 10, with 10 being the highest. Do you highly agree or highly disagree with each of these statements regarding your Internet marketing agency?

This agency has a lot of experience in my industry.
   Strongly disagree **1   2   3   4   5   6   7   8   9   10** Strongly agree

This agency is very careful about not taking on competitive accounts and would not design a Web site for a competitor of mine while working on my account.
   Strongly disagree **1   2   3   4   5   6   7   8   9   10** Strongly agree

They know what I'm trying to accomplish on the Internet and work well within those parameters.
   Strongly disagree **1   2   3   4   5   6   7   8   9   10** Strongly agree

They have a diverse and impressive roster of currently satisfied clients.
   Strongly disagree **1   2   3   4   5   6   7   8   9   10** Strongly agree

Figure 5.5   *(Continued)*

They are able to adapt to any style on the Internet, as shown by examples of their work, in order to meet my needs or corporate personality.

Strongly disagree **1 2 3 4 5 6 7 8 9 10** Strongly agree

They provided me with several client referrals whom I was able to contact and interview to help support my hiring decision.

Strongly disagree **1 2 3 4 5 6 7 8 9 10** Strongly agree

They have both the ability and the interest to service any size account, big or small.

Strongly disagree **1 2 3 4 5 6 7 8 9 10** Strongly agree

They exhibit an equal degree of professionalism, regardless of the account size.

Strongly disagree **1 2 3 4 5 6 7 8 9 10** Strongly agree

This agency always completes my projects on time.

Strongly disagree **1 2 3 4 5 6 7 8 9 10** Strongly agree

Account executives warn me well in advance of any deadline problems so that I can make other arrangements.

Strongly disagree **1 2 3 4 5 6 7 8 9 10** Strongly agree

This agency respects my expertise and never tries to make me feel that I don't understand marketing.

Strongly disagree **1 2 3 4 5 6 7 8 9 10** Strongly agree

I rarely, if ever, have any miscommunications or misunderstandings with this agency's staff.

Strongly disagree **1 2 3 4 5 6 7 8 9 10** Strongly agree

This Internet marketing agency currently offers all the services any company would need to implement an Internet marketing program.

Strongly disagree **1 2 3 4 5 6 7 8 9 10** Strongly agree

The agency rarely outsources projects or portions of projects to other agencies or consultants.

Strongly disagree **1 2 3 4 5 6 7 8 9 10** Strongly agree

Figure 5.5 *(Continued)*

This Internet marketing agency has a strong staff with excellent skills and experience.

   Strongly disagree **1** **2** **3** **4** **5** **6** **7** **8** **9** **10** Strongly agree

This Internet marketing agency has retained a loyal staff and they do not experience much turnover.

   Strongly disagree **1** **2** **3** **4** **5** **6** **7** **8** **9** **10** Strongly agree

This Internet marketing agency has account executives that are always available whenever I need assistance.

   Strongly disagree **1** **2** **3** **4** **5** **6** **7** **8** **9** **10** Strongly agree

My opinion of this agency's account executives is that they are courteous, helpful, and resourceful.

   Strongly disagree **1** **2** **3** **4** **5** **6** **7** **8** **9** **10** Strongly agree

This Internet marketing agency prices its services fairly, competitively, and consistently from project to project.

   Strongly disagree **1** **2** **3** **4** **5** **6** **7** **8** **9** **10** Strongly agree

This Internet marketing agency doesn't low-ball bids to land projects or accounts and rarely has cost overruns as a result.

   Strongly disagree **1** **2** **3** **4** **5** **6** **7** **8** **9** **10** Strongly agree

This Internet marketing agency came highly recommended by a personal colleague of mine.

   Strongly disagree **1** **2** **3** **4** **5** **6** **7** **8** **9** **10** Strongly agree

Overall reputation of this Internet marketing agency (this answer is the average of the above answers):

   Low **1** **2** **3** **4** **5** **6** **7** **8** **9** **10** High

Completed by: _____ Date: _____

Figure 5.5 *(Continued)*

- Know exactly what you want and what you're going to get *before* you sign on the dotted line.
- Make sure both your company and your agency agree on the deadlines.
- Get plenty of recommendations and see plenty of examples of the agency's work.

If you're looking for an interactive marketing agency or a traditional advertising agency that has expanded its capabilities, here is a short list:

- The U.S. Creative Directory at uscreative.com

  From the home page you can search by keyword or locate a multimedia agency in the Atlanta area, if that is your preference. The U.S. map graphic lets you click on your state for an immediate list of possibilities in such areas as advertising, media, printing, graphic design, graphic support, illustrators and artists, photographers, photography support, multimedia/Internet.

- Agency ComPile at agencycompile.com

  This site offers online work samples from listed agencies. Currently there are over 1,200 profiles online. A quick search allows you to research by agency, client, or individual name.

Hiring a Web Boutique

Before you decide *who* to hire, you should decide *what* you're hiring the person for. If you've already identified Web page development as one of the services you plan to outsource and you don't feel you need a big agency to meet your needs, look at a smaller shop to handle some of your Web development projects. You can use the agency evaluation form to evaluate a Web design boutique or similar service firm.

Once you've selected a Web boutique, start requesting bids on services. Before you can get bids, understand what you need or want for your Web site. You'll also need to understand what you can afford. There are a variety of price ranges on the Internet for Web development options, anywhere from free to fee to high fee.

It's getting harder and harder to find someone who will actually tell you up front what a typical Web package costs. Many agencies dance around this issue until you're worn down with defining your requirements. But you need a starting point, especially if you don't want to keel over from sticker shock.

Some smaller Web boutiques can create a nice entry-level five-page Web site for under $500. If you want something fancy, like CGI scripting, you'll have to pay more or search for free scripts on the Web to install.

For small businesses, here's a place to start: Banana Graphics at banana-graphic.com (Figure 5.6). Here is a quick look at its current pricing, which you can use to get an idea for what it costs to develop a very simple Web site.

- For $115.00, a Personal Page includes 1 Web page, up to 3 graphics, 1 e-mail link, and up to 1,000 words of text.

- For $275.00, a Starter Site includes 2 Web pages, site navigation links, 5 hyperlinks to other sites, 1,000 words of text per page, up to 3 graphics per page, and up to 3 e-mail links.

- For $495.00, a Full Site includes 4 Web pages, site navigation links, 6 hyperlinks to other sites, 1,000 words of text per page, up to 3 graphics per page, and up to 4 e-mail links.

- For $695.00, a Deluxe Site includes 8 Web pages, site navigation links, 10 hyperlinks to other sites, 1,000 words of text per page, up to 3 graphics per page, up to 4 e-mail links, and 1 form page.

Sometimes deciding how big you want your site to be is like putting the cart before the horse. I'd recommend that you do the following:

1. Define user and market needs.
2. Specify content.
3. Decide what's reasonable to launch within the next three months.
4. Make a short laundry list of your immediate needs.

Once you've done these four things, you can start shopping around for someone to develop your site. More about this later in the book.

Meanwhile, to get another feel for what you can expect to pay, check out NetMarketing's Web Price Index at netb2b.com/wpi. This resource, updated monthly, provides information on what you can reasonably expect to pay for your online presence. For example, in the June 1999 edition of WPI, you can

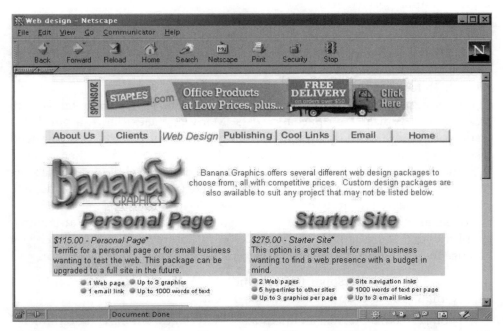

Figure 5.6 Banana Graphics offers several different Web design packages with competitive prices.

find that the median price for developing a community site is $45,000 USD, with a low of $5,000 and a high price tag of $175,000. A very helpful aspect of this site is its case studies of what a sample company might need for each project. The Web Price Index rate card even details what you can expect to pay for such services as database programming, Java/shockwave, strategy formulation, CGI scripting, design, copywriting, and basic HTML.

Hiring a Graphic Artist

If you need only some graphics designed for your Web site, you could hire out this portion of your program to a graphic artist. It helps if that artist has the following qualifications:

- Knowledge of various file formats
- Ability to create simple as well as detailed graphic banners for your Web site needs
- Equipment resources, such as scanners for flat artwork, photos, slides, and transparencies
- Connection to the Internet
- Willingness to do work for hire

If you don't know what *work for hire* means, you're in for a big shock. A work-for-hire agreement means you had a job, you bid it out, and the person you hired completed the work on your behalf. As long as you pay your bill, you have met your obligation. Copyright ownership of the work is now yours. You may reproduce it and modify it at will.

Some graphic artists and photographers require you to sign a copyright statement up front stating that you have only initial rights to the art or photos. Subsequent reproductions or use requires additional fees. If you're purchasing one-time reproduction rights from a photographer or stock photo agency that has previously created the work, this situation is totally understandable and acceptable. After all, you're asking to use work that was produced for another purpose and whose original concept you had nothing to do with.

However, if you own the logo the artist is incorporating into your Web design, if you plan to supervise the development of new graphics for your site, or if you own the product the photographer is shooting, you have a right to demand a work-for-hire agreement. There are just too many hungry artists and photographers out there who can do a good job and are willing to let you own what you pay for.

Now that you've made some preliminary decisions about the whats and wherefores of your Internet marketing team, it's time to move on to implementation concerns. Up next: Designing Advertising and Direct-Mail Campaigns.

Implementation: Fitting the Internet into Your Marketing Communications Mix

Designing Advertising and Direct-Mail Campaigns

Our Web site and our banner ads have a consistent look and feel.
They identifiably belong to each other.
Brian Alpert, Manager, Telogy Networks, Inc.

In Part One of the Internet marketing plan, Creation: Building Your Internet Marketing Plan, you developed the first section of your Internet marketing plan.

In Chapter 2, Preparing the Business Overview and Executive Summary, you created an introduction that set the stage for your program.

In Chapter 3, Analyzing Internet Market Statistics, you reviewed different Internet marketing demographics and surveys, selecting applicable statistics, and applied them to your company's target market.

In Chapter 4, Formulating Marketing Communications Strategies, you discovered why your company wants to market online and determined company-, product-, and market-specific strategies.

In Chapter 5, Forming the Internet Marketing Task Force, you made managerial decisions regarding the composition of your Internet marketing team and wrote an assessment of your team's organization for your plan.

Introduction to Part Two: Implementation

In Part Two of the Internet marketing plan, Implementation: Fitting the Internet into Your Marketing Communications Mix, you will continue to write your Internet marketing plan. You will also keep track of additional expenses needed for your budget. We'll have a chapter on budgets later on in the book.

In Part Two, we will discuss the options for fitting the Internet into your marketing communications mix. The programs you select in Chapters 6 through 13 will comprise the next section of your Internet marketing plan.

Chapters in this section include the following:

Chapter 6. Designing Advertising and Direct-Mail Campaigns

Chapter 7. Utilizing Collateral Materials/Sales Literature

Chapter 8. Developing a Corporate Identity

Chapter 9. Conducting Market Research

Chapter 10. Executing Public Relations and Promotional Programs

Chapter 11. Incorporating Sales Support Functions

Chapter 12. Planning Trade Shows

Chapter 13. Measuring Internet Marketing Results

Internet and Traditional Marketing: The Perfect Marriage

There are two main ways to marry your traditional marketing to the Internet:

1. Integrate the Internet into your marketing communications mix.

2. Integrate your marketing communications mix into the Internet.

Any bricks-and-mortar retailer who uses its Web site to draw customers to its mall store and uses in-store coupons to attract visitors to the Web demonstrates an example of this type of integrated marketing at work. For example, during a recent visit to a local bookstore, the help desk person offered me a discount coupon good for purchases made through the store's secure Web site. While surfing for craft project ideas on the Web, I found an Internet coupon that is good for use in a retailer's national outlets. (See Figure 6.1.)

What Exactly Does This Involve?

The majority of users, or for that matter, your off-line customers, are not going to know that you're on the Internet unless

- You tell them yourself, through your on-line and off-line advertising and PR efforts.

- You tell them through a third party such as through listings placed in printed or Web directories.

- You let others tell them for you, because word-of-mouse marketing has the clout you need.

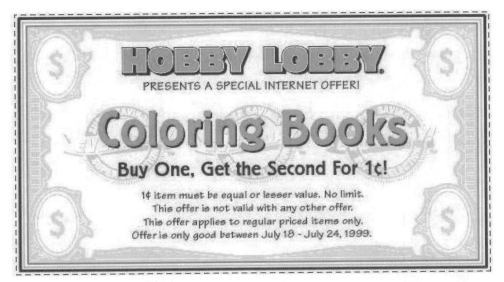

Figure 6.1   Hobby Lobby supplies a Web link to and/or e-mails an embedded graphic with a coupon to opt-in e-mail list subscribers. The coupon can be printed out for use at one of its local stores.

- You let luck be the guide, since some customers are interested enough to plug your company name into the browser, add a "dot-com," and it happens to be your domain name.

No single approach to advertising your online presence will work. You must tap into everything, wherever and whenever you can.

Reminders of the Blatantly Obvious

"Advertise that you're advertising," that's what I always say. And since the Web is a jam-packed marketing and sales vehicle, you must tell people how to find you online. Include your e-mail address and Web URL in every traditional marketing activity you manage. Be ready and prepared to reproduce your URL on anything that comes your way in the future. I'm talking about every little piece of paper, every scrap of cloth, every reproduced photograph, every audio or video production, and every physical object within your reach (Figure 6.2). Consider ordering a batch of temporary rub-on tattoos for the forearms of your employees, especially if your company name is Harley-Davidson. Still not sure what I mean? You'll get plenty of help in Part Two.

Suggestions for the Not-So-Obvious

In support of your marketing communications program, you may have relied strictly on resources that were available only in print. Now you can reduce

```
        THE DISNEY STORE
   Atlanta Airport #706 (404) 762-3800
        http://www.disneystore.com

       43 CASH-1        8674 0706 201

   WMNS S/L WVN/CHMBR          19.00
   421017421143
   WMNS S/L WVN/DENIM          19.00
   421017422393
                  SUBTOTAL     38.00
       GA 7% TAX               2.66
                  TOTAL        40.66

                            $40.66
```

Figure 6.2 The author's receipt from the Atlanta Airport's Disney Store provides a subtle reminder of this entertainment company's online presence.

your marketing budget in selected areas simply by taking advantage of the wealth of free information found on the Internet. Throughout Part Two, you will find out about some of these resources that are designed to make your traditional marketing communications life much easier.

Find new places and ways to publicize your Internet presence that you haven't included in your programs until now. This could mean developing and distributing an interactive software program on disk that just happens to promote your Internet presence while it's introducing a new product. Or it could mean something entirely different. Still not sure what I mean? You'll get plenty of help in Part Two.

Uncover ways to enhance your traditional marketing communications program by using the Internet as an automated partner. This could mean offering a scheduling function on the Web to editors who you might meet in person at a conference. It could involve allowing your in-print advertisers the opportunity to place advertising insertion orders through a secure form on the Web. Or it could mean something entirely different. Still not sure what I mean? You'll get plenty of help in Part Two.

Think about how you can use the Internet to point to your traditional marketing communications activities. This could mean posting your show schedule on the Web as a reminder that you are exhibiting in various locations throughout the year. Or it could mean something entirely different. Am I being a bit vague? Keep reading.

Section Five: Internet Marketing Program Implementation

Chapter 6, Designing Advertising and Direct-Mail Campaigns, begins Part Two of the Internet marketing plan, the segment on implementation. Here is where we get down to brass tacks about how to use the Internet and advertising together. As part of your advertising responsibilities, get ready to select which activities to include in your Internet marketing plan. Include costs associated with each activity in your budget. If you are in charge of actually purchasing different types of media for your company's advertising program, then you are already familiar with the duties associated with advertising planning and placement. This chapter will contain some review material for you. If you have never placed advertisements for your company before, you will begin to develop a basic understanding of traditional print advertising.

In this chapter you will become familiar with different aspects of advertising and direct mail as it appears on the Internet. Advertising, being a subset of Internet marketing, assumes many different forms. You can pay for placement of a graphical ad banner at someone's Web site, you can sell advertising on your pages, and you can pay for a brief text-based message to be included at the beginning of a mailing list digest, to name just a few. There are even opportunities for you to advertise on the Internet without spending any money at all. This chapter contains a brief overview of these options, along with tips for developing this section of your Internet marketing plan.

What This Section of Your Plan Might Include

Including all data that reinforces your decision to market on the Internet best supports your Internet marketing plan. This next section of your plan may include any combination of the following:

- Brief paragraphs on each advertising expenditure
- Your rationale for selection of advertising programs
- A discussion of how each activity complements your overall program
- Strategic ideas for launching a program to accept banner advertising at your site
- An assessment of the impact of your Internet advertising on your traditional advertising

Media Planning with Internet Resources

If you're responsible for media planning, your library or office probably contains the following:

- Bulging files of advertising media kits
- Rat-torn, thick volumes of *Standard Rate and Data Service*
- Sample issues of your favorite publications
- A disk and/or print subscription to your favorite media directory

You gathered these resources by the following methods:

- Telephone calls or faxes to a publication's regional advertising manager
- Postcards sent in from direct-mail postcard decks
- Luncheon meetings sponsored in your city by the publishing company
- Subscriptions purchased with marketing communications funds
- Materials brought in from your home or your previous job
- Lists of regional or neighborhood Web sites where you can get the most bang for your local advertising buck
- Former advertising left in your office by another manager before he or she took that promotion

Nothing replaces having your own finely tuned media list, whether you use it for advertising, public relations, or both. Today you can enhance your advertising planning activities by using the Internet to create a new media list or to enhance one already in use. The result may be a cost saving in the traditional advertising portion of your budget.

A few newspaper networks offer software to facilitate the planning process. Search the Web and you'll find a newspaper rates and data database of U.S. dailies that you can search by circulation and state, online media kits, or an ad placement service that allows you to submit both insertion orders and materials on the Internet.

Several sites include pointers to media-kit libraries for major consumer magazines. Such Web directories also include telephone and fax numbers, e-mail links to ad sales departments, and links to available online media kits.

Traditional Advertising and the Internet

How is advertising on the Internet different from traditional advertising? Furthermore, how is it similar? Webmasters are usually referred to as Internet publishers mainly because it's a text-based medium. There are video and audio capabilities on the Internet, but the current technology doesn't support their transmission as well as broadcast media does (e.g., television and radio). Therefore, I've limited my comparison of the Internet to print media. Take a look at how print is compared to two of its online cousins: mailing lists and Web pages (Figure 6.3).

Print	Internet
Subscriptions and Circulation Records	
Subscriptions are ordered by mail, direct mail, association memberships, publisher's reps, and telephone calls to toll-free numbers, accompanied by a delay in receiving first issues; individual copies are regularly purchased from newsstands and at checkout lanes; local newspapers are delivered in person by newspaper carriers.	Subscriptions are ordered to mailing lists by sending an e-mail message to the list server; subscriptions or registrations at Web sites are usually instantaneous, with forms completed and submitted on the spot for subscriber access.
Circulation lists include subscriber names and addresses, with city, state, and country; circulation lists are used frequently for direct-mail purposes without subscriber's direct consent.	Mailing lists include subscriber e-mail addresses and sometimes subscriber names; lists are rarely used for commercial purposes without subscriber's consent; Web sites that require registration frequently compile e-mail addresses for bulk e-mail activities.
May be distributed free, via controlled circulation, or by paid subscription.	The majority of mailing lists are distributed free of charge; selected electronic newsletters have subscription fees; electronic versions of print editions vary in price; the majority of Web sites are free to visit; some Web sites limit free access to registered visitors.

Figure 6.3   Print advertising versus the Internet.

Controlled circulation publications prequalify and regularly requalify free circulation lists via reader surveys or qualification cards; readers who do not provide complete data risk being deleted from the publication's subscriber list.

Mailing lists usually do not prequalify or renew readers; multiple bounced messages should trigger removal of subscribers from distribution list; the majority of Web sites do not requalify their visitors or require registration to continue access; requalification of a sort may occur through user-transparent software.

Market Demographics

Outside service bureaus, such as the Audit Bureau of Circulation, verify actual subscriber numbers for many magazines; subscriber audit reports for these types of publications include breakdowns in job titles and other demographics.

Outside service bureaus rarely audit mailing list demographics; outside service bureaus, such as the Internet Audit Bureau, may audit hits, clickstreams, and other aspects of Web site visitors; a variety of server-side software packages audit Web sites as well.

Editorial Calendars

Editorial calendars are usually planned and printed in advance to aid the placement of ads in special or focused issues as well as public relations efforts.

Editorial calendars do not exist for the majority of mailing lists, electronic newsletters, or Web sites; those resembling an off-line print edition are the exception.

Figure 6.3 *(Continued)*

Readership Surveys: Retention and Interest

Publishers do not know exactly which articles have been read and which ads have been seen unless they survey the readers immediately after the issue has been distributed; readers may not always remember exact details.

Webmasters can find out exactly which pages users visited, how long they stayed, which pages they clicked in which order; where they came from before visiting the site, which ad banners they clicked on, and so forth; all of these options require prior system installation of some type of clickstream log-analysis tool.

Advertising Insertions and Premium Positions

Premium ad positions may include front cover, back cover, spine, bellyband, or special sections; page positions may include upper right-hand corner, lower right-hand corner, etc.

Premium ad positions for mailing lists are limited to headers and footers; Web sites may offer special positions on selected pages but limit graphics to tops and bottoms of pages.

Specially printed inserts, such as business reply cards, may be bound or included in issues.

Web sites are linked to ad banners; files can be attached to mailing lists, but are rarely included.

Insertion-order closing dates coincide with publication schedules, such as a few days, weeks, or even months prior to the date of issue.

Advertisements are usually accepted anytime and can be run immediately if space is available.

Figure 6.3 *(Continued)*

Mechanical Specifications

Mechanical specifications for ads may include printed copies of ads, pasted-up layouts, film negatives; some publishers accept file formats.

Mechanical specifications for Web ads include graphical file format; list messages are usually text, sent to the list owner by e-mail.

Materials for advertisements may be black and white or color; preprinted advertiser inserts allow even more leeway.

Materials for advertisements are not color-based for mailing lists; materials for Web site ads may be as high as 256-color.

Consecutive ad-page placements are common; full-page ads and fractional ads may be placed.

Consecutive page placements are encumbered by the visitor's choice of links; only the Internet equivalent of "fractionals," a portion of a page or a header, are available; by definition, on the Internet a full-page ad is your own home page.

Artwork is usually sent to the publisher via mail or overnight courier; publishers accepting file formats allow the advertiser to upload files to an FTP directory or deliver it on disk, but they must usually follow up with a print of the advertisement by regular mail or courier.

Artwork is usually uploaded to an FTP directory or sent to the Web site attached to an e-mail message.

Figure 6.3 *(Continued)*

Advertising Sales

Recognized ad agencies may take a 15 percent commission on placements; in-house agencies deduct 15 percent from the ad space costs.

Ad agencies, whether independent or in-house, may still have to negotiate for commissions with most Webmasters and list owners.

Advertising sales offices for national publications are sometimes located worldwide.

Advertising sales office is usually located in the same city as the Webmaster or list owner; Internet ad brokers may serve as sales brokers for placements; geographically diverse sales offices are unnecessary on the Internet.

Reader Service Inquiries

Reader service inquiries are forwarded to the advertiser.

Visitor inquiries culminate in a mouse click and a transfer directly to the advertiser's Web site.

Advertisers know from which magazine their reader service labels came; incoming telephone inquires and trade show booth visits require human intervention to determine the source.

Log-analysis tools, such as referral logs, identify the domain name of the visiting user; cookies can identify even more; Web sites that require passwords know exactly who is visiting.

Figure 6.3 *(Continued)*

Now for a Few Definitions

If you're not familiar with advertising on the Internet, here are some definitions to get you started.

Ad Banners

Banners are those small graphical rectangular or boxlike colored elements placed on Web pages (Figure 6.4). Banners may appear on either the top or bottom of the page, or both. Usually, the Webmaster who accepts an ad banner placement will include some wording near the graphic to encourage visitors to "click here" or

Shell Chemical Company
*Never underestimate what we can do together.*SM

Figure 6.4 Shell Chemical Company uses a clean animated banner layout with a boldly colored URL to attract visitors to its online catalog.

"visit our sponsor." Additionally, Webmasters will include an alternate description in the HTML code for those users who either do not have graphic capabilities or have deselected the image-loading function of their browsers.

Good Web marketers wish to maintain a consistent look throughout their marketing programs, so they will usually select a theme that blends in well with their image. At times, a traditional marketer "let's her hair down" when she takes her company online. In a recent ad banner promotion for Procter & Gamble's Gain laundry detergent, interactive agency iMC2 used the Enliven/Impact rich media solution to create a "scratch and smell" ad campaign. (Figure 6.5)

Good Webmasters wish to maintain a consistent look throughout their sites, so they will usually provide some parameters for banner specifications. Some sites are very particular about specifying banner sizes, while others allow some leeway for individual variations. The size of an ad banner will vary with the Web site it's placed on. Some typical banner dimensions, in pixels, are as follows:

400 by 40

460 by 55

468 by 60

230 by 33

A few Web sites and banner exchanges limit banner dimensions to 400 by 40 in order to guarantee a uniformity of sizes among advertisers. The banner exchanges specify these dimensions in order to leave room for the attachment of a logo on every banner placed. There are also restrictions on file sizes in order to minimize download time. Some sites will put restrictions on the number of colors (maximum of 64 or perhaps 256), as well.

But now that I've outlined the basic banner dimensions, I have to admit that a new variation in online advertising crops up every day (Figure 6.6). Banner ads aside, America Online has a unique position in the online advertising arena, offering a placement on its logon screen (Figure 6.7).

Hyperlinked Banner

The majority of banners placed on Web pages contain a link to the advertiser's Web site for additional information. This link is actually HTML code within

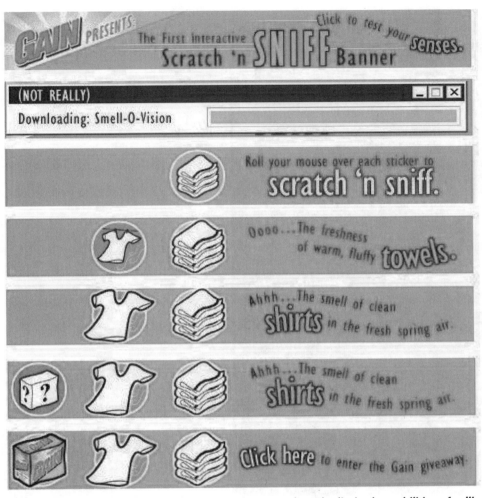

Figure 6.5 Gain presents a tongue-in-cheek approach to the limited capabilities of selling products electronically.

the document. The code allows the user to jump to another Web location by clicking on the linked banner. The ability to transport to the advertiser's Web site is the primary advantage of most ad banners over other forms of advertising, but you'll soon find out that clickthrough is not the only reason to place ads.

To call attention to ads at their site, Webmasters have the option of putting a border around a banner by specifying this preference in the Web page code. The appearance of a border outline could affect your rate of clickthroughs from your ad. But then again, so could just about anything.

Figure 6.6 Capitalizing on its strong traditional branding, American Express promotes its SkyGuide with an unusual banner height and width.

Clickthrough Ratios

This represents the number of times a user has actually clicked on your ad banner to visit your site. Some ad networks report this as a percentage of total appearances of the banner. A clickthrough ratio of 12:43 would mean that 12 people clicked on the banner out of 43 that viewed it. A clickthrough ratio of 24:43 would show better results, since your purpose in advertising is to attract visitors. The Link Exchange at www.linkexchange.com reports clickthrough statistics to its members in this format:

```
We have registered 4322 visits to your site.
You have been advertised on other sites 2161 times so far.
You have received 31 visits through your banner.
This gives you an exposure to click-thru ratio of 69.7:1.
```

Clickstreams

This is the path that the user has taken through your site. Clickstream analysis can contain any number of variations, including the length of time a user spent on a page and where he or she went upon leaving the site. Users are still concerned about the privacy issues associated with compiling such data, and can be reluctant to really roam around your Web site if too much tracking interrupts and derails surfing anonymity.

Headers

This term can refer to a mailing list, also known as an e-mail discussion group. In reading the multiple messages distributed by lists, subscribers use different systems and different e-mail programs. As a result, graphics are not usually attached to or included in the messages distributed by lists. While this may change in the future, currently a list advertiser or sponsor places text for an ad to be inserted in the header or footer of e-mail list messages.

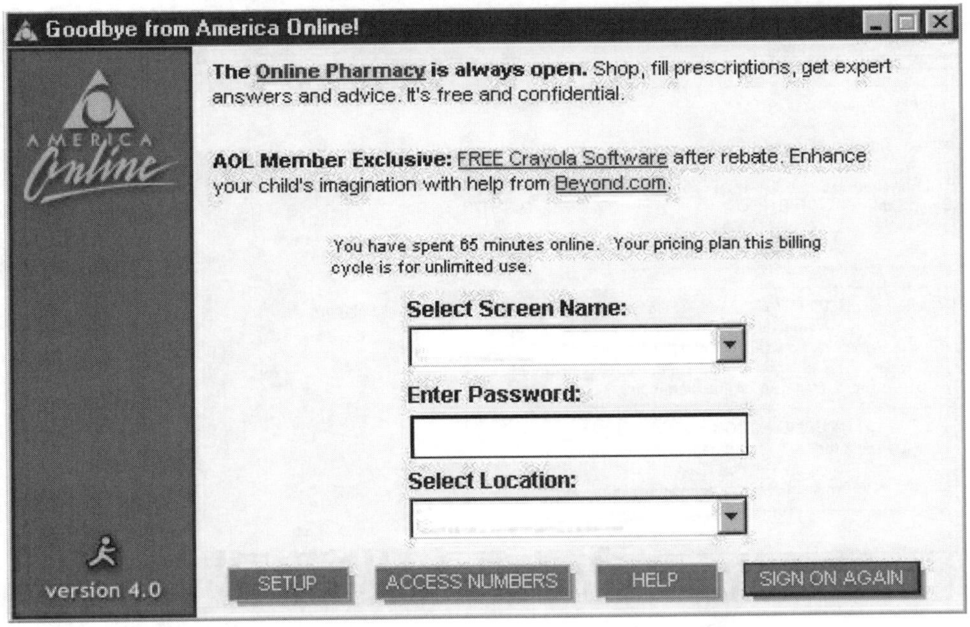

Figure 6.7 Beyond.com and Crayola take "center screen" through the logon window of the AOL software.

The amount of text available for a message varies with the list. Sometimes a paragraph of up to 10 lines is available to the advertiser for an advertising message (Figure 6.8). Usually, this paragraph is attached to the beginning or end of the list digest. A digest can be a consolidation of all the single messages posted to the list over a predetermined period. Advertisements placed on digest headers receive a lower frequency than those ads placed on single messages. However, ads on single messages are usually shorter.

As demonstrated, advertisements on the Internet consist primarily of two main types:

1. Text-based advertising
2. Graphics-based advertising

Text-based advertisements take copywriting skill; however, they are the fastest to implement. Create them by rewriting or repurposing content from preexisting advertisements and changing the writing style or length to fit the Internet audience. Enhance the copy with a "grabber" or headline to get the reader's attention if the Webmaster or list owner allows it.

Text-based advertising can consist of any of these possibilities:

1. E-mail messages containing advertising copy
   a. Messages created in response to a request for information
      (1) ASCII-based text files stored in an online directory

```
matthew@maven.co.il                    http://www.maven.co.il
- - - - - - - - - - - - - - - - - - - - - - - - - - - - - - - - - - - -
Maven, The Virtual Know It All

Toll Free from USA: 1-888-472-7635 x169    Global Fax: 1-212-214-0553
Direct Dial: +972-2-568-9169               Israel Fax: 568-9173
- - - - - - - - - - - - - - - - - - - - - - - - - - - - - - - - - - - -
              * The Jewish/Israel Index *

YOUR TICKET TO ISRAEL- WIN A FREE TRIP EVERY WEEK AT www.vjweek.com
                    Virtual Jerusalem
              -- We're Everything Jewish Online --
    News. People. Israel. Living. Torah. KotelKam. Shops.
              http://www.virtualjerusalem.com

                  PUBLIC ACTION NOTICE
    Demand the Release of the Imprisoned Iranian Jews
                  Sign the Petition Now!
          http://www.vjnews.com/iranpetition.htm
```

Delete   Prev   17 of 185   Next   Help

Figure 6.8 The Maven Announce list publicizes Virtual Jerusalem's Israel trip giveaway in an August e-mail newsletter sent to 11,000 subscribers.

        (a) FTP files available for downloading

        (b) Text inserted automatically into a response generated by a mailbot script or program

    (2) Manually created e-mail messages

        (a) Reused boilerplates from other text files

        (b) Customized sections of the message to personalize it

        (c) Personalized responses created entirely from scratch

  b. Posts to appropriate newsgroups, lists, and forums

  c. Signature blocks within e-mail messages

  d. Sponsorship sentences or paragraphs placed in the headers or footers of a mailing list

  e. Text-based promotions on the login screen of commercial service providers

2. Descriptions of your site on other Web sites, with or without hypertext links

3. Hypertext links on other Web sites, with or without graphics

4. Content at your own Web site in various forms

  a. Documents converted to HTML

  b. Text-only files linked to your Web pages, such as list digests

  c. Scrolling text displayed through Java script on a browser bottom or in the middle of a Web page

Graphics-based advertising can consist of any of these possibilities:

1. Graphics files attached to e-mail messages

2. Graphics files incorporated into downloadable software or demo disks, such as screensavers and search engine applications

3. Graphics files on Web sites

  a. Logos or icons on other Web sites with hypertext links

  b. Banners on other Web sites with hypertext links

4. Banners at your own Web site in various forms

  a. Logos or icons within your site directing visitors to other parts of your site

  b. Advertising banners within your site directing visitors to other parts of your site

5. Banners or logos in off-Web software, such as those found in a customizable application (Figure 6.9)

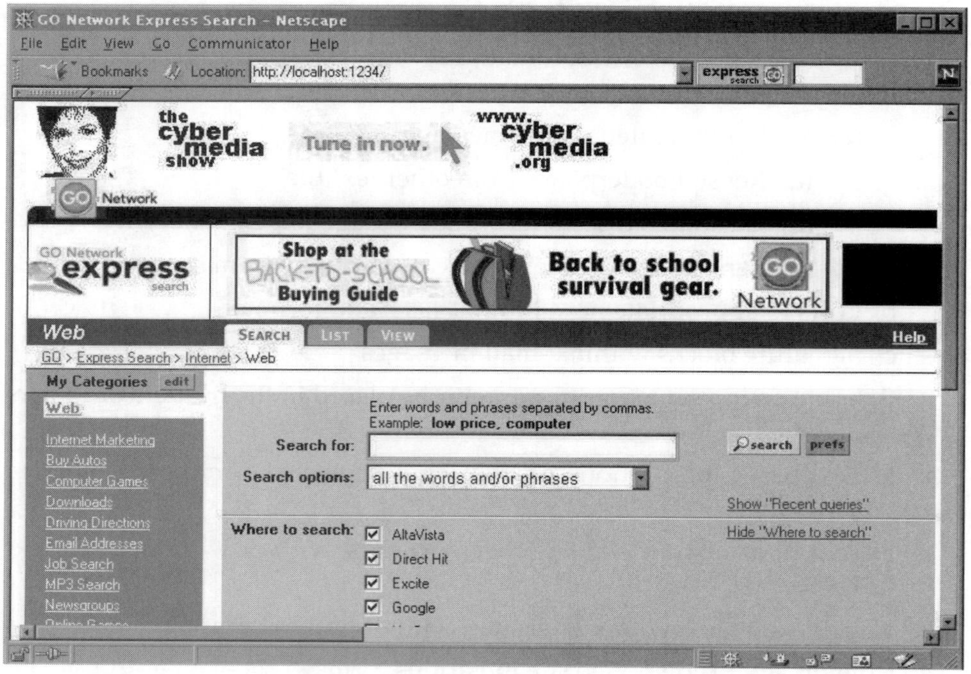

Figure 6.9 The GO Network Express search tool allows marketers to co-brand search software by adding a 1,000-pixel wide by 60- high banner ad to the top of the screen and linking to the download from any site.

Whether the online advertisement you place resides on a page or a list, on your company's site or another's, Internet advertisements usually serve three purposes:

1. Attract the user to a Web site (yours or someone else's).
2. Coax the user through the different pages of the Web site.
3. Encourage the user to return to the Web site.

As part of your Internet marketing program you can choose any combination of advertising activities to supplement your traditional advertising program. These include free advertising, fee-based advertising, and revenue-generating options.

Some Activities You Can Do Now

Free or low-cost online advertising options will have little to no impact on your Internet marketing budget, other than saving funds that you can use on other programs. I'll take you through finding and capitalizing on these opportunities.

1. Create an informational file in ASCII text for use by a mailbot or e-mail autoresponse program. Remember to update this often, as mailbots are forgotten and become obsolete.

2. Contact Webmasters individually and offer to exchange hypertext links. This is harder to do than it used to be, mainly because there are so many sites and too many requests for sharing links. Your best bet is to focus your efforts on sites with which you have established a business relationship, rather than surfing the Web looking for a fit.

3. Place sponsorships or advertisements on other mailing lists managed by your company. Look around at some of your competitors' e-mail discussion lists to get ideas for how to construct a header or footer ad. The best ones are under five lines and get right to the point.

4. Exchange reciprocal links by registering in a link or banner exchange directory. If you can control the placement of your link or banner, or at least suggest an appropriate area, then it's a good match for you. Otherwise, if you place the exchange's link or banner in a good place on your site and the rest of the advertisers place their links in hidden areas, you're not getting your value for the exchange. Although banner exchanges try to encourage advertisers to keep site placement consistent, you really have no control—and the management of banner exchanges don't have time to police the Web for you, either.

5. Exchange sponsorships or advertising space with partner companies. If you manage more than one site, you don't have to ask anyone to arrange this. If not, get on the phone or Net and close the deal!

6. Include ads at your own site, such as banners and scrolling browser text. Sometimes all this takes is adding the banner created by your advertising agency to your own site. With hyperlink text that states what's coming up, you can tell the user that the link goes to a special area.

On the other hand, fee-based online advertising options will have to be tallied for inclusion in your budget.

1. Include an estimate of the costs for creating one or more ad banners for Webwide placement opportunities. Unless you're a graphic designer, you won't want to create your own banner ad, no matter how easy the animated GIF maker software is to use.

2. Place sponsorships or advertisements on other mailing lists at other companies. Sometimes the cost is minimal. Sometimes you can negotiate an exchange.

3. Place sponsorships or advertisements on other Web sites within your company. If every penny has a pocket, then you may be forced to pay for intracompany or intranet advertising. I hope this is not the case.

4. Create and distribute software or disks for promotion of your Web site. In the battle to get the Internet users' attention, more and more companies are finding ways to get the users' attention before they go on the Web. This means customized browsers, new desktop applications, and embedded browser buttons will become commonplace in a very short time (Figure 6.10).

The Reality of Internet Advertising

Advertising on the Internet is now a reality. Have users accepted it? That's debatable. Either out of respect for the Internet's former "no advertising" policy or merely in a euphemistic approach to selling space, some Internet marketers will refer to online advertising as "sponsorship." Sugarcoated politically correct label or not, it is clear that Internet advertising has stimulated a lot more than just income.

Littering the Information Superhighway

Some Internet users believe that the cost of online services and information retrieval will increase if companies are not allowed to recover their expenses for Web site development. Under the best of circumstances, advertising sales generate enough revenue to not only offset the costs of a Web site's operation, but also surpass it.

Meanwhile, other users believe that advertising online is a nuisance—a modern canker sore on the Internet that they once knew and loved. To some extent, these users are right. Along with the thousands of companies who respect the culture of the online world, there are thousands of companies who feel that any visibility is good visibility, "Internet etiquette be damned." These so-called Internet marketers bombard individuals with countless untargeted e-mails. They

Figure 6.10 When downloaded and installed by the user, the GO Search software adds an easy-access button to the Netscape browser.

place the responsibility on the user to request removal from their databases. They claim that the Internet is a public thoroughfare, free of speed limits. They challenge anyone who would deny them the right to use it as they see fit.

In any society, there exist a few rogues whose sole purpose lies in taking advantage of situations. The Internet is certainly no exception. Fortunately, the industry is comprised of conscientious individuals who self-police and educate in an effort to maintain the quality of life in the online community. With a vigilant Internet marketing cooperative effort and any luck, the responsible marketers will triumph over the irresponsible ones in the long run.

Acceptable Online Advertising

There are acceptable and unacceptable methods of advertising online. As young as the Internet is, there are already some established norms for advertising online. Unsolicited advertising is still met with opposition. Recipients go out of their way to punish inconsiderate e-mailers with flames or notices to their Internet service providers. On the other hand, discreet and well-crafted signature blocks, those brief paragraphs or favorite sayings found at the end of e-mail messages, appear to have reached total acceptance by the online community.

Graphical ad banners are still receiving mixed reviews. Some users like seeing these colorful advertising messages. They serve as constant reminders that there are other exciting places to visit online. Some users feel that advertising in its various forms has littered the Internet and downgraded its quality. Rather than submitting themselves to an advertiser's message, users choose to change the options on their Web browsers so that graphics do not load automatically. This change allows users to view only the Web page text. Webmasters have adapted to that tactic, including descriptions in the HTML source code, known as ALT tags (Figure 6.11). The advertiser's message or company name still appears on the page, but in text. So much for circumventing an ambitious advertiser's intentions.

Advertisers Prevail

All that is Internet advertising is not bad. Naysayers of all types of Internet advertising, regardless of content, have forgotten one thing. Where there is advertising, there is operating revenue. It is the successful development of the Internet economy that will either make or break the Internet, of which advertising is a big and growing portion. Without some type of ongoing subsistence, the Internet will cease to exist as it does now. It does not appear that advertising on the Internet will go away soon. There are too many financial issues at stake and too many interested individuals to let that happen. When there's money involved, businesses have been known to defend their territory with a vengeance. Internet advertisers will not give up without a fight.

Figure 6.11   Virtual Jerusalem's Webmaster includes brief ALT tags with banner ad graphics, which causes a text box under the Presto! Card banner to appear when the cursor hovers over the area.

It's a Competitive World out There

It's getting increasingly difficult to make an *impression* on the Internet these days. If you're dying for online traffic, you realize it takes more than launching a Web site and peppering the Web with a few registrations to get people to visit. It takes advertising and lots of it. If you don't have an advertising budget, you'll have to come up with one . . . or make do.

There are many different ways that can be used to get the word out online. You can sign up for free advertising banner services at a banner or link exchange; but to tell you the truth, sometimes these services are nothing more than exercises in spinning your wheels, at least for businesses. Advertising on the Web isn't going to do you any good if you can't get people to click.

How Can I Get People to Click on My Banner Ad?

That's an interesting question—one that's been posed, debated, bandied about, and somewhat addressed by tons of online marketers, Internet advertising gurus, and industry pundits. For an article on this topic, visit Webreference.com at www.webreference.com/dev/banners/ and read "Banner Ad Placement Study" by Kim Doyle, Anastasia Minor, and Carolyn Weyrich. The major findings of this study address placement strategies for improving click-through. If you're more interested in first-hand data on what works for banner ads, that is, something more closely related to your industry, consider doing your own audience studies—online focus groups are great for this. Focus groups allow you to get results in your online advertising campaigns based on customized information.

In spite of well-conceived placement strategies, your online advertising campaign could still fail. It may fail due to any number of reasons: demographic fudges by an unscrupulous Webmaster, Internet users who aren't buying this month, or even a competitive Web site launch that blows your online advantage to smithereens. It could even be as simple as forgetting to include those often seen and simple instructions for Web users on how to click on a banner (Figure 6.12). What else can go wrong? You could have the right message, the right audience, and still not get what you need . . . sales on the Web.

But don't give up yet. It's really not your fault. One of the biggest barriers to closing the gap between Internet marketing and Internet sales is actually the user. Many users just don't want to surf anymore. Users are tired. There's too much to see. They've got their favorite Web sites and keep visiting the old familiar places. They get too much "spam." They don't have time anymore. Bandwidth is a problem. They've seen your message before and they don't care. More importantly, if they have to click one more time to get to honest-to-goodness content, they just won't.

Sure online users want to buy goods and services, but that's hardly a motivating factor. No, the real truth is, if you want someone to buy on the Web you have to make it easy. It's like this.

1. Tell the user you have something for sale.

2. Tell the user to buy it.

3. Help the user buy it.

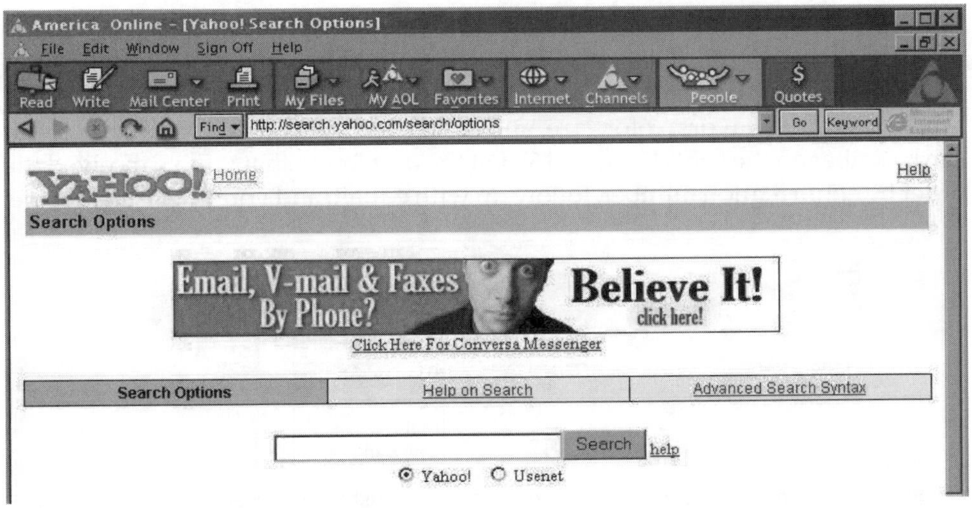

Figure 6.12   Yahoo! prompts the user with a hyperlinked reminder under the banner.

Yes, it's a bit simplistic, but are customers going to part with money unless you find a way to quickly and easily appeal to their needs? The Web is no different. With the increasing numbers of Internet newbies logging on each month, making it easy is what really counts.

Enter Rich Media

Here's where rich media comes in. It's an opportunity to interest and entertain your customer, then close the sale immediately, all at the same time. Rich media on the Web is better than plain vanilla banners, because it is truly interactive. A real interactive advertisement is not a static e-mail header or boring banner that sits there hoping the user will know what action to take. It offers choices to the user (Figure 6.13).

Interactive advertising is not simple animation that catches the eye for about two seconds. It doesn't require a Webmaster at a hosting site to tell anybody what to do, such as remembering to put hyperlinked words like "Click Here" in place.

Rich media interactive advertising is the Web's answer to why people don't buy or click through on the Web. Rich media brings not only the message to the user, but the means as well, on a silver platter. If your product lends itself well to simple selection, impulse buying, and credit card purchases, you've got it made. If your Web site needs a jump-start with navigation, you're looking at the right solution (Figure 6.14). If your Web site is thick with content, you can interest users by placing a search box in your banner ad (Figure 6.15).

A Quick Way to Demo Products

With certain types of rich media advertising, you can demonstrate as much, if not more than the average mail-order catalog, all in a fraction of the space. With a rich media banner ad, you can take your user through a brief commercial message. You can point to flavors, color, size, and style selection and then capture a credit card number on the spot (Figure 6.16). Let the user know that you've received the order by confirmation number, follow up with e-mail, and you've closed the sale.

Figure 6.13 Lands' End's holiday banner ad helps customers select a department before entering the virtual store.

Figure 6.14 The Plastics Network, an electronic commerce site for the plastics industry, includes a drop-down menu in its banner ads to aid users with precise site navigation.

Now, if my Web site is being driven by advertising revenue, I may not be quite as happy as if I'd managed to attract one more visitor to my pages. But, like most things in business, you often have to make choices and compromises.

So the next time someone complains about not making money on the Web, ask this: Do you want visitors or do you want product sales? You can have both, but one's got to take priority. And interactive advertising is but one way to make your decisions to place banner advertising really pay off.

Internet Advertising Is Not Alone

The growth in advertising is certainly not unique to the Internet. The last several years have witnessed a tremendous expansion in advertising in many different forms. It's not enough for companies to place a yellow pages ad, a spot on the radio or television, or even run a series of ads in consecutive Sunday newspapers. Telephone and utility companies now include advertising inserts with their monthly bills. Dairies accept advertising placements on the sides of their milk cartons. Elementary schools send home flyers advertising a back-to-school skating night at a local roller rink. School districts and airline companies accept ads to be painted on the sides of their buses and airplanes. Marketers say, "Where there's a space, there's an ad." The Internet is only one small part of this trend.

Bribes and Other Goodies

Over the past few years, hundreds of companies have emerged to capitalize on the advent of Internet advertising. Web sites such as CyberGold (www.cybergold.com) offer Internet users payment for viewing advertisements and/or

Figure 6.15 MusicFile.com encourages users to search its millions of titles before they even visit the site.

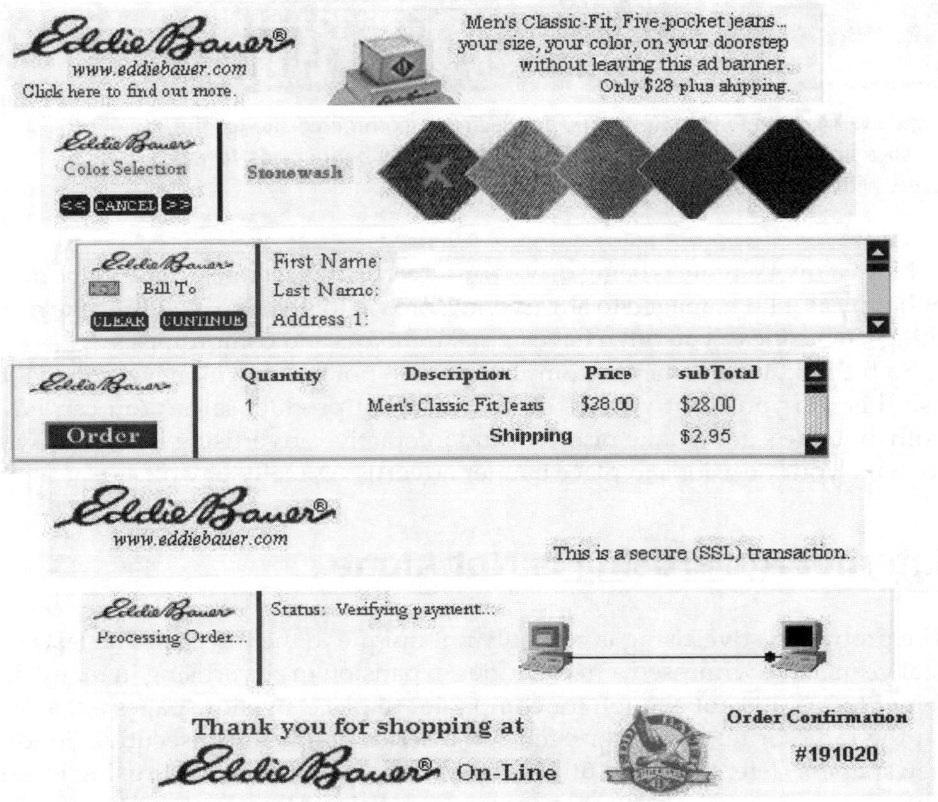

Figure 6.16 Eddie Bauer's banner runs an animated product selection feature, then presents a secure form for instant ordering.

surfing the Web. This Web advertising approach entices many Web sites to use incentives to attract more visitors (Figure 6.17).

Creating Your Own Ads

If you choose to create your own advertisement in-house, you have several options. You can repurpose or rewrite content from a company brochure or news release for an Internet ad. You can write entirely new copy. Whatever your approach, avoid hackneyed headlines. Internet users will tune you out. Empty self-praise, such as "we're number one," has little meaning for the customer. Declaring that you're the "number one" anything is more self-serving than it is customer-oriented. Maybe you're number one because you're good at fooling people until they click through to your Web site or order your products.

Figure 6.17   CyberGold attracts Web sites such as E*Trade that place minibanners at the CyberGold site.

I lean toward short statements that tell me how I will benefit by visiting a Web site and buying. But I'm also attracted to ads with personality—not the obnoxious "operators are standing by" approach, but the clever ones based on humor. Do these preferences conflict? Maybe. Your experience and industry may differ.

Here's a list of advertising banner ideas that I don't like very much. They trick the user, whether intentionally or not. The disappointment associated with creating and placing such banners is not worth the reputation damage.

- Radio buttons that act like they do but *don't* click
- So-called drop-down menus of choices that don't drop down
- Text that's cut off so the user can't read it, plus a nonfunctional scroll bar
- Blank fields that don't accept input
- Solutions for problems that scare the user (remember all the snake-oil salespeople spawned by the Y2K bug?)
- Great come-ons that don't follow through when you click
- Discounts that can't be entered into the order form when you buy

- Animated graphics that catch your eye but you can't tell what's being advertised
- A link to a page that no longer exists or never did
- Too-good-to-be-true offers, such as "free money," whatever that means
- Any kind of ad copy that smacks of a sideshow

Internet advertising design and copywriting is a style issue. Don't let anyone tell you otherwise. What works for your industry and company may not work for someone else. I'm a computer and electronics marketing communicator. My rules for business-to-business advertising are threefold:

1. Know the audience.
2. Emphasize features and benefits.
3. Inject a little personality.

Look less like an online carnival barker and more like a class act. Skillfully brag about your company, products, and services in terms that fit well within your market. Take advantage of the Internet by encouraging users to ask for additional information.

I used to take the wimpy approach to Internet copywriting by eschewing personality. I counseled marketers to tone down copy for the Internet by stripping out anything that even vaguely resembled advertising. I felt that a straight-as-an-arrow slant was more acceptable. At the time, this advice suited the educational aspects of the Internet's history. Advertising on the Internet hadn't been accepted yet. It certainly wasn't as far-reaching as it is today. Fortunately, I've evolved, and so has the Internet.

Here is a great article written by Ivan Levison in *The Levison Letter* (www.levison.com, 1996).

> *A lot of Internet gurus are giving out lousy advice about writing Web sites.*
>
> *Believe me, if you're selling software on the Internet, the last thing you want to do is sound like the new cure for insomnia.*
>
> *O.K. I agree that you shouldn't sound like you're selling Ginsu knives, but let's get real! As I mentioned before in my newsletter, the Web today is a text-based medium and you've got to quickly capture the reader's interest and attention. In other words, as always, you have to establish a relationship with the reader and therefore write with energy, enthusiasm, and personality.*
>
> *If you don't, you may wind up sounding like . . . flatter-than-a-pancake Web copy.*

To paraphrase the author: Balance is the key. If you're a business marketer, you don't want to develop an image more fitting for a late-night infomercial. However, you do want to stand out in a crowd. Still too vague for you? Honestly, copywriting is an art, not a science. If you can't write balanced, professional, Internet copy that grabs your audience, hire a skilled copywriter. It's just that simple.

Banner Design Services

If you include Web advertising placement in your Internet marketing plan, you need to design, or have someone design, a banner. If you are trying to keep costs to a minimum, a few tools can help you generate the banners yourself, such Ulead GIF Animator (Figure 6.18). If you decide to have your Web advertising banner created by an outside firm, your budget will include these costs. Check with your Web design firm for additional charges.

Placing Advertising on the Web

Several market research firms have predicted that advertising placement on the Internet will be the primary Internet revenue-generating force by the year 2000. If you haven't taken a look at these studies yet, go to Chapter 3, Analyzing Internet Market Statistics, for some excellent resources in this area.

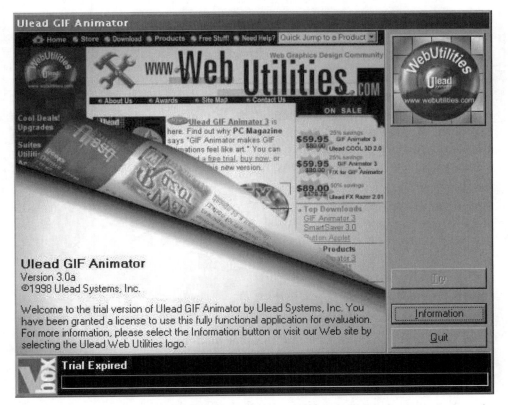

Figure 6.18 Ulead GIF Animator offers a trial version for users interested in trying out the software's features.

Where are the resources for placing advertisements on the Internet? If you have seen an ad at a favorite Web site or on a list, you already know at least one contact point. However, if you're interested in placing your ad on several different Internet properties simultaneously, think about working with an advertising network. Visit Adbility.com. A good page to check out is "Ad Networks, Brokers, and Reps," by Mark J. Welch. Welch pulls no punches in telling you exactly what he thinks about some of the players in the industry. He'll help you decipher some "fine-print" documents before you sign contracts for your ad campaigns.

Selling Advertising on the Web

Before you decide to offer your site for sponsorship, think about what the advertiser has to gain by advertising at your site. Once you've decided that your site is a worthwhile Internet property, start gathering data for your advertising rate card. A rate card tells the prospective advertiser what it costs to place an ad, among other things. By addressing this issue, you will also determine whether it is worth it to you to take on this responsibility.

Attracting and Retaining Advertisers

In order to attract advertisers, your site must fulfill certain criteria. Your site must be targeted to a specific audience; that is, your site attracts members of this audience and they return often. How do you know if your site meets this standard? If you haven't defined your audience, you have a problem. If you don't know who your audience is, then neither will potential advertisers. Compare your site to other sites in your industry that also offer sponsorship for the following key points:

- Features
- Interactivity
- Ease of navigation
- Graphics
- Content quality
- Frequency of updating
- Promotion on other sites and in other media

Some Activities You Can Do Now

1. Visit other sites in your industry that offer advertising.
2. Note why you believe these competitive sites are attracting advertisers.

3. Think about how you can improve your site along the same or better lines.

4. Use the form in Figure 6.19 to review any Internet property that will accept ads.

Instructions

Visit other sites in your industry that offer advertising.

Note why you believe these competitive sites are attracting advertisers.

Think about how you can improve your site along the same or better lines.

You can use this form for any Internet property that will accept ads.

Internet Marketing Goals Review

Why do you want to accept Internet marketing, and how do your overall Internet marketing goals support this activity?

_____

_____

_____

_____

_____

Competitive Analysis

Who are your competitors in offering advertising on the Internet?

_____

_____

_____

_____

_____

What do your competitors' sites offer? (Check all that apply.)

❑ Large customer base
   Unimportant   1   2   3   4   5   6   7   8   9   10   Important

❑ Highly targeted customer base
   Unimportant   1   2   3   4   5   6   7   8   9   10   Important

---

Figure 6.19 Offering advertising on the Internet.

❑ Audio   Specify: _____

❑ Video   Specify: _____

❑ Java   Specify: _____

❑ VRML   Specify: _____

❑ Searches   Specify: _____

❑ Other   Specify: _____

❑ Other   Specify: _____

In the above list, circle all the features your site provides.

Drawbacks to Accepting Advertising

How much time per week do you want to devote to integrating ads into your Web site?

_____

How much time per week do you want to devote to billing activities?

_____

How much time per week do you want to devote to site maintenance issues, such as content and improvements?

_____

Current Site Value

Publishing frequency: How often do you update your site?

_____

How does your site compare to other advertising sites on the Internet?

_____

_____

_____

_____

_____

Why would someone want to advertise at your site compared to your competitors'?

_____

_____

_____

_____

_____

Figure 6.19   *(Continued)*

Based on your answers to this point, how likely is it that you will offer advertising at your site?

Highly unlikely   **1**   **2**   **3**   **4**   **5**   **6**   **7**   **8**   **9**   **10**   Highly likely

If you selected a rating of 5 or less, stop right now. You are not ready to accept advertising.

If you selected a rating of more than 5, you are ready to accept advertising. Continue this form.

Sponsorship Information for the Media Buyer

Rate card: What would you charge for an ad?

Compare your site with others in your industry and determine a competitive rate.

Adjust your rate up or down depending on your site's competitive position.

Fixed fee rates are based on (check all that apply):

❑ Impressions (number of audited hits per ad)

Insert guaranteed minimum number of impressions per ad: _____

❑ The period the ad will run:

Insert rates per week _____ Month _____ Other term _____

❑ The position of the ad in the Web site or on the list:

Insert rates per position standard _____ Premium _____

Other position _____

❑ Frequency discounts

Please describe: _____

_____

_____

The variable rate is based on (compare your site with others in your industry and determine a competitive rate):

❑ Impressions (number of hits per page)

Figure 6.19 *(Continued)*

Insert anticipated impressions per ad: _____

❏ Clickthroughs (number of users clicking on the advertiser's ad)

Insert anticipated clickthroughs per ad: _____

Will you pay a commission to a recognized placement agency? ❏ Yes ❏ No

If yes, typical commissions for advertising agencies are 15 percent if paid within 30 days.

Circulation demographics (traffic)

Note: You must have analysis software or an auditing bureau in place before you can answer this question.

How many unique users visit your site?

_____ per _____ ❏ day ❏ week ❏ month

Circulation demographics (audience)

Describe the type of your targeted audience, readership, subscribers, or visitors.

_____

_____

_____

_____

_____

Who actually visits your site?

Visitor Description	Visitors per Time Period	Percentage of Total Visitors
_____	_____ per _____	_____ %
_____	_____ per _____	_____ %
_____	_____ per _____	_____ %
_____	_____ per _____	_____ %
_____	_____ per _____	_____ %

Figure 6.19   *(Continued)*

Is your site audited?   ❑ Yes   ❑ No

If no, stop right now. If advertisers cannot verify your claims, you may not be able to convince them to buy.

If yes, continue.

How will you manage ad placements at your site? (Check all that apply.)

❑ Accept and manage ad placements entirely in-house.

❑ Hire an outside firm to advertise or list my site. Cost to add to budget: _____

❑ Hire an outside firm to manage billing and invoices. Cost to add to budget: _____

❑ Hire an outside firm to manage site content and maintenance. Cost to add to budget: _____

❑ Install a feature to rotate advertising banners. Cost to add to budget: _____

❑ Limit banner dimensions and file sizes.

Specify: Dimensions _____ by _____ File size _____

❑ Limit placement of the ad throughout the site.

Specify: ❑ Top of page   ❑ Bottom of page   ❑ Other _____

State your policy for accepting or rejecting advertisements.

_____

_____

_____

_____

_____

_____

_____

_____

_____

_____

Figure 6.19   (Continued)

Income Potential

Keep in mind that your site may not sell ads immediately or fill all available ad space 100 percent of the time.

Number of Web pages available for ad placement _____

Multiply by number of ads rotated per page   × _____

Multiply by average price per ad   × _____

Estimate maximum gross advertising revenue _____ per _____ (period)

Minus expenses to upgrade or operate site   − _____

Estimate maximum net advertising revenue _____ per _____ (period)

What is your target or goal for advertising sales in the following time periods?

The next month _____

The next two months _____

The next three months _____

Figure 6.19   *(Continued)*

Why Should You Place Advertising on the Internet?

From a marketer's viewpoint, analyzing why, where, and how to place an advertisement on the Internet requires reviewing your objectives and comparing them to several other factors unique to your organization. Before you decide to purchase Internet advertising space, ask yourself several questions. Use Figure 6.20 on the accompanying media to evaluate your choices in this area.

Review the various options of Internet advertising and determine which activities would be the best fit. Try to anticipate any biases that others in your company might have to this particular Internet marketing activity. If you are convinced that Internet advertising would be a beneficial program for your Internet marketing plan, you must be prepared to defend your position.

Selecting a site to sponsor involves the following steps:

1. Visit sponsorable sites in your industry.
2. Compare various sites for audience, demographics, site statistics, and pricing.
3. Be realistic about what you can accomplish.

Instructions

Complete each question as briefly as possible, using bulleted and concise statements.

If you are unable to answer a question, brainstorm with others in your organization.

Excerpt portions of this form for use in evaluating multiple options.

Use the statements from this form to draft supporting or opposing paragraphs on Internet advertising for your Internet marketing plan.

Why Do You Want to Advertise?

List five overall marketing benefits that you will realize from placing advertisements on the Internet.

_____

_____

_____

_____

_____

Based on these benefits, list five company-specific reasons why you should place advertisements.

_____

_____

_____

_____

_____

List five overall marketing risks that you might take from placing advertisements on the Internet.

_____

_____

_____

_____

_____

Figure 6.20 Placing Internet advertising.

List five company-specific reasons why you should not place advertisements on the Internet.

_____

_____

_____

_____

_____

Take a look at the answers given in the previous question. Are any of the following reasons related to (check all that apply):

❑ Lack of budget   ❑ Reputation   ❑ Competitive influences

❑ Staff capabilities   ❑ Management resistance   ❑ Marketing plan objectives

❑ Traditional media   ❑ Past experience   ❑ Other _____

Do you believe any of these risks are insurmountable?   ❑ Yes   ❑ No   ❑ Unsure

If you answered yes, stop right now. Come back to this form after you have completed evaluations of other Internet marketing activities.

If you answered no, continue.

How would you counter or challenge each of the above objectives to Internet advertising?

_____

_____

_____

_____

_____

Based on your answers, how likely is it that you will place advertisements on the Internet?

Low probability   **1   2   3   4   5   6   7   8   9   10**   High probability

If you selected a rating of 5 or less, stop right now. You are not ready to advertise.

If you selected a rating of more than 5, continue.

Figure 6.20 *(Continued)*

Ad Positioning

Who do you want to target with your Internet marketing ad? (Be specific.)

_____

_____

_____

Have you identified your online market?   ❑ Yes   ❑ No

If no, stop right now and research this question.

If yes, continue.

Have you identified specific Internet properties for ad placement?   ❑ Yes   ❑ No

Selecting a Site to Sponsor

Which of the following Internet advertising activities are you considering?

❑ Web site ad banners   ❑ Signature blocks   ❑ Link exchanges

❑ Banner exchanges   ❑ List messages   ❑ Other _____

❑ Other _____

❑ Other _____

If you narrowed down your selection, complete this portion of the form for all sites under consideration. What does this Internet property offer? (Check all that apply.) Rate their importance to your industry.

❑ Large customer base
  Unimportant   **1   2   3   4   5   6   7   8   9   10**   Important
❑ Highly targeted customer base
  Unimportant   **1   2   3   4   5   6   7   8   9   10**   Important
❑ Audio
  Unimportant   **1   2   3   4   5   6   7   8   9   10**   Important
❑ Video
  Unimportant   **1   2   3   4   5   6   7   8   9   10**   Important
❑ Java
  Unimportant   **1   2   3   4   5   6   7   8   9   10**   Important
❑ VRML
  Unimportant   **1   2   3   4   5   6   7   8   9   10**   Important
❑ Searches
  Unimportant   **1   2   3   4   5   6   7   8   9   10**   Important

Figure 6.20   (Continued)

❑ Other
   Unimportant   **1   2   3   4   5   6   7   8   9   10**   Important
❑ Other
   Unimportant   **1   2   3   4   5   6   7   8   9   10**   Important

Statistics Reporting

Is this site audited?   ❑ Yes   ❑ No

If yes, explain: _____

How are statistics at this site reported to the advertiser?

_____

_____

_____

_____

_____

Based on this information, how likely is it that you will advertise at this site?
   Highly unlikely   **1   2   3   4   5   6   7   8   9   10**   Highly likely

If you selected a rating of 5 or less, stop right now. Evaluate another site.

If you selected a rating of more than 5, put this site in your plan. Complete this portion of the form for any additional sites. Continue this form.

Designing Your Advertisement

Using features and benefits, state how you will differentiate your products and services from those of your competitor.

_____

_____

_____

Using your previous answer as a reference point, what do you want your ad to emphasize?

_____

_____

_____

Is price important to your customer?   ❑ Yes   ❑ No

Figure 6.20   *(Continued)*

If yes, how much does this product or service cost?

_____

Do you have any photography or illustrations that you can incorporate into a banner? ❏ Yes ❏ No

If you are placing a graphical banner and you answered no, consider ordering product photography and/or graphic design services.

Completed by: _____ Date: _____

Figure 6.20   _(Continued)_

Being realistic means looking at how you can fit the Internet into your marketing plans and writing a feasibility statement that you can include in your marketing plan. You may have a long list of great ideas, but only enough staff or time to launch a small percentage of your ideas. Don't worry. The future holds your expansion plans.

Some Activities You Can Do Now

1. Review your company's Internet marketing plan objectives.
2. Using the form in Figure 6.21, evaluate all Internet advertising activities that support these objectives.

Instructions

Review your company's Internet marketing plan objectives.

Evaluate all Internet advertising activities listed below that support these objectives.

Evaluate all Internet advertising implementation activities that complement or enhance your traditional marketing plan.

Prioritize these selected Internet advertising activities in the order in which they will be the easiest for you to implement. Start with number one (1) for the activity that you can implement immediately with the least amount of preparation and cost.

Figure 6.21   Fitting Internet advertising into your marketing communications mix.

If you choose to place fee-based advertisements, start collecting rates and other information.

If you choose to offer fee-based advertisements, start estimating anticipated revenue from selling sponsorships to other companies.

Prepare an estimate of your Internet advertising expenditures and income.

Add this cost information to your Internet marketing budget.

Summarize these advertising activities for your Internet marketing plan.

Free Internet Advertising Options

❑ Creating companywide standard for signature blocks to appear on all outgoing e-mail messages

❑ Creating an informational file in ASCII text for use by a mailbot or e-mail autoresponse program

❑ Placing sponsorships or advertisements on other mailing lists managed by your company

❑ Exchanging reciprocal links with other sites

❑ Exchanging sponsorships or advertising space with partner companies

❑ Other _____

❑ Other _____

Fee-Based Internet Advertising Options

❑ Place sponsorships or advertisements on other mailing lists at other companies

❑ Place sponsorships or advertisements on other Web sites within your company

❑ Place sponsorships or advertisements on other Web sites at other companies

❑ Other _____

❑ Other _____

Figure 6.21 *(Continued)*

> **Revenue-Generating Advertising Options**
>
> ❑ Offer fee-based sponsorship or advertising space on your company's mailing list
>
> ❑ Offer fee-based sponsorship or advertising space on your company's Web site
>
> ❑ Other _____
>
> ❑ Other _____

Figure 6.21   *(Continued)*

3. Evaluate all Internet advertising implementation activities that complement or enhance your traditional marketing plan.

4. Prioritize these selected Internet advertising activities in the order in which they will be the easiest for you to implement.

5. Start with number one (1) for the activity that you can implement immediately with the least amount of preparation and cost.

6. If you choose to place fee-based advertisements, start collecting rates and other information.

7. If you choose to offer fee-based advertisements, start estimating anticipated revenue from selling sponsorships to other companies.

8. Prepare an estimate of your Internet advertising expenditures and income.

9. Add this cost information to your Internet marketing budget.

10. Summarize these advertising activities for your Internet marketing plan.

Advertising Specialties

Using the Internet in your advertising program includes publicizing its presence in the physical world. Leveraging established marketing programs for your Internet advertising is a good way to stretch your budget. When using imprinted specialty items for customer gifts and incentives, include your Internet addresses. Alan's Shoes Superstores at www.shoes.com, GTE at www.gte.net, and PeopleSupport at www.peoplesupport.com hand out free pens imprinted with their respective URLs.

Remember, functional items have a longer shelf life than cute gadgets. If you're using ad premiums as booth giveaways, consider having your visitor "earn" the gift by sitting through a presentation or completing a qualification form.

Give very important customers something functional and wearable . . . a watch. Whenever they check the time, they'll be reminded of your Internet presence (Figure 6.22).

Figure 6.22 Wonder what time it is? It's time for the Internet.

(Photo courtesy of Lynx Marketing Corporation at www .logotime.com and the Tenagra Corporation at www.tenagra .com.)

Leveraging Direct Mail for Your Internet Presence

As a hobbyist, I receive fliers from local crafts store merchants informing me of upcoming sales. I've noticed lately that more and more retailers are including their URLs in their direct-mail materials in an effort to encourage me to visit their Web sites (Figure 6.23). Even traditional coupon direct mailers are getting into the act by teaming with well-known Web properties (Figure 6.24).

Direct Mail and How to Make Online Enemies

Well there's egg and bacon; egg, sausage, and bacon; egg and spam; bacon and spam; egg, bacon, sausage, and spam; spam, bacon, sausage, and spam; spam, egg, spam, spam, bacon, and spam; spam, spam, spam, egg, and spam; spam, spam, spam, spam, spam, spam, baked beans, spam, spam, spam, and spam; or lobster thermidor aux crevettes with a mornay sauce garnished with truffle pâté, brandy, and a fried egg on top of spam (Monty Python's Flying Circus).

If you're ever wondered why unsolicited e-mail is referred to as "spam," well, now you know. There's nothing more annoying than being continually bombarded with either an unwanted menu choice or unwanted electronic

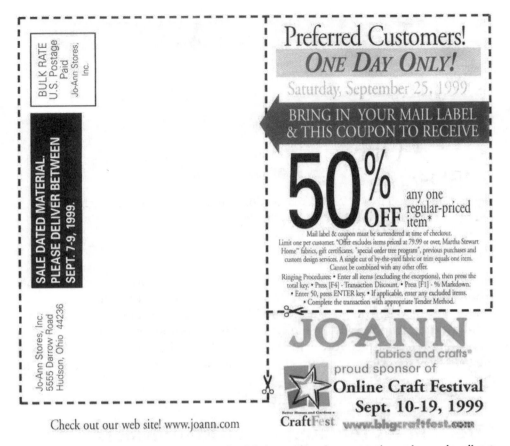

Figure 6.23 Jo-Ann Stores promotes its fabrics and crafts stores through regular direct-mail brochures, including the URLs for both its site and a strategic partner's.

mail. Yet some advertisers on the Internet have justified to themselves that it's open season on everyone who has an e-mail address. If you have ever posted a message to a newsgroup or joined a mailing list, you are now fair game in their eyes.

Compare this to the e-mail you may have received as a result of signing up for a discussion list. You started a subscription to a list for the purposes of networking with your peers by discussing marketing communications issues. Now every list broker that retrieves that list of e-mail addresses from the list server will assume that anything that has to do with marketing will appeal to you.

American Express regularly sends out notices to its cardholders allowing them the option of being removed from traditional mailing lists. It screens

Figure 6.24 Direct mailer Val-Pak teams with Web directory leader Yahoo! to offer consumer coupons both in print and on the Web.

advertisers and accepts only those that it believes offer a product that would appeal to its customer base. Unfortunately, anyone can request the e-mail addresses from a public mailing list on a public server without authorization from the list owner. No one is screening its use. When a direct e-mail broker assumes you want to receive his or her customer's mailings, the broker is making an assumption that doesn't necessarily ring true on the Internet.

Three Cheers for Internet Service Providers

Most Internet service providers have woken up to the customer inconvenience caused by e-mail marauders. E-mail server security has been tightened in the past few years, preventing users from faking Reply-To addresses and sending out unsolicited garbage through distant servers (Figure 6.25).

But all is not rosy. It's still too easy to use ISP servers to send out junk, and forge someone's e-mail address in the process. Recently, someone started using a colleague's domain name to "spam" the Net, and he could do nothing about it, since the mail was relayed or distributed through a different server which allowed such nonsense.

As evidenced by the annoying offers I receive in my in-box every day, it's safe to say that many online marketers still haven't gotten the message about respecting users' e-mail preferences (Figure 6.26). Part of the problem lies in the number of free Web-based e-mail accounts that are now available. It's too easy for someone to establish an account and reestablish one somewhere else, even if multiple accounts are removed for Terms of Service violations.

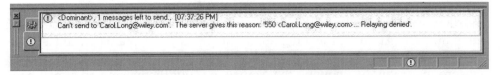

Figure 6.25 While logged on to AOL, the author is unable to send an e-mail through her regular ISP, due to security measures preventing such relayed transmissions.

The Impact of Unsolicited E-mail

Although paper-based direct-mail campaigns are essentially "unsolicited mail," the impact on the user is not the same. Traditional direct mailers cost the advertiser money. The advertiser must pay for printing and pay for postage. As a result, advertisers can be very picky about which lists they purchase. Under pressure from the paying customer, direct-mail list brokers can be very picky about which lists they offer for sale. Many list brokers offer customer rebates when obsolete mailing addresses are found. This allows them to keep their lists as clean as possible, but it also costs them money.

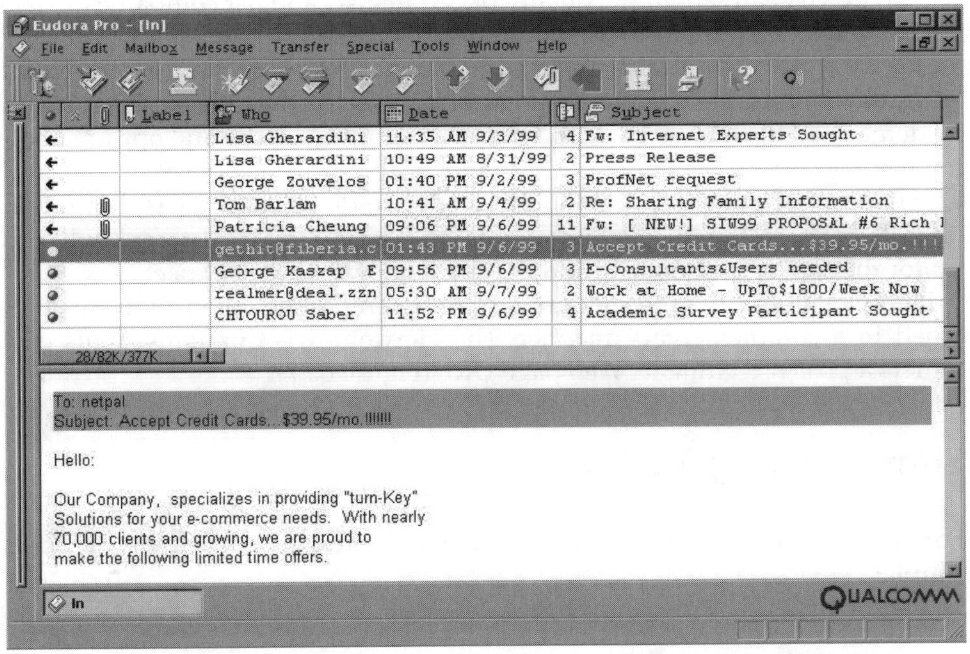

Figure 6.26 One company's turnkey solutions for e-commerce alienates online businesses with its unsolicited advertising approach.

Due to the low cost of e-mail distribution and the technology used to gather these lists of names, bulk e-mail houses are not as picky about the addresses they gather and sell. At times, I wonder about the privacy statements posted at Web sites—are they really honoring my preferences or not? And I hesitate to post to newsgroups anymore, knowing that someone is out there using an e-mail harvester that gathers addresses for bulk e-mail purposes. The method by which some list brokers sell e-mail addresses is questionable, as is the quality of many of these lists. I receive duplicate e-mail ads every day, often addressed to old addresses that have been forwarded and for multiple accounts I've established for various business purposes. I get tired of hitting Ctrl-D all the time, which is the sophomoric answer many bulk e-mail companies counter with to your complaints about the hordes of e-mail you don't want. Unsolicited e-mail costs the recipient service fees, connect time, and impacts workflow negatively.

Deciding to Use Bulk E-mail Lists

If you choose to use bulk e-mail addresses, determine how the list was compiled. If it was compiled from the names of users who specifically asked to receive more information on a certain topic, you have a better chance that your message will not offend. But not all lists are reputable, so ask your colleagues what they've heard about the quality of certain lists and list companies.

I received a mailing from one company that claimed I had been voluntarily added to a list they purchased, but I had never heard of the list compiler. I wasn't even interested in the product. I let the advertiser know about it and he demanded his money back on what was supposed to be an "opt-in" mailing list.

If you establish an e-mail announcement list, do not add users, but rather offer them the option to join and un-join on demand. Your customer will sign up for this service voluntarily and therefore knows what to expect.

Direct mail and the Internet are the most compatible when they are combined in a complementary manner. The Herringtown Company mails customers a postcard citing its Web page URL (Figure 6.27).

Some Closing Advice

For marketers who wish to use e-mail in their Internet marketing, my advice is simple:

- Build individual relationships and a reputable Internet marketing presence first.
- Inquire about a customer's contact preference (e.g., e-mail, mail, fax, telephone) and honor it.

Figure 6.27 The Herringtown Company announces its Web page with a simple card mailed to established customers.

- Ask customers to voluntarily provide e-mail addresses. Provide an incentive such as product giveaways or access to a password-protected portion of your Web site.
- Always keep initial e-mail messages as brief as possible.
- Do not automatically add users to a list just because they requested information.
- Offer the recipient a choice to retrieve additional information.
- Do not automatically place the burden of being removed from a list on the user. If a user has voluntarily subscribed to your distribution list, remind that person of the options for removal.
- Do not give away, trade, or sell a user's e-mail address without explicit permission.

Figure 6.28 KenTech helps marketers determine the cost of ad placements.

Resources

Here are selected resources to assist you in planning and budgeting for the advertising portion of your Internet marketing plan.

Ad calculators:

- WDFM's Media Tools at www.wdfm.com
- KenTech's Cost-Per-Sale Ad Calculator at www.kentech.com/marketing/costpersale.html (Figure 6.28)

Some banner exchanges allow you to target your ad geographically and by types of sites. Web site parodies continue to poke fun at the phenomenon (Figure 6.29).

- Advertising placement: Banner Mania at www.banner-mania.com
- BannerSwap at www.bannerswap.com
- Disney Banner Network at www.disneybanner.net

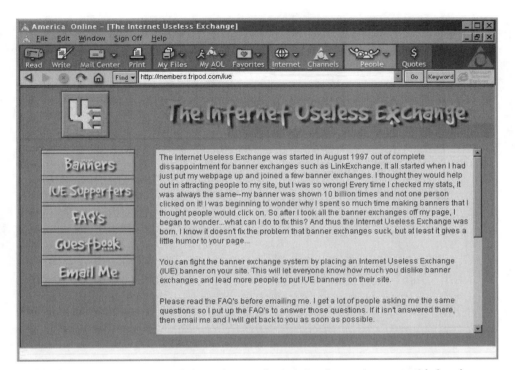

Figure 6.29   The Internet Useless Exchange displays its disappointment with free banner exchanges on the Web.

■ Free Banner Exchange at free-banner-exchange.com

■ LinkExchange at www.linkexchange.com

Direct mail:

■ Direct Mail Marketing Association at www.the-dma.org

References

Ivan Levison & Associates. 1996. "Ideas for Better Direct Mail & Advertising." *The Levison Letter*. September. Ivan Levison & Associates, Marketing Communications, 14 Los Cerros Dr., Greenbrae, CA 94904. Tel. (415) 461-0672, fax (415) 461-7738, ivan@levison.com, www.levison.com. Reprinted with written permission.

Crispen, Patrick Douglas, list operator. 1994. Excerpt from a skit by the comedy troupe Monty Python's Flying Circus as it appeared in the Roadmap Workshop Distribution List. October 18, 1994.

Utilizing Collateral
Materials/Sales Literature

The first thing people did was make brochureware, then they made superbrochureware. I think it's essential that Web sites are interactive, one way or another.
Louise Kirkbride, president and founder of
Acme Software, Inc., creators of FAQtory™

This chapter will discuss collateral materials, also known as literature or printed matter, as it relates to your development of your Internet marketing presence. To leverage your company's collateral library, you must publish at least some of it on the Internet. If you're new to this process, your first thoughts will be of sales literature. You'll soon discover that there's more to publishing online than repurposing content and graphics from glossy brochures.

You will inventory all documents in your sales literature library and determine which pieces, if any will be included in your online library. You will provide your online customers with options for obtaining your product literature in a variety of forms, including the most popular. You'll think about how to make your literature interactive, possibly by adding demonstration capabilities on the Web through the use of audio and video tools.

Using the Internet in your collateral programs may involve little more than adding an action item or two to a long list of print development activities. You will simply change a few production choices when working with the various suppliers, printers, illustrators, and photographers who produce your printed pieces. A few activities will involve an investment in order to update your literature for use on the Web. Remember to obtain costs for any additional services or equipment for your Internet marketing budget.

In Chapter 6, Designing Advertising and Direct-Mail Campaigns, you evaluated a variety of advertising-related activities. You determined whether you would place advertising on the Web, or if you would generate income for your company by accepting advertising yourself. You reviewed the differences between traditional advertising and Internet advertising, and became familiar with related terminology. You even learned about some Internet tools designed to make your traditional media planning activities easier.

In Chapter 7, Utilizing Collateral Materials/Sales Literature, you will learn how to distribute your sales literature or collateral materials on the Internet. Company literature, commonly referred to as Web publications, assumes many different forms. You can convert individual document files to HTML. You can publish an entire searchable database on the Web. There are even opportunities for you to publish on the Internet through pure sweat equity and no additional budget. This chapter contains a brief overview of some of these options.

Effective Supporting Materials for the Plan

Including data that reinforces your decision to market on the Internet best supports your Internet marketing plan. Including any combination of the following can expand this portion of your Internet marketing plan:

- Plan of action for converting selected collateral materials to the Internet

- Suggestions for incorporating Internet addresses into your literature

- Ideas for transforming your literature into more than just HTML, including new ideas for demonstrating your products' features on the Web

- A brief overview of the need for converting preexisting databases for use on the Web

- A list of needed document conversion software and equipment for incorporation into the budget portion of your plan

- A summary of how incorporating the Internet into literature activities will improve your marketing communications program

Integrate the Internet into Your Collateral Materials

In Chapter 6, I talked about some of the blatantly obvious ways to include the Internet in your traditional marketing communications program. If you fail or forget to take advantage of these free or almost-free opportunities, you're spending more money than you should to promote your online presence. The same holds true for printed literature, since collateral materials are often the best place to inform the public about your online presence. Any piece of paper used to promote your company is fair game when it comes to getting the word out and leveraging your printed matter for the Internet. Similarly, any Web site that fails to provide traditional contact information in a conspicuous location is missing out on connecting to customers in real time.

There are plenty of good examples of this canon in action. If you advertise your toll-free and fax numbers on your literature, there's no reason you can't do the same for your Web address. In fact, nothing frustrates a potential buyer more than wanting to research a company online and not seeing a URL in an obvious location on printed matter. Sometimes a user will just go online and either guess at or search for your Web site address, but many times, it's a lost opportunity to draw that person in and introduce your company in a way no printed material can.

Integrate Your Collateral Materials into the Internet

Webmasters are often referred to as Internet publishers, because the Internet is a content-packed environment. You include graphics at your Web site, just as you do in your printed sales literature, but the major portion of your Web document is in text. The major difference between the physical world and the Internet is the absence of paper from online literature. Well, there's supposed to be an absence of paper. People print out your data sheet and Web pages to show a colleague or take along while shopping at a local store.

There are other differences between the two media, print and online, as well. This is where many novice Internet marketers get into trouble. They expect to be able to take that data sheet and duplicate it exactly on the Web. There are some aspects of printed literature you will give up when you convert to online. There are also some nice features of the Internet that printed literature doesn't have, such as interactivity (Figure 7.1).

In traditional printing, what you envision at the start resembles what you see at the finish. Green is green. Blue is blue. A paragraph on the left side of the page balances a chart on the right. On the Internet, what you see is not always what you get. If anything can go wrong or can be changed by the Internet or the user, it most certainly will be. If anything controllable does go wrong, such as a mistake in HTML coding, a graphics file that was uploaded to the wrong directory, or a script that doesn't work, it's your responsibility to correct it immediately.

Printed Literature	Online Literature
Colors and Inks	
Printing processes include black and white, two-color, three-color, four-color; identical colors, even when specified by exact PMS number, can appear different on various papers; anything printed on paper can appear in color; during the prepress stage, colors may be separated into plates; printers can compensate for color imbalances before producing the final printed piece; subsequent print runs may not always match ink color.	Browsers can display most colors, but variations in browsers and incompatible TSR software on the user's computer will cause color shifts; users can set browser preferences to override Webmaster's choices; HTML allows some color specifications, including fonts, backgrounds, frames, and links; color imbalances can occur; subsequent downloads can match in color due to page caching.
Format	
Margins and layout are predetermined by a graphic artist and executed by the printer; software programs can be set to specify page layout, including columns, page sizes, pagination, etc.; print jobs are run vertically and horizontally; paper can be folded and opened by the reader to view text.	Margins and layouts are predetermined by a Webmaster; Web authoring tools can be used to create layouts that are close to print; pagination is not an internal document issue; browsers can scroll to view both vertical and horizontal formats; vertical formats are preferred on the Web because browsers open to a default setting that most users do not change; documents that overextend monitor dimensions simply frustrate users as they scroll left and right to read.

Figure 7.1 Print collateral versus the Internet.

Art

Materials can include typesetting, photography, and illustrations combined into a "comp"; negatives and transparencies are converted to film and stripped in place; printers can accept comps on disk, such as a PageMaker or PostScript file, but may still convert to plates for printing presses.

Materials can include photography and other illustrations; art appears on the Internet in a variety of graphical file formats, however *.GIF is the most commonly used one for the Web; documents are converted into text, HTML, or other formats and uploaded; photography and illustrations are converted to file formats and uploaded into place.

Typography and Copy

Graphic artists or designers specify the typeface and fit the copy before printing; there are thousands of typefaces a designer can choose from.

Webmasters can specify the typeface, but the user has the final say; copyfitting is not a problem for plain HTML; some Web page layouts, including tables and frames, may require copyfitting corrections; there are several fonts a Webmaster can choose from, but the user has the final say by setting browser options.

Binding and Pages

Multipage documents are usually printed in even numbers (such as four-page, eight-page) due to signature or page-group binding; full-color literature is run in quantities of a few thousand or more.

Multipage documents can be any length; long documents take time to download and are best viewed when broken into several files; literature appears in quantity one on the Web.

Figure 7.1 *(Continued)*

Paper

Papers come in a variety of stock: coated, uncoated, recycled, laser-compatible, etc.

Paper is an issue only when the user prints your Web page or text for viewing off-line, but the Webmaster has absolutely no control over paper.

Size

Standard paper sizes for individual sheets are 8½ by 11 inches, 8½ by 14 inches, 8 by 5 inches.

Standard page sizes for the Web are equivalent to a screen, with multiple screens making up a document.

Special

Spot varnish, metallic colors, die cutting, inserts, foldouts, embossing, scoring, perforations, binding, deckled edges, fluorescent inks, watermarks.

Not currently transferable to the Internet, there are some HTML and graphics features which can simulate special effects, such as animated and transparent *.GIFs and wallpapers.

Prepress Proofs

Graphic artist, agency, and/or customer must sign off on inspection sheets, such as bluelines and color keys, before print job is run; mistakes must be corrected before production; mistakes noticed after production are tolerated until the next print run.

Webmaster should view the finished page off-line with a browser before uploading; HTML, typographical, or other mistakes noticed after publishing can be corrected immediately; publishing can be corrected immediately; Internet users are not very forgiving when mistakes remain online.

Figure 7.1   (*Continued*)

Why Put Your Literature on the Web?

Here are some of the reasons to duplicate part or all of your company's literature on the Internet. Use some or all of these reasons to justify your creation of product literature on the Web and include these reasons when you write this portion of your Internet marketing plan. By publishing literature on the Web, you can do the following:

- Distribute product information worldwide with none of the incremental reproduction and fulfillment costs associated with print
- Add search capabilities to the current product literature library, allowing potential buyers to find what they need more easily
- Automate tracking of Web sales leads generated by literature to evaluate the effectiveness of your collateral distribution and associated Web marketing program
- Demonstrate selected product features to potential customers when your business is closed
- Expand your site content to include more of your product line, especially if your print catalog can't possibly accommodate all your current and future offerings for whatever reason
- Provide links to technical information for immediate technical support, such as linking to downloadable software fixes
- Post price breaks or volume discounts as they occur, including e-mailing a notice of critical pricing data to registered mailing list subscribers
- Reach a larger geographical audience than current literature distribution efforts can afford
- Reduce current literature development and production expenditures, including redesigns associated with expanded catalogs and printing house charges
- Reduce literature-fulfillment expenditures, including personnel, outside mailing houses, and incremental postage costs
- Update changed product specifications on the fly

If you wish to reduce printing costs, you may decide to publish your documents on the Web to save that portion of your marketing budget. You probably won't realize cost savings immediately, and you may not realize cost savings at all. In some cases, your literature distribution costs will increase, since more people will have access to your literature, and more people will want your literature in their hands. If you succeed, reducing literature costs can make a big difference in your budget, especially when you take into account literature development, revisions, storage, and ongoing fulfillment.

More people worldwide are accessing your literature than ever before. That may or may not be a good thing for your company. The Web may open up the floodgates, attracting more customers or potential customers than you are ready to serve. For competitors or other individuals who are conducting research on the Internet and have no intention of purchasing your product, your Web publishing activities have avoided the costs associated with mailing literature packets to them. On the positive side, new customers can locate your sales materials on the Web immediately, especially if you've done a good job of promoting your Web presence, both online and off.

Large data books, such as those distributed by computer and electronic companies, are bulky, difficult to ship, and expensive to print. By converting your data books to the Web, you are able to reduce the number of people who receive your printed data book to only the most serious buyers. Searching for the right product in your data book may be a time-consuming job. By installing a search capability and/or an index at your Web site, you allow users to search your literature library by keyword or concept. They locate product information faster, and many times without the help of your customer-service personnel (Figure 7.2).

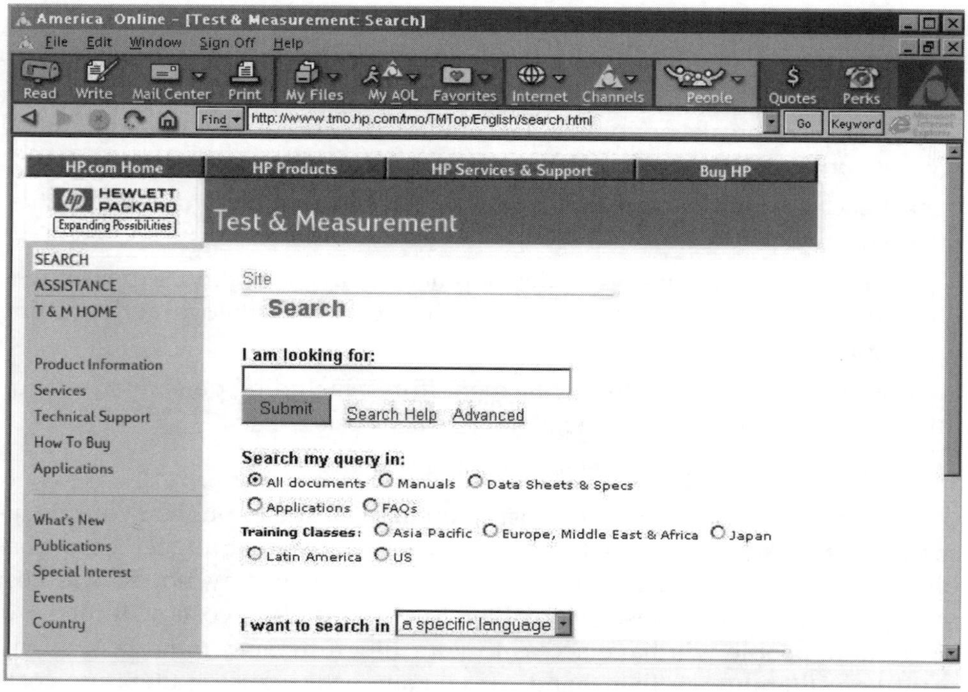

Figure 7.2 Hewlett-Packard's Test & Measurement Division provides a search capability to an extensive cache of product sheets in a variety of languages.

What Should You Publish on the Web?

Think of the Internet as an adjunct to your literature printing and distribution activities. Imagine that you're going to use the Internet to not only distribute your literature electronically, but it's going to help you close the sale in a way no other marketing media has been able to before. On the Web, you'll want to publish the following:

- Annual reports—to reach financial analysts and Internet-savvy investors
- Application and technical notes—to encourage OEMs (Original Equipment Manufacturers) and VARs (Value Added Resellers) to incorporate your product into theirs
- Brochures—to provide links to similar products or accessories for cross-selling and up-selling opportunities for buyers who need such sales assistance
- Catalogs—to either duplicate print editions or expand versions to the point where no budget can go, especially important if your company and product line is constantly growing
- Company brochures—for easy browsing in the widely used HTML format and for those times you need to adhere to corporate identity guidelines, in another format, such as PDF (Portable Document Format)
- Data books—in an effort to prequalify "tire kickers" and to severely reduce expensive production and distribution costs for such bulky books
- Data sheets—to enhance their presentation interactively, with more than just text and pictures
- White papers—to widely publicize the expertise of your company's senior-level executives

Some of these documents will be easy to adapt to the Web, while others, such as large catalogs, will be cumbersome. You may decide to either divide your document into manageable files or publish it in a form other than HTML.

How Should You Publish on the Web?

It's more difficult to publish online than it used to be, especially if you're trying to "keep up with the Joneses." New and exciting ways to distribute literature on the Net emerge every day. With all the millions of pages on the Web, it's no wonder that once users drop on by in cyberspace, they expect you to both inform and entertain them. Knowing that, you'll want to brainstorm about how to get your customers to stay longer. Perhaps you'll link your product photos to a nice interactive feature, such as a guided tour of features and some short video clips.

Too often, however, product literature on the Web is merely an exact duplicate of its print cousin. Too often, it's not even that good. All the salesmanship is stripped out in exchange for the Internet's "politically correct" version—a boring, uninviting, low-budget production. But if a visitor has come to your Web site, you've already gotten over the first hurdle associated with selling on the Web—pitching interested prospects. If you're still having trouble visualizing what possibilities exist, read on.

For example, many technology product manufacturers enhance their Web distribution of literature by including some or all of the following at their Web sites. These items are often linked directly from individual literature pages and/or from shopping carts during the purchase process:

- Animated graphics giving a basic demonstration of a product's functionality
- Clickable call buttons for immediate telephone call-back by the customer service department to the customer's place of business or residence
- Downloadable or Web-resident product demos in streaming video, perhaps for products requiring a more realistic portrayal than static illustrations or animated graphics can handle
- HTML-to-e-mail inquiry forms for requesting additional literature by return e-mail, fax-on-demand, or regular postal mail
- HTML-to-fax capabilities, for sending the text of a Web page to a distant colleague. (According to an August 16, 1999, news release, Fax4free.com offers Web sites "the ability to enable its users to fax Web content for free with a single click.")
- Links to inventory databases to check product availability before ordering
- Links to customer order databases to check the shipping status on a previously ordered product, including related links to the customer's shipping data at a freight company's Web site
- Online contests or quizzes to test visitors' product knowledge and increase product identification and branding
- Slide show presentations of product features and benefits, through PowerPoint presentations converted to HTML
- Screen captures of products, configured as clickable images, that highlight features in a low-bandwidth manner
- Translations of product information in languages other than English, for attracting and serving a wider range of international customers

Choosing Document File Formats

Documents are published on the Internet in a variety of formats, the most widely used being both ASCII or plain text, as transmitted in e-mail messages, and HTML or Hypertext Markup Language, as posted on Web pages. PDF or Portable Document Format makes up a growing number of financial documents, such as annual reports. There is also a growing movement of linking product databases to Web pages that generate on the fly, based on the customer's search parameters. Keep in mind that if your final result produces documents that are not easily read by most users on the Web, then you aren't reaching the largest possible audience.

Many decisions to publish in a certain format are made due to cost. Converting materials to the Web is not just for deep-pocketed marketers, but it is true that some of the more sophisticated options will require an investment you're not ready for. For low-end publishing options, the budget hit can be minimized because conversion can be automated. For simple text-to-HTML conversion, wordprocessing, and other applications, publishers include Web publishing tools as a matter of course. For example, after creating a conference presentation in Microsoft PowerPoint, I often convert it to HTML for publishing on the Web. This only takes a few minutes, if that, and allows seminar attendees to review my presentation long after the event has concluded and allows nonattendees to see what they might have missed.

Sometimes you must review whether converting certain documents to a Web format will diminish or weaken your marketing message. Beautiful formats and vibrant colors lose their luster in cyberspace, so you either have to bite the bullet and live with the Web version or find a way to enhance your online presentation. In that case, you may choose to offer documents in more than one format. Perhaps you'll decide to publish in HTML, but provide links to other documents for downloading.

The Portable Document Format allows hypertext features to be added to PostScript documents. Web documents using PDF require the user to have the additional software installed before viewing text. To read PDF documents, you need a reader, such as Adobe Acrobat Reader at www.adobe.com. Of course, I didn't have to spend time downloading it to my computer. The CD-ROM with the latest upgrade for Qualcomm's Eudora Pro E-mail included the Adobe Acrobat Reader, which I installed on my computer. With many software installations and upgrades, I've received the latest version of Adobe Acrobat Reader as well.

While readily available and downloadable from the Web, PDF readers are not experiencing the same widespread use among Internet users as browsers. This fact is not a reflection on the quality or features of different less-popular products. The decision to use one format over another is a variation on the old "VHS versus Betamax tape" debate. If you produce videotapes in a format that's incompatible with the majority of players in use, you risk losing sales. If you publish your Web documents in formats other than HTML, you risk losing your audience to sites with browser-compatible literature.

I can't tell you how many times I've been in a hurry to research information on the Web, only to be stopped cold by a nonstandard format or one that required additional time to access or download. When time is short, I bookmark the page for possible review later and browse to another site. Given the choice, Internet citizens will take the easy route and bypass your site altogether. Installing one more piece of software to view Web documents is a matter of convenience and priorities. It's incredibly arrogant to assume that the "real customers" will adjust to your Web publishing decisions. Cover all the bases and don't twist your visitors' arms. If you publish your company literature in a format that is not used by the majority of visitors, provide additional formats, such as HTML or plain text, as well.

Some Activities You Can Do Now

1. Read the article on creating browser-optimized content at www.webreference.com/dev/automatic.html.

2. If your market dictates that you create a Web site that is "universally browser friendly," visit the "Campaign for a Non-Specific WWW" at www.anybrowser.org/campaign for some helpful guidelines.

3. If you're concerned about people with disabilities who visit your site, go to the Web Accessibility Initiative (WAI) at www.w3.org/WAI to find out how to make your Web site more useful.

4. CAST, the Center for Applied Special Technology at www.cast.org, offers a Web-based tool called Bobby for analyzing preexisting Web pages for accessibility to people with disabilities. Click on Bobby from the home page and enter your Web site address to rate your pages. Bobby will rate each section of a page, providing specific guidelines for improving your site's access, including a summary of browser compatibility errors and download time.

Annual Reports and Other Financial Data

The past few years have seen an enormous increase in the number of annual reports published on the Web. When this book was first written, few companies were aware of or capitalizing on the Web to reach potential investors or financial analysts. A recent search of the Web using the keywords "annual report," "quarterly report," "financial report," "10-K," "10-Q," "offering," and "prospectus" produced a wealth of third-party Web publishing and competitive research choices. In spite of this trend, federal law still requires that print versions of these reports remain available, mainly because Internet use by investors is still in its infancy. Restricting publication of your company's annual report to just the Internet doesn't fulfill SEC requirements.

If you're inexperienced in publishing an annual report online, companies such as StockProfiles.com, VirtualWallStreet.com, and the Investor Relations Information Network (IRIN) at www.irin.com (Figure 7.3) can assist you. In addition, these sites provide additional online visibility by cataloging financial reports of multiple companies, making each a one-stop online shop for potential investors interested in researching the market.

Marketers who have taken their annual reports independently to the Web use just as many variations as they do for their other Web pages. Baxter International at www.baxter.com allows its visitors to search its annual reports by keyword through the last few years (Figure 7.4). Systems & Computer Technology (SCT) at www.sctcorp.com points to its SEC filings on the Web, as found on the SEC site, but allows potential investors to receive a print copy in the mail (Figure 7.5). GE at www.ge.com includes all of the sections of a typical standard report, with simple graphics and an easy-to-navigate look, but delays immediate investor gratification by requesting customer feedback (Figure 7.6).

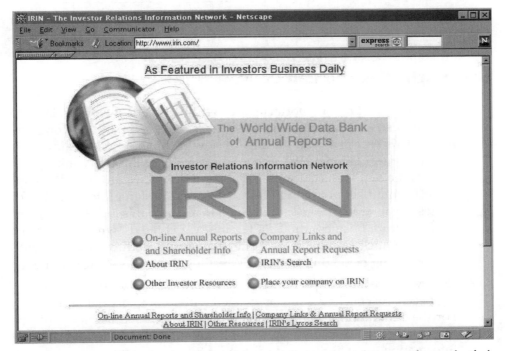

Figure 7.3 IRIN provides instant access to annual reports and news releases in their original format.

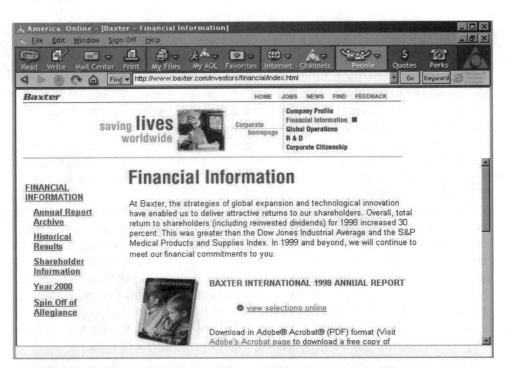

Figure 7.4 Baxter International provides a home page link to corporate and investor information and an annual report archive.

Some Activities You Can Do Now

1. Go to an annual reports portal on the Web and enter keywords related to your industry, complementary businesses, or a competitor's company name. This will give you an idea of how companies are posting their financial information on the Web, either directly or through a third party such as the SEC. I started with 10k Wizard at tenkwizard.com. Wondering if I should get out of high technology and design glittery outfits for professional wrestlers on TV, I decided to research this industry to determine a future business model's feasibility. I entered "wrestling" in the field for "Quick Search Filings." The total results produced were 62, with the top listing belonging to World Wrestling Federation Entertainment.

2. Review the results, applying selected data to your own unique marketing needs. Just click on a link associated with a company name and read. For the Federation, I found its main business address as filed with the SEC, along with area code and telephone number. I added this contact information to my industry database for future reference.

3. Look for hidden advertising and sales opportunities, as well as ideas for publishing your own company's investor relations' material online.

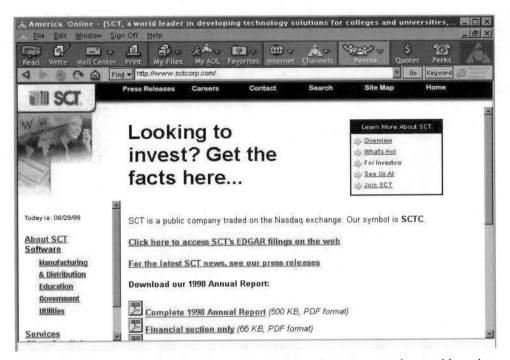

Figure 7.5 SCT publishes its financial data in HTML and PDF to appeal to a wide variety of visitors.

A brief description of the Federation's initial public offering included a prospectus summary describing the Federation's "ability to offer consumers an affordable and exciting entertainment experience." As an aside, now that I understand what amounts to Federation's business overview and executive summary, I can adjust my marketing plan accordingly. The information at tenkwizard.com reveals that the Federation's roster includes "approximately 110 talented performers" which could be a potential untapped market for my proposed apparel line.

4. Review competitors' S-1 and related documents to enhance selected areas of your Internet marketing plan. For example, an analysis of SEC filings can help you improve your plan's business overview and executive summary or formulate better marketing communications strategies.

5. Continue your search for industry- and company-specific information at other related financial Web sites, such as Hoover's Online. You'll find that many companies do little more than file electronically, then point from their Web site to their financial data found elsewhere on the Web. For example, searching for a public company often produces links to cur-

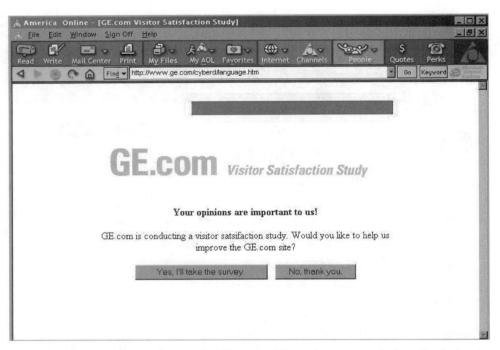

Figure 7.6 GE asks its Web site visitors to participate in a survey before displaying its home page.

rent stock prices and other financial data, and companies throughout the Web often link to these financial sites for reference.

Continue your search for online financial data by reviewing how others in your industry disclose information on the Web. If I were a marketing manager for a company in the home appliance business—for example, if I worked for a company that manufactured vacuum cleaners—I would check out the Dirt Devil Web site and online store at dirtdevil.com. Here, I'd find a link to company information from the main page, which would eventually lead to The Royal Appliance Manufacturing Company's annual reports in HTML and a 10-K in PDF format at *www.dirtdevil.com/annual.cfm*.

Resources

Here are a variety of useful resources to use when deciding how to use the Web to meet disclosure requirements for your company's financial reports. If anything, these resources will demonstrate that your financial information may already be on the Web, even if your company didn't put it there.

News

- PRN Market Focus: Financial at www.prnewswire.com/financial

  Daily updates from "banks, brokers, investment and insurance companies, and other financial institutions"

- Businesswire.com's IPOs on the Net through businesswire.com

  Includes electronic media kits, a list of sites cataloging IPOs, and corporate profiles

IPO Portals

- U.S. Securities and Exchange Commission at www.sec.gov

  The SEC is the regulatory agency that administers U.S. federal securities laws. You can search an archive of SEC-related documents here. The SEC site links to the SEC EDGAR (Electronic Data Gathering, Analysis, and Retrieval) Database of Corporate Information at www.sec.gov/edgarhp.htm and the SEC's Small Business Information at www.sec.gov/smbus1.htm.

- Hoover's Online: The Business Network at www.hoovers.com

  Contains links to Hoover's IPO Central at www.hoovers.com/ipo, where you'll find information on the latest filings and pricings, view IPOs, IPO news headlines, stock quotes, and charts. If you're new to Investor Relations, this site provides "The Beginner's Guide to IPO Investing" to answer frequently asked questions, "Meet the S-1" to introduce you to the content and format of an S-1 SEC filing, and "Definitions of Investment Terms and SEC Forms."

- The Annual Reports Library at www.zpub.com/sf/arl/

  The Library offers an overview of "How to Find a Company's Annual Report Online" and "Tips for Reading an Annual Report."

Organizations

Professional associations are the best source of information on creating an online presence for company financial data.

- National Investor Relations Institute at www.niri.org

  Vienna, Virginia-based NIRI is a professional association of corporate executives and investor relations professionals. It has over 4,200 members in 29 chapters around the United States.

- Canadian Investor Relations Institute at www.ciri.org

  Formerly NIRI Canada, CIRI is Canada's investor relations professional society. CIRI's online resource library catalog lists a publication titled "Standards and Guidance for Disclosure," which addresses Web site publishing.

- Investor Relations Society at www.ir-soc.org.uk

  The Investor Relations Society (IRS) includes about 300 members who are company executives involved in investor relations in the United Kingdom.

Equipment Needs

If you're converting any of your documents in-house, regardless of the format, you'll need to incorporate existing artwork. A scanner would be helpful, unless you plan to rely on your interactive agency or an outside service bureau to convert documents.

I recently purchased a Hewlett-Packard ScanJet Scanner, which has been very helpful in converting my small library of simple documents for use on the Web, in e-mail, and in facsimile transmissions. The accompanying software allows me to choose a scanned file destination, such as Microsoft Power-Point, Microsoft Paint, or Adobe Acrobat Reader. I can tell the software that I wish to save the image and text separately or together in a file, use it with an application, or print it out on my laser printer (Figure 7.7). The optical character recognition software converts recognizable regions to text for editing. HP's online documentation provides more information on scanning for the Internet.

Scanning technology isn't perfect for converting text, so I wouldn't recommend this as a first step in converting documents. Nothing replaces using the original files and graphics. However, if you're caught in a bind, such as being unable to locate your marketing predecessor's materials or a former ad agency that can't locate your transparencies from that last job, using a scanner is the next best thing.

Regardless of how you get your material to the Web, such equipment can save time and money. Start comparing costs for services versus equipment. Inventory all of your document files, slides, photographs, transparencies, and other collateral materials to see which new equipment can best handle your needs. For future product photo sessions, consider establishing at least one standard format, such as making sure that all products are photographed in 35mm slides, besides any additional formats you may need for trade show signage or other reproduction activities. This allows you to narrow down your choices for capital equipment to one "must have" device.

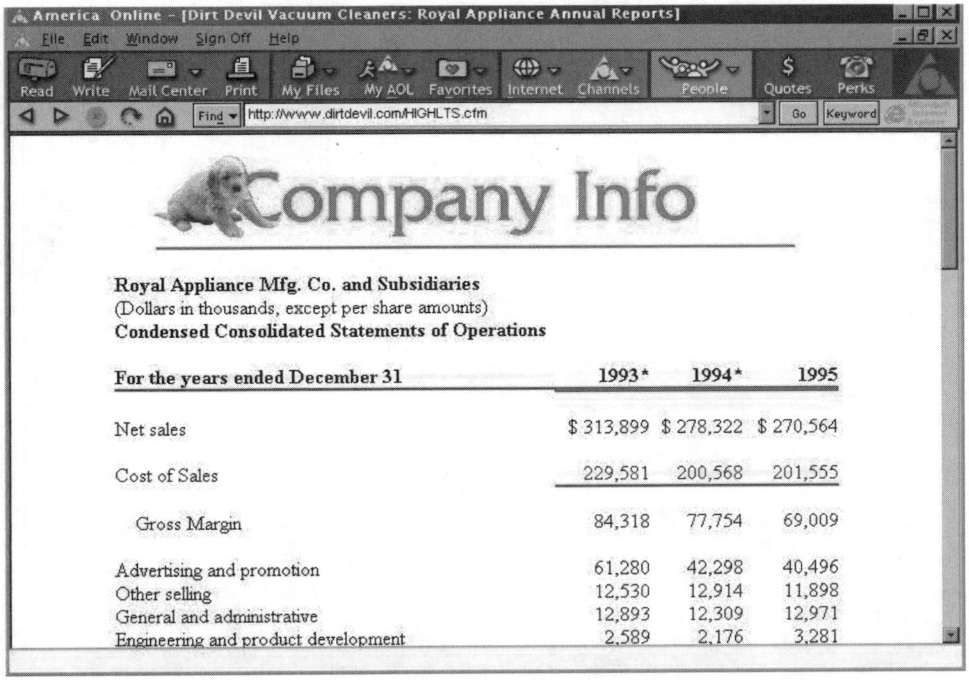

Royal Appliance Mfg. Co. and Subsidiaries
(Dollars in thousands, except per share amounts)
Condensed Consolidated Statements of Operations

For the years ended December 31	1993*	1994*	1995
Net sales	$ 313,899	$ 278,322	$ 270,564
Cost of Sales	229,581	200,568	201,555
Gross Margin	84,318	77,754	69,009
Advertising and promotion	61,280	42,298	40,496
Other selling	12,530	12,914	11,898
General and administrative	12,893	12,309	12,971
Engineering and product development	2,589	2,176	3,281

Figure 7.7 HP PrecisionScan scans to files for use with HTML editors, image editors, word processing programs, or e-mail clients.

Some Activities You Can Do Now

1. Start pricing basic equipment to include in your Internet marketing budget. Go to your favorite auction, comparison-shopping, or buyers guide site. For example, I entered Amazon.com and searched its auction area by keyword "scanner."
2. If your search yields too many hits, don't forget to narrow your search. I found too many links, including one to a Star Trek Picard Figure. I included more words, such as "hardware" and "computer," and searched again. By the way, the matching Amazon.com category for the keyword "scanner" is "Computers & Software / Hardware / Scanners." After scrolling through scores of listings, I was frustrated at not being able to find a desktop scanner immediately, so I gave up on searching the auction sites for capital equipment, at least for now.
3. Another place to window shop is also a computer magazine publisher's site, such as *PC World* Online at pcworld.com (Figure 7.8) and *PC Magazine* Online at pcmagazine.com. At such sites, you can find third-party

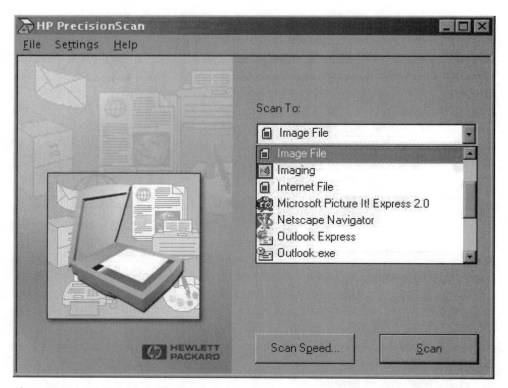

Figure 7.8 *PC World* Online includes a section on scanners with several individual product reviews and comparative reviews in one location.

equipment reviews, which kills two birds with one stone—gathering prices and looking for features that meet your Web publishing needs.

Software Needs

Yahoo! Shopping lists over 750 different products for Web publishing, including several good books on teaching yourself Web publishing quickly. Rather than provide you with an exhaustive list that will soon be outdated, here is a short list for your quick reference.

HTML editors are used to create new documents and convert preexisting documents for use on the Web. Many products serve double duty, so I've lumped them together under this heading. These can include Adobe PageMill, BBEdit, Claris Home Page, Corel Web Designer, Hot Dog, HoTMetaL Pro, and Microsoft's Internet Assistant for Word, to name a few.

HTML converters are also used to convert databases for use on the Web. For example, TILE, a software program, converts Lotus Notes databases into HTML.

WYSIWYG Web publishing tools are for maintaining the look (colors, fonts, layout, and images) of your original sales literature, especially important if you are concerned about corporate identity violations or compromises, hence the acronym WYSIWYG (What You See Is What You Get). These tools can include Adobe Acrobat, ATRAX, and Microsoft Front Page.

Graphics- or image-editing programs, such as Paint Shop Pro, can take a scanned image and convert it into such widely used formats as GIF and JPG for use on your Web pages.

Clickable image map generators are used for mapping out regions of an image, such as a graphical navigational bar, and designating areas for linking to other pages. These include Mapedit or Map This.

Animated GIF creators, such as Ulead GIF Animator or GifBuilder, are used to create advertising banners with action. It's also an inexpensive way to demonstrate product features in a relatively simple but entertaining way.

Bundled Web publishing packages such as Netscape Publishing Suite and Adobe GoLive offer multiple publishing features. Some of these turnkey packages include drag-and-drop features for pictures and other elements, the ability to view the hierarchy of your Web site to evaluate the logic of your site navigation, and site management features such as the ability to check the validity of links.

XML-based content management solutions include BladeRunner for e-commerce applications. According to an August 11, 1999, product announcement, "BladeRunner enables companies to create, manage, and publish structured e-business information . . . for Web-enabled applications using XML as its technology backbone and Microsoft Word for content creation."

How Much Are You Going to Put Online?

Now is the time to create a master document list of your company literature (Figure 7.9).

Regardless of who will convert your print literature for you, this inventory list will help you understand how much work is involved in translating everything to the Web. And you'll also be able to prioritize your literature needs, perhaps in smaller batches, since it may be either too costly or labor intensive to put everything up on the Web at once.

No, there's no unwritten law that you must have every single data sheet online the first day your site goes live. This is a strategic publishing decision your company must make. For more reasons than I can list here, the "all or nothing" Web publishing strategy is not feasible for many companies.

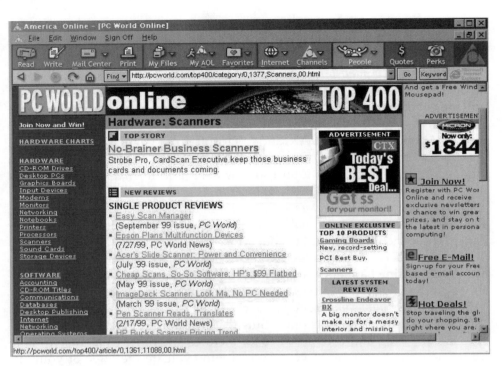

Figure 7.9 Master document list.

Finally, remember to keep track of where the original text files and associated graphics for all your literature reside, in both off-line and online form. Don't discard anything, even after you upload duplicates to the World Wide Web.

Password-Restricted Access

If your Web site contains proprietary or sensitive information, you risk access by individuals who don't have a need to know. If you publish current pricing information in a special area of your site that only employees know about, you'll want to create a password-protected area, because someone will stumble across it sooner or later. Perhaps you've decided that not every Tom, Dick, or Harry.com should have access to all of your literature, including your very special product development notes. So now you have a need to create password-restricted access to selected areas of your Web site.

If you create a password-restricted area, you can use this feature to offer access to your library to one or more types of visitors:

■ Editors and reporters
■ Very important customers

MANUFACTURING.NET

As publisher and executive director for Cahners Business Information's Manufacturing Marketplace, at www.manufacturing.net, Jerry Steinbrink has struggled with overcoming the hurdles of Web publishing. He knows firsthand what it takes to adapt internal publishing procedures to a new technology. In spite of the fact that Cahners has been working with what Steinbrink calls an "antiquated database that requires quite a bit of fiddling," the publishing company is very dedicated to publishing on the Web. Meanwhile, Steinbrink has watched Web publishing change over the past few years from hard-wired HTML to basic databases.

Like most online companies, Cahners's budget has been tapped to keep up with Web development changes, but it's been well worth the effort as the publishing company develops and fine-tunes "a series of standards for both our editors and developers." In the process, Cahners has had to automate some of its front-end procedures and move into an XML-based content management system. Of course, there are much better tools for content management than existed when Cahners first started publishing online. Still, changing from an established form of publishing to a new one can be stressful when the HTML conversion technology isn't yet there to support your unique needs. Each of Cahners's 128 magazines uses Quark to produce hard-copy print pages and the final edited results must be converted to the Web.

"Quark is not compatible with any Web technology, so someone has to manually extract the information out of Quark and into HTML," says Steinbrink. When you have five years of archived material to translate to the Web, it's too much to even fathom. These days, Cahners's magazine editors write articles in a format that tags the information. Those tags are used for both print production and Web publishing. "We pioneered so many of these technologies—and it was so painful for so long," says Steinbrink. "It was extremely primitive and in many ways, it still is."

- Registered visitors
- Your friends at the CIA
- Off-site or traveling sales personnel

Password-protected sites evoke different responses from Internet users. Password-protected sites with easy entry gained through a simple registration procedure can be viewed as a bonus to the registrant, especially when the content is unique or helpful. Password-protected sites can also be viewed as intimidating, annoying, and downright rude. There are still plenty of people who feel that information on the Internet should be free. *Free* means I don't have to provide you with my identity, either. Still, Web publishing shouldn't require you to spend your budget feeding information to the wrong people, either.

Your choice to create this type of site may include a need to track exactly who is reading your online literature. Many users will reregister at a Web site several times using an assumed name and free Web-based e-mail address, thereby skewing your results. This happens often, especially when there are so many password-protected sites around. Users just can't keep track of all the different user names and passwords or don't care to. Previous visitors reregister because they can't remember their password and you've provided no easy way for them to retrieve it.

Another consideration for password-protected literature is cost. If you are a publisher who regularly charges for subscriptions to or copies of your magazine or newspaper, you may not want to freely publish all of your documents on the Web. Web publishing may reduce the income you receive from selling copies of the printed work. You may choose to excerpt portions of your documents. Decide on your strategy for recreating sales literature online beforehand. Creating a password-protected site is big business. It may involve additional technical development costs you didn't consider. Obtain these cost estimates for your budget beforehand.

Different traditional print publishers have different strategies when it comes to republishing print editions online. *Advertising Age* at www.adage.com requires a registered account name and password to search its site. *Ad Age* Online makes it clear that the entire print edition is not available on the Web, which I've personally found to be true. Some of the articles I wrote for *Ad Age* were indexed in a magazine indexing database found through the Northern Light Web site, but didn't appear on adage.com. Presumably, this selective Web publishing strategy helps maintain a loyal print subscription base.

But maybe some of the material you give out is only available to prequalified customers, that is, those with whom you've either developed a relationship or ones who've demonstrated an affiliation with an established customer. In this case, you'll still want to publish on the Web, but you'll want to restrict access to registered parties.

Security Issues and Web Publishing Mistakes

The news is full of stories of companies who have had their security or business plans compromised. It happens simply because IT (information technology) personnel underestimate the skills of disgruntled employees, competitors, site-cracking loners, or some young geniuses with too much time on their hands.

But it's simpler than keeping noncustomers and nonemployees out of areas where they don't belong. Effective site management plays a big role in knowing what to publish on the Web and when. Energetic marketing personnel often upload material to Web servers before it's ready. I always see half-constructed pages on sites under construction, some laughably missing crucial data.

Too many people still don't understand the concept of search engines and robots which catalog Web pages even if you don't specifically register them. The bottom line: If it's on the Internet, it's open season. A word of advice: Don't publish anything on the Web you don't want seen.

I'm not a hacker or a cracker by any stretch of the imagination, and my skills in corporate espionage are easily upstaged. Still, I can tell you that over the years I've found plenty of strange files by accident, including someone's job resume that should have never been uploaded to his company's Web server. I often read the contents of unprotected graphics directories, simply because the Webmaster forgot to put an index page in place to redirect straying visitors. Often, I reach a Web dead-end or a 404 Error (File Not Found). I'll backspace and erase portions of the URL in my browser location, in a low-tech attempt to still find the information. With hardly any effort, I'll uncover log files and gain access to nonpublic documents, all because someone didn't cover all the Web publishing and security bases. Maybe I just want to look around the site on my own terms or I'm trying to save time associated with using poorly designed navigational aids. Now imagine how much information someone can uncover with a corporate research mission or personal agenda in mind.

So how do you know if you should put it up on the Web? Easy. If you distribute it to unqualified customers in print, whether in person, by fax, or by regular mail, it's safe to assume you can publish it on the Internet. Think about it. If someone, possibly your competitor, can walk into your trade show booth and walk out with your catalog without even talking to anyone, then why would you think you shouldn't put this literature up on the Web? If, on the other hand, you don't distribute a certain booklet unless customers fork over some money, you've got a good reason not to let the average Joe find it while surfing the free-for-all spots on your site.

The Web Demands More

When it comes to attracting visitors to your Web site, by way of your printed literature, give them a reason to visit and ongoing reasons to return. Those reasons define your Web site's "stickiness." Stickiness means more than having great content. After you decide on your strategy for converting or republishing your company literature on the Internet, ask yourself again whether the Internet has added anything to the mix. If you are limiting your conversion of documents to a few HTML lines of code and several linked graphics, then your product literature will remain static in an interactive environment. Investigate how you can use hyperlinked screen shots, video clips, VRML, Java, or something else to invigorate your literature and demonstrate product features. Involve your visitor instead of adding more links to other documents. Capitalize on the unique properties of the Internet and you'll succeed in bringing your products to life on the Web.

CHAPTER 8

Developing a Corporate Identity

Corporate branding challenges the company's character, not its pocketbook.
G. Jarvis Coffin, III, President and CEO, BURST! Media

This chapter discusses the use and application of guidelines for your Internet presence in both on- and off-line activities. When you apply consistent standards to your corporate identity programs, you clearly communicate to your market and encourage better recollection of your company, its products, and its image.

The true measure of a company's market identification is in its recognition. Few companies command it without some type of uniform message, whether it includes a company name or nickname, a corporate logo or identifiable graphics, a slogan, or simply a clearly defined communication style. That's why it is so essential to apply the principles of corporate identity to your Internet marketing presence.

In Chapter 7, Utilizing Collateral Materials/Sales Literature, you reviewed your sales literature, such as corporate brochures, product catalogs, folders, and data sheets for content that could be repurposed and enhanced for the Internet. You also reviewed examples of how other companies were recreating their literature libraries.

In Chapter 8, Developing a Corporate Identity, you will continue to strengthen your marketing mix by adding Internet elements into your corporate identity. We will also explore ways to use the Internet to strengthen your off-line identity. This chapter will contribute to the further development of section six of your Internet marketing plan.

Effective Supporting Materials for the Plan

Including data that reinforces your decision to market on the Internet best supports your Internet marketing plan. This section of your Internet marketing plan can be expanded by including any combination of the following:

- Plan of action for teaming portions of selected corporate identity activities with Internet activities

- A preliminary draft of your corporate Internet style manual

- Cost estimates and schedules for adding your URL to building exteriors and signs, company vehicles, product packaging, corporate stationery, and business cards

- A summary of how incorporating the Internet into the corporate identity function will improve your marketing communications program efficiency

Getting the Most out of This Chapter

The activities in this chapter include reviewing and comparing one or more options for enhancing your corporate identity activities. If you have a traditional corporate identity style manual, now is the time to dig it out. It will contain practical information on guidelines that you have already applied to your marketing programs. A style manual will help you incorporate some of your company's style methods into your Internet marketing. It will also keep you from overlooking anything that may create a problem later on. Finally, you should include any Internet marketing guidelines that you have developed as an addendum to your corporate identity manual. That way, you can be sure that it gets the attention it deserves.

Applying the Internet to Your Corporate Identity

Part of the fun in developing a company image lies in watching that image take on a life of its own. How many times have you glanced at the logo of a nationally known company and recognized it immediately, even without the company name nearby? Do you ever refer to one company's name as similar to another's? The companies that have earned your recognition did so for the following reasons:

- They uniformly applied their identity to their marketing communications programs.

- They regularly reviewed its application.
- They updated its use to suit the times.

In applying corporate identity principles to the Internet, do not establish rigid guidelines that require the use of a ruler, a magnifying glass, or some other type of exacting physical measurement. Many of the corporate ID guidelines you are accustomed to, such as color selection and typeface specifications, are lost causes on the Internet. You can attempt to duplicate these elements online, but the ultimate decision maker on some of these choices may turn out to be your users.

Many marketers salute an unbending adherence to identity guidelines. Unfortunately, these same marketers experience culture shock when entering cyberspace. Corporate identity guidelines are just that . . . *guidelines.* They are not a doctor's prescription that must be filled precisely. Corporate identity guidelines are a blueprint. They help you maintain a certain look and feel in the marketplace—one that can't or won't be confused with any other company. Corporate identity guidelines shouldn't be used as a ruler to slap the hands of creative marketers. Corporate identity guidelines shouldn't be used to force a size 8 foot into a size 5 shoe. In many cases, the Internet *is* that size 5 shoe.

How Corporate Identity Guidelines Change Online

Application of your established corporate identity program to your Internet programs is hampered by several factors. These factors are a combination of the technological restrictions, the culture, and online management issues. If you become better aware of them, you can best address how you are going to circumvent corporate identity issues online.

The majority of documents on the World Wide Web are formatted in HTML. HTML approximates formats found in print documents, but currently cannot duplicate them exactly. For text, the range of colors, font types, and sizes is comparatively limited. If your company has a specific corporate typeface and PMS (ink) color, you may have to accept some substitutions during your Internet development. Decide on which substitutions will be made and include this information in your Internet style manual.

The ability to create special effects in HTML, such as those afforded by the use of wallpapers, may create readability or recognition problems when used alongside your company logo or wordmark. Your traditional corporate identity manual may specify restrictions on the types of paper or paper color on which you are allowed to reproduce your company logo. Make note of this and reference a similar policy for the Internet. At the end of this chapter, you will draft your Internet style manual.

Take Advantage of Your Identity

If you are in charge of applying your corporate identity guidelines to marketing communications, such as advertising, sales literature, packaging, or trade shows, then you are well aware of the importance of your logo or company name in the physical world. Companies who are marketing on the Internet have already taken the obvious approach in applying the Internet to their traditional marketing materials, such as stationery and business cards. Some companies incorporate their addresses into company letterhead with a unique flair for Internet style (Figure 8.1). Some marketers find a way to take a standard corporate identity vehicle, such as the business card, and give it an entirely new look and usefulness. Still other corporate identity administrators, fully aware of the Internet's influence, allow it to drive their entire off-line image.

Why is it so important to watch your identity on the Internet? After all, you don't use your company logo in your e-mail messages (at least not yet). That Web site you're designing is one of a few online places where you're reproducing these company-specific graphics. You're controlling how your logo is being created and used, correct?

Well, the Internet is a public thoroughfare. You may put up a sign that says NO SPITTING, but sometimes it just doesn't do any good. The Internet continues to grow at a tremendous rate. As with most growing entities, there are growing pains. The users are testing the Internet's limits, again and again. The users are also testing the limits of the companies who are marketing online. That's why it's not only important for your company to apply its corporate identity to the Internet consistently, but to monitor its application as well.

The Shortest Distance between Two Points

If your department's Web pages are buried in the middle of your company's superlarge Web site, you may have a Web identity problem—a long URL that is bulky and impossible for your customers to remember. No one wants to type www.your-company-name.com/your-division/your-department.html, and you can bet that few will. Users truncate Web addresses all the time, betting that the company's home page will point the way. If you're in this situation, you know that users get lost everyday. You may have been fighting to get your department featured on the corporate home page, or at the very least, easily found through the aid of a site-specific search engine. Meanwhile, no one is visiting your pages and you're desperately trying to build online visibility.

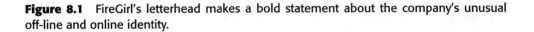

FIRE FG GIRL

FIREGIRL, INC. PROVIDES..

Spicy WEB SITE DESIGN

FireGirl, Inc. is the only web site design firm specializing in the fiery foods industry. Visit out online portfolio at http://firegirl.com/services/portfolio.htm

Robust STOREFRONT PACKAGE

Includes "shopping basket," secure checkout, flexible product inventory structure, five types of shipping calculation, built in search capability, and sales tracking. Designed for computer novices, it's super easy to use.

Gigantic CHILEHEAD EXPOSURE

Want more chile-loving, money-wielding visitors hanging out at your web site? FireGirl's web site gets between 8000 and 10,000 hits everyday! Advertise with us and we guarantee your hits will go up!

Superior WEB SITE HOSTING

All web sites must be hosted somewhere. Our hosting is fast and reliable, plus we have lots of cool geek goodies like 10mb of space, multiple T-3 lines, Unix or Windows NT, your own cgibin, true virtual hosting, and more. A complete list of features is available on the web at http://firegirl.com/services/virtualfeatures.htm

1 - 8 0 0 - 3 4 4 - 8 8 8 2

HTTP://WWW.FIREGIRL.COM

Figure 8.1 FireGirl's letterhead makes a bold statement about the company's unusual off-line and online identity.

You do have some solutions, depending on how daring you are. You can pay to register your own unique domain name through InterNIC and negotiate with the technically savvy to have it point directly to your departmental pages. You can sign up for one of those free domain name redirect or Web site forwarding services. There are advantages and disadvantages of both approaches.

Redirect Service

By signing up for a free Web site referral or URL redirect service, you'll have a much shorter address to publicize. Of course, you'll have to tolerate creating and living with marketing material associated with its use. That means that your content will appear as though it belongs to someone else; someone else who is making money at your expense. If the trade does not offend you—you gain a new URL and the URL provider gains advertising revenue—then select the free redirect service. Since giving away your hard work in exchange for a small service doesn't scare you, the look of these domain names should. Most of these URLs are not pretty. These domain referral services are great for personal pages, such as the page of a local clown (Figure 8.2). But if you're thinking about reprinting that new address on company literature, think again. Even with the permission of the redirect service, these new URLs have the potential to damage your credibility, pegging your Web site as a low-class operation. It's okay for *some clown*, but if you work for a corporation, I'd advise you to stay clear. Here are a few examples of domain name referrals and what they'll do to or for your marketing program.

V3, the Internet Identity Company at v3.come.to, offers a simple registration process. In about 24 hours or less, you can have a shorter, easier-to-remember

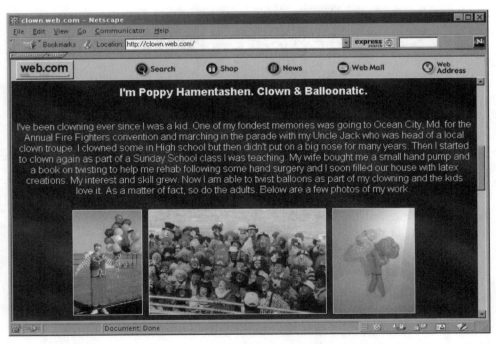

Figure 8.2 Poppy the Clown shows off his home page, complete with pictures of his balloon creations. His long URL has been changed to a simple one (clown.web.com) through the aid of a URL redirect service.

Web address to replace the clunky one that everyone mistypes or forgets. V3 allows Webmasters to choose from a dozen or so V3 URLs, enter their current home page addresses and e-mail addresses, and they are on their way to a better corporate identity on the Web (Figure 8.3). Interested? Choose carefully.

One disadvantage to this service is that a V3 address brands V3, rather than your department, even if the extension spells it out for your customers. Your new Web site will look like "come.to/our-company" which is cute, but hardly fits in comfortably with recognizable Internet address standards. As you can see by the example, these URLs don't look like typical Web site addresses because they're missing the "www" and they'll have a ".to" suffix in the domain name. Visitors may think the address is an error and they won't always recognize your address on printed matter if they don't see that familiar "http://."

At the www.web.com Directory, you can sign up for a subdomain name such as clown.web.com. In this case, your department or company name appears in the beginning of the URL, which is a little better than the path name or Web subdirectory aspect of V3. A domain name such as web.com has a certain special quality, because it is generic enough for users to remember. Web.com is the type of address we've all come to know and love. It even

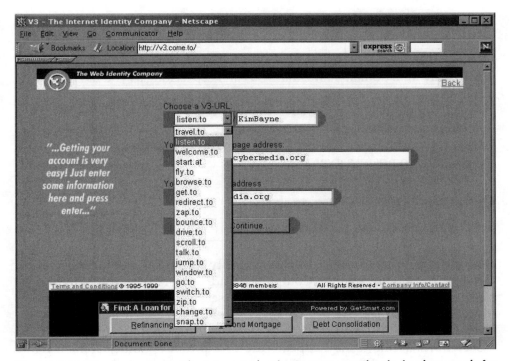

Figure 8.3 V3, also known as the Internet Identity Company, makes it simple to apply for a new Web site address.

sounds like a strong Internet company as well, which puts it in the category of a "vanity" URL, not unlike a vanity license plate for your automobile. But once again, everyone knows that web.com doesn't belong to you, so you're back to square one with regard to branding your company on the Web.

Web.com gives the registering Webmaster two choices. In Package A, "you agree that Web.com may frame your Web site with links to Web.com's Web site or other locations." In Package B, "you agree that Web.com may frame your Web site with advertising of Web.com's choosing." By the way, you can't use your new domain name for commercial purposes unless you first obtain Web.com's written permission, which is a fair and typical request for these free domain name providers.

Can I Get There from Here?

Aside from the branding issues of borrowing someone else's domain name, the server accessibility issues might foil you. Your site takes longer to load because the hosting redirect server has to route requests to and through your server and then back again. If the redirect server is down, so is your site. If the Web service goes out of business, you're out of luck and will have to start anew with your Internet branding efforts. I hope you didn't print up a year's worth of letterhead, if that's your fortune.

Unique Domain Name

I believe that the best solution is one that you own and control. It's a small price to pay for a domain name that you can keep as long as you like. Costs are minimal to own your own Web address and you can pay by credit card on the Web, if you're in a hurry. Many domain registration services offer "free domain parking" until you have your own server or the technical people at your company figure out how to configure your new address to point to your pages on the company server.

Domain Name Ownership and Trademark Issues

One of the biggest areas of corporate identity confusion on the Internet is in the area of domain names. Companies and university administrators are often upset by unscrupulous domain name services trying to make a buck off of their good names. These domain hawkers offer e-mail accounts resembling the names of well-known and respected universities, companies, and associations. While it may appear cute or a prank to some, domain name confusion can be the source of lost revenue or a damaged reputation for many organizations. At the least, watching someone else grab your online customers, because his or her domain name is dangerously close to yours, can cause you to fruitlessly pour dollars into a branding campaign that doesn't work.

I recently performed a search on the keyword "drugstore" at www.whois.net, which produced plenty of matches. I selected a few to demonstrate how confusing it is to maintain a strong online identity. Compare the following domain names and list of owners and see if you can match them up correctly. Look at the domain name on the left and find the correct company name on the right. They are *not* matched correctly as shown here. (By the way, it's not fair to look up the registrants online first.)

DOMAIN NAME	REGISTERED TO
24-7DRUGSTORE.COM	SavvyStuff Property Trust in Massachusetts
AMADRUGSTORE.COM	Open-Web-Net in New York
AMAZON-DRUGSTORE.COM	Drugstore.com, Inc. in Washington
AMERICANDRUGSTORE.COM	Greg Pittman in Kentucky
BESTDRUGSTOREUSA.COM	Robert M. Judge in Portland, Oregon
DRUGSTORE.COM	OneSource Institute, Inc. in California

Interested in checking out your answers? Go to Whois.net and look up the domain names. You can also find the answers at the end of this chapter.

Now imagine how confusing this must be to the customer. Webmasters routinely receive e-mail addressed to postmaster@this-domain-name.com or webmaster@that-domain-name.com rather than the address the company publicizes. Sometimes it's very obvious to the receiving Web site that the user is looking for another drugstore. Sometimes it's not. Some of these messages *could* be intended for drugstores in other cities. There's no way to know for sure, unless the customer is very specific. If you're a sick individual at home trying to get drug-related information that is critical to your health, you've got more concerns than a minor Web identity mix-up. When the Webmaster or company responds, users will know whether they have reached the right company, especially if the customer service department is smart enough to include a standard signature block with company name, street address, and telephone number in all responses. Meanwhile, precious time has been wasted in meeting someone's medical needs.

Domain name confusion is rampant throughout the Internet, and these days, it's often intentional. Domain name registrants know that customers don't care as long as they're being served. If you're selling a common product, such as shoes, you have to compete in every way you can to get the market's attention. Loyal fans of Birkenstock shoes are usually looking for replacements when they start shopping for an Internet retailer. They don't really care if they reach the right shoe store in Tucson or not, just as long as the selection exists, the price is reasonable, and the order is filled promptly. Wouldn't this problem be eliminated if Internet users were more careful? Internet users are as careful as the technology helps them to be.

Why Can't the Government Do Something?

If you think you had copyright issues beat by enlisting your country's trademark officials, think again. In the United States, trademark applications for domain names are often rejected if the Web address is too generic or too similar to others. Even if the federal government *could* manage to extend protection to all domain names, no matter how similar, the problem still isn't solved.

If you have a company or product name that you'd like to register, go ahead and apply for a registered trademark with your local government. It couldn't hurt. In the off-line world, trademark registration is but one formal solution to protecting your identity. You may think this is foolproof, but it's not. A company called Travel Bug located in New York can still register its trade name with the state. Across the country, another Travel Bug in Colorado can register that same name there (Figure 8.4). Are these companies related? It doesn't matter. If neither of them engages in interstate commerce, then no one will be financially harmed by the duplication.

In anticipation of an expanded market, many business owners choose to register a trade name that doesn't conflict with either government registrations. They hire a trademark lawyer who determines whether and where an identity conflict can occur.

I once worked for a company that was interested in securing a trademark for one of its tape drive products, called "The Independence." Having experience in searching online databases, I conducted a trademark search for this name in anticipation of my employer's registration of it. I limited my search to U.S. federal records, and yet I came up with 34 different products named Independence. I wonder what I would have found had I researched further, extending my search to other countries? Most of the products named Independence were in different industries. A few, however, were in the computer industry. Eventually, after consulting a trademark lawyer, company management decided against attempting to register the name.

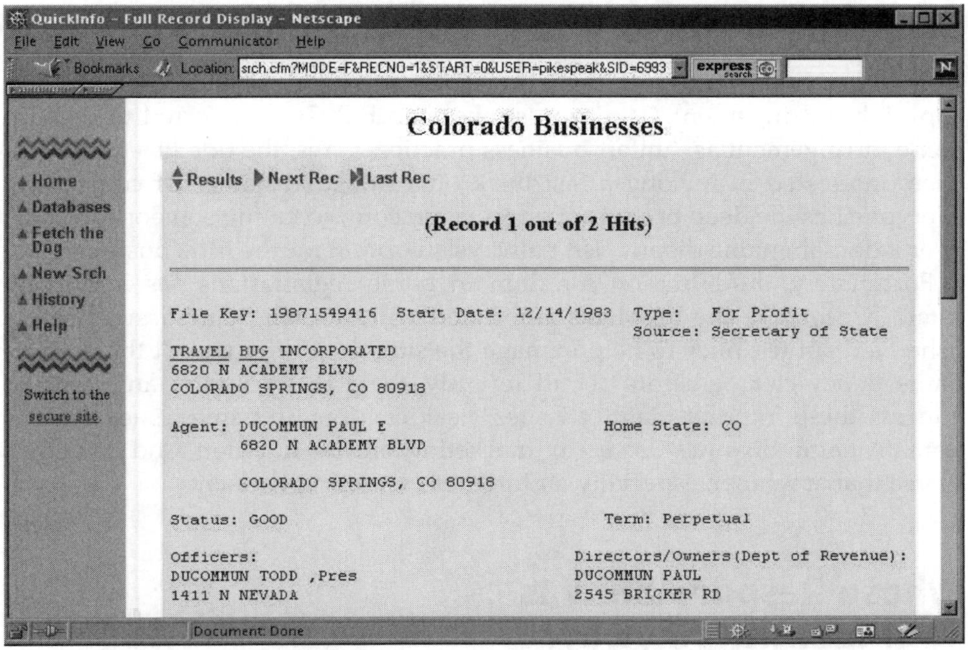

Figure 8.4 QuickInfo.net offers a search of Colorado businesses to determine a company's registration with state authorities.

How Did Everything Get So Messed Up?

Certain Internet users, anticipating the growth in domain registrations, took advantage of the situation. They registered names as fast as possible in order to scalp potential registrants. We have a name for these scoundrels: *cybersquatters*.

As if the cybersquatter problem wasn't enough, the variations in domain name extensions (for example, *.com, *.org, *.net) make it impossible to stop anyone from claiming almost any unregistered name they chose. With enough creativity and some Internet gymnastics, your competitor can wear an Internet name similar to your own. For the marketer, this is equivalent to having directory assistance operators point your customers to someone else. For the customer, this is equivalent to trying to locate a store at 1701 Star Trek when Star Trek Drive, Star Trek Lane, and Star Trek Street are all in the same neighborhood.

Amazon Calls Someone's Bluff

The August 18, 1999, issue of InternetNews.com's E-Commerce News covered the case of Amazon.com's lawsuit against a Web site owner in Greece. Amazon didn't stop at a minor slap on the wrist. According to the article, the lawsuit specified charges such as "extortion, mail fraud, wire fraud, and other racketeering activities" plus "trademark infringement, trademark dilution and copyright infringement." Amazon spokesman Bill Curry referred to domain name infringement as "unfair business practices." Yes, the tide has turned for users interested in making a fast buck on your good name. Of course, not everyone has the deep pockets of an Amazon.com, so taking someone to court over a domain name dispute isn't always an option for the little business.

Fortunately, the situation for domain name registrations *has* improved. InterNIC, tired of the problems associated with domain name issues, established a dispute policy to help manage the situation. Why wasn't the domain name policy clearer before? Until recently, there really wasn't any need to address these Internet identity issues. Besides, domain name issues became domain name disputes *because of* marketing on the Internet. And nothing's worse than a whiner, especially an Internet marketing whiner.

Whose Responsibility Is Your Identity, Anyway?

When it comes to locating your company on the Web, it's not the customers' responsibility to make sure they reached the right store. It's the responsibility of your company to make sure the path to your door is easy to find. Having the right domain name, such as one closely related to your company's trademark, will help a lot. But it's better not to rely exclusively on that avenue for securing your place on the Internet.

No matter what, the government, the courts, and even the domain name registries won't help if you don't take preventive steps. Sleazy individuals will always find a way to take advantage of your conscientious efforts to establish or maintain a market identity, whether it's on the Internet or not. The courts and lawyers' offices are full of business owners who are trying to stop someone else from intentionally capitalizing on their previously established names.

If you're hoping someone else, such as InterNIC or the government, will solve your Internet identity problems for you, you're going to be waiting a long time. You can complain all you want about things you have no direct control over, such as company or product name confusion, intentional or otherwise. You can complain about the thousands of duplicate company names in the world. You can gripe about the way domain names are issued. You can blame any of a number of different governing agencies for this mess. It doesn't really solve anything. You have a job to do. You have to get the word out that you're on the Internet. It's time to take some action.

Action Item One

If you're going to establish an Internet presence, you need to create your own domain name (Figure 8.5). A company-specific domain name is portable. You can take it with you regardless of where your Internet access originates. A company-specific domain name says you are serious about your Internet presence. If you are marketing on the Internet for the long term, you'll want your customers to find you easily.

Internet marketers without a domain name send a different message to the marketplace. For example, think about the message a company like UPS would send if it had its customer packages delivered by the post office. If you work for a company with a large market presence or one that would like to have a larger presence, you don't want to do anything online that detracts from the company's image. Companies that use an access provider's address on company literature make a nice statement . . . for Internet service providers. As a marketer, you want to promote *your* company's presence, *not* someone else's.

The most obvious choice for your domain name is your company name. You may decide not to register your company name due to preexisting Internet conflicts, whether they are by accident or intentional. You may not be able to register your company name as a domain name because someone else may already have taken it.

Many large companies have circumvented the problem by registering as many variations on their company name as possible. By doing so, they shut out all other companies who may have a legitimate claim to a variation. Domain name registration isn't free, like it once was. It costs money—a small amount, but money just the same. Multiple registrations are an option that is feasible only for the large company. Meanwhile, the opportunity to be a hog about registrations takes advantage of the small company. Some domain registry restrictions will limit your ability to register multiple domains, even if they resemble your company name, by requiring a separate server for each.

Creating an Internet Style Manual

In the Internet addendum to your corporate style manual, or in your Internet style manual, you will specify two main items (Figure 8.6):

1. How your Internet presence will be publicized through your traditional corporate identity program

2. How your traditional corporate identity elements will be incorporated into and modified for the Internet

Instructions

◆ Review Chapter 2, *Preparing the Business Overview and Executive Summary,* for examples of companies and their domain name choices.

◆ You may choose to complete this form with full sentences, bullets, or a combination of the two.

◆ Include all currently used and former versions of your company and product names, whether legal, formal, or casual.

◆ Include all versions of company and product names used in verbal or written communications by management, employees, sales personnel, vendors, and the press.

◆ Include all versions that appear on signage around your company.

◆ Include all former company names, including those appended, truncated, or changed in some manner.

◆ Include all frequent misspellings that may have appeared in the press.

◆ Include all abbreviations, letters, or nicknames.

◆ Include all company names that are similar but unrelated to your own.

◆ Include anything that a potential customer might use to locate your company on the Internet, whether you think it's even remotely possible or totally unappealing (you can eliminate the unappealing choices later, if you like).

What type of domain name would you like to create? (Check all that apply.)

❏ Company-specific (e.g., hp.com, ibm.com, microsoft.com, mcdonalds.com, fedex.com)

❏ Product-, brand-, or service-specific (e.g., laserjet.com, shoes.com, huntclub. com)

Figure 8.5 Brainstorming for domain names.

❏ Industry-specific (e.g., marketing.org, electronics.com, finance.com)

❏ Image-specific (e.g., targeting.com, ingenious.com, creative.com)

❏ Geography-specific (e.g., colorado.com, wintergreen.com, southcarolina.com)

❏ Other _____

Company-Specific Domain Names

What is the name of your company?

Your company's complete name:

_____

_____

Name variations

By your employees:

_____

_____

By your customers:

_____

_____

By members of the press:

_____

_____

By others:

_____

_____

Circle all of the names listed above that are trademarked by your company.

Figure 8.5 *(Continued)*

Image problems

Other companies whose names are similar to that of your company:

_____

_____

Any known translation problems in foreign languages:

_____

_____

Circle all of the names listed above that generate concern.

Product-, Brand-, or Service-Specific Domain Names

List your company's product names, brand names, or service marks.

_____ _____ _____ _____ _____

_____ _____ _____ _____ _____

_____ _____ _____ _____ _____

_____ _____ _____ _____ _____

Industry-Specific Domain Names

List keywords for your company.

_____ _____ _____ _____ _____

_____ _____ _____ _____ _____

_____ _____ _____ _____ _____

_____ _____ _____ _____ _____

Figure 8.5   *(Continued)*

Image-Specific Domain Names

List words, such as adjectives, that describe your company, products, or image.

_____ _____ _____ _____ _____

_____ _____ _____ _____ _____

_____ _____ _____ _____ _____

_____ _____ _____ _____ _____

Geography-Specific Domain Names

List streets, cities, states, regions, or other areas identifiable with your company.

_____ _____ _____ _____ _____

_____ _____ _____ _____ _____

_____ _____ _____ _____ _____

_____ _____ _____ _____ _____

Note: _Once you have selected a domain name, register it immediately with the appropriate issuing authority. Include the costs to register and renew it in your Internet marketing budget. If you're unsure who is responsible for domain name registration, start with InterNIC, http://rs.internic.com/, or contact your Internet service provider for assistance._

Completed by: _____ Date: _____

Figure 8.5 _(Continued)_

You may incur some costs for incorporating your Internet addresses into preexisting materials. You may choose to wait until your inventory of letterhead and business cards is depleted before reprinting. You may decide to use an interim solution. I wouldn't recommend using rubber stamps on your letterhead to signal your Internet marketing presence. Nothing ruins the professional image of a nicely designed set of company stationery more than a poorly inked, stamped impression of an e-mail address.

Establish formats for displaying your e-mail addresses on business cards, letterhead, interoffice memos, news releases, and so on. Your decision to include an identifying prefix, such as "e-mail," is up to you. Examples:

Instructions

- ◆ Review your traditional corporate identity manual, if you have one. If not, locate all art directions and type specifications for re-creating your company artwork.

- ◆ Adapt any applicable sections of your traditional identity guidelines for the Internet.

- ◆ If Internet substitutions are not available, for example, for corporate typefaces or colors, choose something close and make note of it.

- ◆ You may need to consult a book on Web design or HTML coding to cover all the possibilities. Check with your Web designer or interactive agency as well.

- ◆ For all cases, explain the guidelines and attach sample layouts, if applicable.

Placement of Internet Addresses on Off-Line Marketing Media

Business cards

_____

_____

_____

❑ Replace all inventory   ❑ Replace selected inventory

❑ Deplete inventory before ordering   ❑ Other: _____

❑ Do not include in program

Cost: _____

Company letterhead

_____

_____

_____

Figure 8.6 Drafting an Internet style manual.

❏ Replace all inventory ❏ Replace selected inventory

❏ Deplete inventory before ordering ❏ Other: _____

❏ Do not include in program

Cost: _____

Envelopes

_____

_____

_____

❏ Replace all inventory ❏ Replace selected inventory

❏ Deplete inventory before ordering ❏ Other: _____

❏ Do not include in program

Cost: _____

Fax cover sheets

_____

_____

_____

❏ Replace all inventory ❏ Replace selected inventory

❏ Deplete inventory before ordering ❏ Other: _____

❏ Do not include in program

Cost: _____

Mailing and shipping labels

_____

_____

_____

Figure 8.6 *(Continued)*

❑ Replace all inventory   ❑ Replace selected inventory

❑ Deplete inventory before ordering   ❑ Other: _____

❑ Do not include in program

Cost: _____

Interoffice memos

_____

_____

_____

❑ Replace all inventory   ❑ Replace selected inventory

❑ Deplete inventory before ordering   ❑ Other: _____

❑ Do not include in program

Cost: _____

News release letterhead

_____

_____

_____

❑ Replace all inventory   ❑ Replace selected inventory

❑ Deplete inventory before ordering   ❑ Other: _____

❑ Do not include in program

Cost: _____

Product literature (*Note:* You may have already addressed these costs in Chapter 8.)

_____

_____

_____

Figure 8.6   *(Continued)*

❑ Replace all inventory   ❑ Replace selected inventory

❑ Deplete inventory before ordering   ❑ Other: _____

❑ Do not include in program

Cost: _____

Employee name badges

_____

_____

_____

❑ Replace all inventory   ❑ Replace selected inventory

❑ Deplete inventory before ordering   ❑ Other: _____

❑ Do not include in program

Cost: _____

Visitor badges

_____

_____

_____

❑ Replace all inventory   ❑ Replace selected inventory

❑ Deplete inventory before ordering   ❑ Other: _____

❑ Do not include in program

Cost: _____

Signage

_____

_____

_____

Figure 8.6 *(Continued)*

❑ Replace all inventory   ❑ Replace selected inventory

❑ Deplete inventory before ordering   ❑ Other: _____

❑ Do not include in program

Cost: _____

Slide presentations

_____

_____

_____

❑ Replace all inventory   ❑ Replace selected inventory

❑ Deplete inventory before ordering   ❑ Other: _____

❑ Do not include in program

Cost: _____

Packaging

_____

_____

_____

❑ Replace all inventory   ❑ Replace selected inventory

❑ Deplete inventory before ordering   ❑ Other: _____

❑ Do not include in program

Cost: _____

Usage Guidelines for Corporate Identity Elements on the Internet

Logo application

_____

_____

_____

Figure 8.6   *(Continued)*

Graphic file dimensions

_____

_____

_____

Color restrictions

_____

_____

_____

Sizing

_____

_____

_____

Whitespace

_____

_____

_____

Address lines

_____

_____

_____

.signature blocks

_____

_____

_____

Figure 8.6   _(Continued)_

info@wolfBayne.com

e-mail info@wolfBayne.com

Contact info@wolfBayne.com

Establish formats for displaying your Web address as well. Your decision to include an identifying prefix, such as "Web" or "http://" is up to you. Examples:

www.wolfBayne.com

URL: www.wolfBayne.com

Web: http://www.wolfBayne.com

Remember that this format won't always work when you reproduce your Internet address on pens, mugs, T-shirts, or anything else. Try to be consistent but be flexible.

Contact Information

When you create pages for your Web site, create a consistent format for displaying your contact information. The page placement and contents of your company copyright statement, company name, address, telephone number, and so forth should be included in your Internet style manual. Don't forget to specify how to display your traditional contact information for customers who want to change communication modes from online to off-line.

Many companies include a link at the bottom of their pages to a contact form and/or list of offices. You can choose to put your headquarters address, toll-free, and fax numbers at the bottom of each of your pages, or link from your copyright statement to a page of multiple office locations (Figure 8.7).

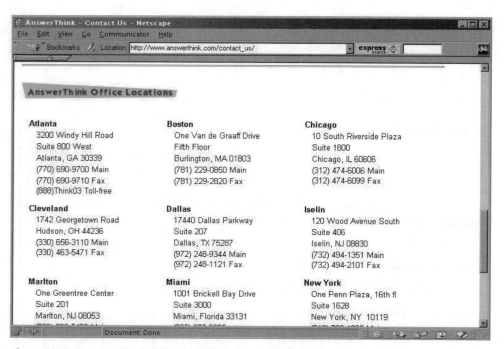

Figure 8.7 AnswerThink offers local help for its U.S. customers.

Signature Blocks

Internet signatures are those blocks of text found at the end of individual e-mail messages. You may wish to establish a consistent look for the messages that are distributed to the outside world through your company's e-mail system. This allows you to take advantage of company communications throughout the Internet, yet maintain and reinforce a consistent look.

Create a boilerplate layout for your company, allowing individual employees to personalize it as needed. If you need some inspiration for generating your own signature slogans, then visit Coolsig.com, a depository for signature files (Figure 8.8).

The following imaginary examples are brief, yet they manage to convey all the key information about the company and its sender, including the company name, traditional contact information, and the sender's claim to fame.

```
------------------------------------------------------
Tim Sturn      http://www.tinkering.com
tsturn@tinkering.com      Tinker Weaving
Author: "World Wide Web Weaving"      580-555-4813
------------------------------------------------------
```

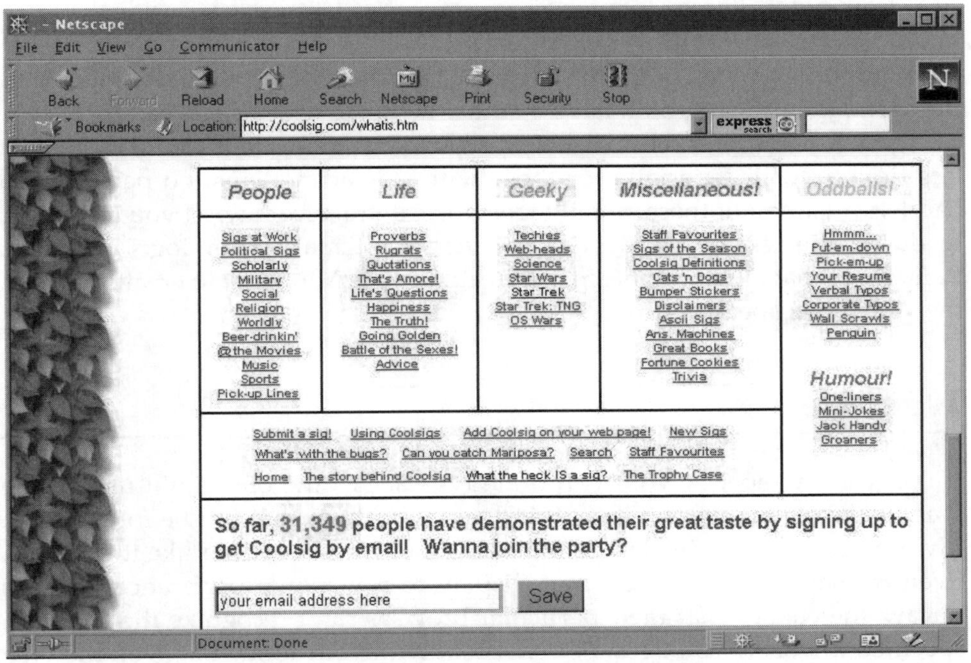

Figure 8.8 Coolsig visitors have a wide variety of signature tastes.

```
=================================================
Jan Danelle           http://www.danelle.com/
Author of "The Marvelous Online Cookbook"
"101 Briskets You Can Cook on the Internet"
501-555-1691              jan@danelle.com
=================================================
```

Your standard company signature block can be any combination of elements, as long as it is not too long and is easy to read. You might consider including an ASCII text version of your logo as well.

Logo

Your logo is that little design, picture, or "bug" that you keep using consistently on your company letterhead and stationery. If you don't have one already, have one professionally designed. A logo that is incorporated into your Web page design can help distinguish your site from many of the low-rent ones on the Web. If you *do* have a logo, you'll be concerned about its sizing.

Two ways to control the size of your logo on the Internet are (1) by resizing the graphics file that contains your logo before uploading it, and (2) by using the image "width" tag in your HTML code to specify how the image will display.

As you're deciding on the size for your logo, make sure you decide the maximum amount of graphics you'll tolerate on a page. You can specify this as the total number of bytes in graphics per page or as a percentage of graphics to pure text. Either way, you'll have a guideline that everyone can easily follow.

A good rule of thumb is to keep your logo relatively small. Small logos take less time to load, especially for those with slower modems, no patience, no bandwidth, or all of these. Small logos don't detract from what you are trying to do on the rest of the page. However, don't make your logo *too* small. Remember that all monitors are not created equal. You want to create a *look* on the Web, not a speck of dirt.

Typeface

If you want to specify your corporate typeface as the one you'll use on the Web, make sure it exists online. If it does, go right ahead. But be forewarned. My browser is set to display all fonts as Times New Roman. I like it that way. Even if users don't set their font display to a personal preference, there is always the chance that their particular browser can't recognize the font face specified in your Web pages. Be consistent with your font choices on the Web site but don't lose any sleep over it.

Horizontal Rule

One of the features of HTML is the ability to include a horizontal rule or line. A rule helps break up large blocks of text and makes a page easier to read. Sometimes it's overused. Actually, many times it's overused. I overuse it myself on occasion. I just can't get over the fact that I can specify its look in so many ways simply by changing a few things in the coding.

The size, shading, alignment, or width of horizontal rules on your Web page might be one of those areas in need of definition. It's certainly easy to say that the standard for horizontal lines in your site is a size 1, no shading, and a width at 60 percent. It's easier to show it this way in your Internet style manual.

```
<hr SIZE=1 NOSHADE width=60%>
```

Navigational Links

Any element you use, such as icons or a special arrangement of text and lines, to help your user navigate your site should be repeated on subsequent pages. If more than one person is designing your site, it's a good idea to provide them with an example of how this should appear, too.

Colors

Nice logo. Funny how it looks green and sickly on my monitor. Did you intend for that to happen? Sorry, but my browser doesn't recognize it as gold. I also like the way you've specified the text color for your page links. Did I tell you that I've set my browser to something different and my choices always override yours? And I can't stand black backgrounds because they always make it so hard to read the text, so I've set my Netscape preferences to always use my colors and override yours (Figure 8.9).

To learn just how much control individual users have over your Web page, check out the help files associated with different browsers. Remember: If you're going to specify backgrounds, links, and other colors, be realistic. Give it your best shot and then get over it.

Signage

You have signs around your company (Figure 8.10) and signs in your trade show booth. You may even have signs on your company vehicles (Figure 8.11).

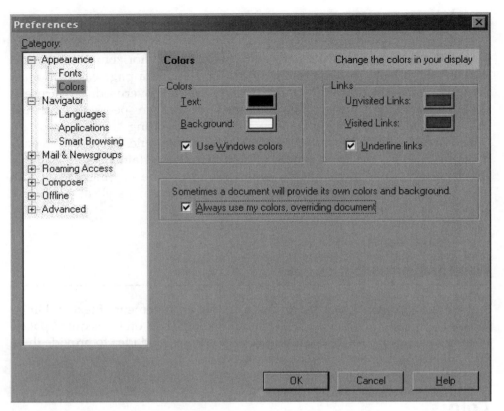

Figure 8.9   Netscape allows users some leeway in deciding how Web pages will display.

Who says you can't publicize your Internet presence on all three? There is no better way to let employees *and* customers know you're serious about Web marketing.

Webmasters Behaving Badly: Designing Browser-Specific Pages

Many companies will tell you that their sites look better with certain browsers. If you insist on designing your Web site to appeal to a select portion of the Internet audience, don't forget to mention it in your style manual.

If you specify that your site will be designed for Netscape Communicator 4.6 or Microsoft Internet Explorer 5, then you've dictated that certain sophisticated users are welcome, while others are not. You might as well hang a sign on your door admitting you treat some customers with less respect than

Figure 8.10 Interse Corporation, www.interse.com, shows its Internet pride by displaying its URL around a doorframe in the company lobby.

others. Web segregation issues aside, you can't solve the problem by "bussing" someone to another Web site to download the appropriate application.

When sites display such a statement as "This site is best viewed with Microsoft Internet Explorer" and provide a hyperlinked button to pick up the latest, greatest version of another browser, I ignore the recommendation. I'm not interested in interrupting my research to download yet *another* application to my computer. If the site looks bad, or text and elements overlap due to some coding error, I decide the Webmaster has no clue. It's not fair, but most users don't have time to look around to figure out why your site looks bad.

Imagine that every time you handed out a printed brochure at your conference exhibit, you had to distribute a special pair of eyeglasses to read it. Imagine that most customers don't want to wear these eyeglasses every time they refer to your literature so they just file your brochure in the trash. Now imagine that customers see your warning about using the "correct" browser but they are either offended by your audacity or don't care. Customers won't change browsers to suit *your* needs, even if you encourage them nicely. They shouldn't have to.

I know how easy it is to develop Web design habits. I empathize with you. I agree that it's hard to keep up on all the HTML variations among browsers, so sometimes you have to choose. But it isn't the customers' responsibility to adjust to your technology preferences in order to be served. It's your responsi-

Figure 8.11   Ryder TRS at www.yellowtruck.com enhances its bright yellow Ford and GMC trucks with the addition of its Web site address.

bility to meet *their* needs. It's your responsibility to check the validity and readability of your Web site pages in multiple browsers before you upload them.

Know Your Users

A decision to design your site as browser-specific may or may not coincide with your visitors' needs. If it does and you can prove it, good for you. Deciding to have a cutting-edge site can be tricky. Just make sure you also define the parameters for alternate versions of your pages.

Maintaining a Consistent Corporate Identity

Your Internet style manual should contain guidelines in several areas, and they should be applied as consistently as possible throughout your site. If your Web visitor tinkers with the color options on his or her browser, at least the colors won't change from page to page.

A list of Web design options could make up another book on HTML. There are several on the market that will help you in that area. This book isn't one of them. If you get a good designer, whether that person is in-house or at an agency, make sure you get documentation for all the specifications used to develop your Web site. Decide if any of these specs conflict in any way with your traditional corporate identity. Then decide what you can live with. Make changes if you prefer, but remember that the user has the final say in how your pages will appear. Take your specifications and integrate them into your written corporate identity manual. Make sure you make plenty of copies to distribute to anyone who has anything to do with your Internet presence.

Answers to the Match Quiz

If you haven't solved the others, here are the answers to the drugstore domain name match quiz posed earlier in this chapter:

DOMAIN NAME	REGISTERED TO
24-7DRUGSTORE.COM	OneSource Institute, Inc. in California
AMADRUGSTORE.COM	Greg Pittman in Kentucky
AMAZON-DRUGSTORE.COM	Open-Web-Net in New York
AMERICANDRUGSTORE.COM	Robert M. Judge in Portland, Oregon
BESTDRUGSTOREUSA.COM	SavvyStuff Property Trust in Massachusetts
DRUGSTORE.COM	Drugstore.com, Inc. in Washington

I bet you didn't know that selling pharmaceuticals on the Internet was so confusing!

Conducting Market Research

I didn't need market research to tell me that the Web was hot. It was obvious.
Karen Dillon, President of KidSource OnLine

This chapter discusses using the Internet to gather competitive and market research information for your marketing communications program. This chapter differs from the one on analyzing Internet market statistics because it is geared toward compiling your own company-, customer- and competitor-specific information, rather than tracking general market trends or accepting someone else's version of the truth. Regardless of how much the industry tells you that your company should be online, you still need to collect personalized information, and do so on an ongoing basis in order to remain competitive.

Keeping track of the image or perception of your company and its competitors is a significant part of managing your company's reputation. If you've already spent a considerable amount of time surfing the Internet over the last few months or more, this chapter is a review of the basics. If you're a novice in online searching tactics and techniques, you'll enjoy learning about the number of free resources now available online.

In Chapter 8, Developing a Corporate Identity, you drafted guidelines for formulating or strengthening your online brand and maintaining a consistent look and feel for your company's online presence. In addition, you applied basic corporate identity principles to your Web presence, specifically adapted for use on the Internet.

In Chapter 9, Conducting Market Research, you will continue to strengthen your marketing mix with the addition of market research. This chapter will support your activities in developing a cohesive Internet marketing plan.

Effective Supporting Materials for the Plan

Including data that reinforces your decision to market on the Internet best supports your Internet marketing plan. Section five of your Internet marketing plan can be expanded by including any combination of the following:

- Plan of action for teaming portions of selected market research activities with Internet activities

- Recommendations for cost savings in traditional market research

- Schedule of regular customer survey opportunities, coinciding with product announcements and other important company developments

- Listings of online resources needed for founding and managing customer beta or focus groups

- Summary of how incorporating the Internet into market research will improve your marketing communications program efficiency

Getting the Most out of This Chapter

This chapter consists of getting online and searching for information. If you don't have the time or the inclination to log on to the Internet right now, come back and read this chapter later. If you're not the kind of person who enjoys online surfing or you can't stay focused enough to tune into relevant information, delegate this task to someone else.

If you're ready, make sure you have decided exactly what you're looking for before you get online. This preparation includes formulating a detailed search strategy before you even open your browser. This is especially important if you're paying for connect time through a dial-up account or still paying incremental costs associated with the number of megabytes downloaded.

Market Research, the Internet, and Business Ethics

Finding information about your competitors couldn't be any easier. When I worked in reference services at an academic library, I remember negotiating time and dollars to log on to a paid database service, such as DIALOG. These days, anyone with Internet access can sit down just about anywhere to log on. Between connecting flights at an airport, I often see travelers with laptops plugged into the data jack of a pay phone. Glancing over a shoulder or two, I notice searches for company information on businesswire.com, Ask Jeeves at ask.com, or Northern Light at nlsearch.com. Market research is as spontaneous as uncovering the five-minutes-old announcement of a company merger just before arriving for an out-of-town company meeting.

Never before has so much business information been contained in one place. I used to think the Library of Congress was the ultimate searching experience. Now, it's the Internet. It's refreshing to be able to gather market data and not have to always trek to the library anymore. And that's because there is a plethora of free information on the Web.

Sometimes there's very good information online. Sometimes the really good information costs money. This chapter will concentrate on how much you can find out without adding to your budget. If you want more than that, there are several companies waiting to serve your needs. I already mentioned some of them in the chapter on Analyzing Internet market statistics.

Competitive Sleuthing

Are you ever concerned about invasions of privacy or competitive espionage? Every person or company is, at one time or another. If you're on the "retrieving end" of competitive research, you should stop and ask yourself this simple question: Where do you draw the line? These are decisions you must make, if you wish to consider yourself an ethical marketer. Here are my personal guidelines for researching information, whether on the Internet or off-line.

The Internet is a public thoroughfare. Any factual, documented information about a public entity, such as a business, is fair game to read and analyze for inclusion in internal market research reports. If a company puts its annual report on its Web site or you find it online in a stock exchange–related database, it's safe to say that you can use that information for competitive analysis and market research purposes.

Opinions can be mistaken as facts. Be careful about misinterpreting and including individual opinions in your Internet marketing plan instead of documented facts. Internet users post convictions, philosophies, and wishful thinking to newsgroups, e-mail discussion lists, and Web sites all the time. Don't take everything at face value. Remember to evaluate all sources for credibility.

Avoid defamatory remarks. Do not repost, reprint, or redistribute any derogatory information about another company or person, even if you quote its source. You're asking for someone to quote you out of context, if you do. Simply forwarding someone else's discussion list post to a friend subjects you to quoting and editing you can't control.

This cautionary guideline is even more important if you e-mail colleagues or others using your company's server. You may think that if your reply-to e-mail address doesn't contain your company's domain, you're safe. If you're using your company's server to distribute the message, the "dirty" or full hidden headers of all your messages will tell the tale. You and your employer could be a party to a defamation lawsuit, even if you weren't the writer of the original derogatory information. If you must bring inflammatory comments or reports to someone's attention, provide the URL so your intended recipients can read and interpret the information themselves right at the source.

Personal data is irrelevant. Any personal information about individuals found on the Internet should *not* be included in market research reports, unless it already appears in a public document, such as a magazine or newspaper. Too many companies are putting marketing databases online, allowing criminals and other busybodies to gather all kinds of detailed personal data for both illegal and invasive purposes. Besides, personal information on the senior-level executive staff of your competitor, such as a recent divorce or a recent illness in the family, has no valid bearing on your company's Internet marketing plan, regardless of how juicy it reads during that "instant messaging" chat with your colleague. Stick to the facts of running a business and avoid sounding like talk show host Jerry Springer.

E-mail messages to individuals are private. If someone e-mails information to you by mistake, don't use it unless you have the originator's permission. Obviously, your competitor is not going to give you permission. In that case, get rid of it. I've received enough misdirected and bounced e-mails to know that sometimes "technology happens." In that case, the only real decision is spelled Ctrl-D.

Some e-mail messages clarify the exact limits of use in the e-mail footer, often through a brief legal notice like this:

This document may contain legally privileged and/or confidential information. If you are not the intended recipient of this e-mail, you are notified that any use (internal or otherwise), dissemination, distribution or copying of this e-mail and/or any attachments is strictly prohibited.

Your competitor is watching you, too. Remember that however you gather and use market research or track your competitors, someone else on the Internet is doing it the same way. Don't publish anything you don't want used by someone else.

Searching Tips

Why would you want to conduct research on the Internet? The Internet is an inexpensive substitute for an outside clipping service, provided you're not reselling this information and only applying it for internal use.

You can easily accomplish competitive tracking activities by bookmarking and visiting a variety of newsgroups, industry newswires, business and trade journals, government and business databases, and related sites. Knowing such sources exist is extremely useful for tracking your own company's editorial coverage as well. Online information exists in every language and covers current news in your industry all around the world. Figure 9.1 lists a few advantages and disadvantages of doing research on the Internet.

What Search Strategy? I Can Just Surf Until I Find It!

Before you get online, decide how and what you're going to retrieve. You do this by developing a good, solid search strategy to save yourself time and money. Become familiar with the terminology in your industry so your search will be productive.

Take the time to become familiar with and use different Internet tools. You won't become versed in online market research until you log hands-on experience and establish your own flow of gathering information effectively. If you need some encouragement, there are hundreds of free tutorials on the Internet. Start by searching in Yahoo! at search.yahoo.com, with the keywords "Internet search tutorial."

The phrases "conducting market research" and "surfing the Net" are *not* interchangeable, mainly because so many users don't understand what it takes to thoroughly uncover useful information. You can begin your market research quest most effectively by developing and documenting your own set of basic search techniques to ensure you cover all the bases.

What Is Boolean Searching?

One of the biggest complaints of Internet users is that search engines rarely produce finely tuned and relevant information. The best way to get around that problem is to become familiar with Boolean searching techniques, which allow you to combine terms or values to find exactly what you want. It's kind of like creating algebraic expressions with words.

Advantages	Disadvantages
Growth is much faster than in print publications.	Links to online resources are outdated quickly.
The amount of free information is unknown.	Free versus fee: The Internet has its share of inconsistent and inaccurate search tools.
You have access to many worldwide resources at once.	Service and access problems can overshadow convenience.

Figure 9.1 Advantages and disadvantages of doing research on the Internet.

Search engines that accept Boolean searches work by interpreting what you want, what else you want (AND), what you'll take instead (OR), and what you don't want (NOT). For more detailed information, tutorials on Boolean searching can be found online at the following sites:

- ADAM: "Boolean Searching Tips" at adam.ac.uk/info/boolean.html
- St. Paul's School: Ohrstrom Library: "Introduction to Boolean Searching" at www.sps.edu/Academics/AIS/Library/Hypertext_tutorial/boolean .shtml
- York University: FAQ: "What is a Boolean search?" at www.yorku .ca/admin/teachtec/faq/boolean.htm

Some Activities You Can Do Now

1. Go to your favorite Internet search engine or directory. Enter a combination of terms that defines your research needs (your search parameters). For example, I was interested in locating information on how to market my radio program to national radio affiliates. I went to Google.com and entered this Boolean expression:

   radio AND syndication NOT music

   I received this response:

   At least 1910 matches for radio AND syndication NOT music

   The AND operator is unnecessary—we do an AND of all search terms by default.

2. Scroll down and read the minidescriptions or abstracts of each link, to determine quickly whether you want to click to investigate further. My results produced too many links, but thanks to my trained eye, I could see that one of them was for a recognizable resource: "RADIO-MEDIA past issues." Too bad the link was outdated!

3. If you run into a dead-end, like I did, refine your search by adding more qualifying keywords, change your search strategy entirely, or go to another site. Trade publication sites are a good place to start, too. For example, I typed in radioworld.com and immediately found that *RW Online* had links to industry organizations and a products and services directory.

4. Finally, if Boolean searching isn't getting you anywhere, use Web sites that allow you to retrieve information as a human being might. Simply ask a question. Go to a site such as Ask Jeeves at ask.com and enter:

   How do you syndicate a radio program?

   Jeeves responded that InfoSeek had found a page with that exact title!

5. If searching at individual Web sites seems laborious, consider downloading and installing a copy of the GO Network's Express Search software from www.go.com. This new desktop application allows you to search multiple search engines and directories, while entering your search scheme just once.

6. Start a checklist of places to visit whenever you start an online search. Lists are great for staying focused. By example, when I started to update this book, I created a personal checklist of resources for retrieving updated information, along with some notes for organizing new material. Here's an abbreviated version of my checklist.

My Documents

Using the chapters of this book as a guideline, I created folders on my computer for each Internet marketing topic. This allows me to easily find all the files I need quickly. As you research material for writing your Internet marketing plan, you may wish to organize your desktop documents the same way.

E-mail Messages

I use the latest version of Eudora Pro, which has a number of very helpful features, such as filters and auto-reply. For example, filters help me sort e-mail into folders and mailboxes divided into a hierarchy of topics and subtopics.

Facsimile Transmissions

These days, all of my incoming faxes are fax-to-e-mail, through such services as FaxWave at callwave.com, eFax.com, or JFax.com. I file all fax documents in my e-mail folders by topic.

Web Browser Bookmarks

I have such an extensive list of Netscape Communicator bookmarks that I've created multiple bookmark files by subject to make topic research easier to manage. Most of the relevant articles found in trade publications can be found online. After reading a helpful article, I often toss the publication and bookmark the online version for reference.

Find Some Private Time

Search time can be pretty hectic. If you don't have a closed office situation or you work on a cubicle-packed floor, negotiate time in a private office for an hour or two per week. Lock the door if you have to. Many times, I've been interrupted in the middle of an expensive fee-based search in a subscriber-restricted database. I've learned not to answer the telephone. Fortunately, you'll be doing your research on the Internet, so most of the resources you use won't have these types of access charges. Interruptions can still be distracting, because you'll lose track of where you are. That's where the bookmarks on your browser come in handy. Use them often.

Now about that search strategy. Figure 9.2 shows my worksheet. Feel free to use it and modify it as you see fit.

Resources

The following sections contain information on resources you can find online.

Mailbot Addresses

E-mail addresses such as info@cybermedia.org are categorized interchangeably as e-mail robots, mailbots, infobots, bots, autoresponders, or even Internet agents. They are the Internet's version of fax-on-demand. Created for the purpose of automated information delivery, the Internet overflows with their existence. Mailbots are often used to automate such mundane e-mail replies as providing a company backgrounder, recent news release, or updated product overview. Unfortunately, at some companies such addresses are a one-way street—your request goes in, but nothing ever comes out. Tag this as another missed customer service opportunity. But, I digress.

Mailbot addresses are normally not accounts that are routed or delivered to any specific individual. These e-mail accounts are set up to manage incoming traffic and are best handled by the server. Bots are supposed to send you boilerplate data without human intervention, but that's not always the case. Some marketing enthusiast may have promoted such an address, but failed to inform computing services of the need to create or route such an account. If your request for information does not respond immediately, this could be the reason. Either your e-mail is bounced, is routed into a black hole, or some poor customer service representative is buried under hundreds of similar requests, trying to process them individually. Of course, a reasonable explanation could also be that Internet and server traffic slowed response time.

So now that you know what mailbots are all about, here's how to use them to your competitive advantage. First, keep in mind that some e-mail addresses *resemble* autoresponders but are really used to weed out competitive snoops or compile databases for unsolicited bulk e-mail purposes. Knowing this, you may wish to create a temporary e-mail account while you conduct your market research. You can always shut it off if the spam reaches obscene levels. Second, if you're ready to gather competitive data by e-mail, send an e-mail to the info@ account at your competitor's domain name just to see what, if anything, comes back. At the very least, you'll get an idea for that company's level of Internet marketing competence, if nothing else.

Instructions

- ◆ Complete this form for each topic before you go online.
- ◆ Once you're on the Internet, make bookmarks for all the resources you find.
- ◆ Go back and search each one individually.
- ◆ If you find another hyperlinked resource, bookmark it and then come back to it.
- ◆ Save files and pages to disk in one separate, but new, directory.
- ◆ Print out information only if you need to and only after you've logged off.

What are you looking for? (State your concept in complete sentences.)

_____

_____

_____

_____

_____

Why are you looking for this information? (Check all that apply.)

❏ Competitive analysis   ❏ Educational purposes   ❏ Statistics

❏ Market research   ❏ Product and service opportunities

❏ Other (specify): _____

What factors will affect this search? (Check all that apply.)

❏ Some information has already been found. Specify: _____

❏ Avoid searches at competitor's sites that require registration.

❏ This data is needed by (specify date and time): _____

❏ Other (specify): _____

Figure 9.2 Search strategy worksheet.

What type of information do you want to find?

❑ Financial data ❑ Case studies

❑ Technical bulletins ❑ Product specifications

❑ Data sheets ❑ News articles

❑ Company background ❑ Data on similar companies

❑ Only information on the Internet (Note: Many Internet resources will point you to off-line resources.)

❑ Other (specify): _____

List keywords, companies, and phrases to *include* in this search.

_____ _____ _____ _____ _____

_____ _____ _____ _____ _____

_____ _____ _____ _____ _____

_____ _____ _____ _____ _____

List keywords, companies, and phrases to *exclude* from this search.

Note: Some Web search engines will allow you to eliminate concepts. This will save you time, especially if you receive too many responses to your search.

_____ _____ _____ _____ _____

_____ _____ _____ _____ _____

_____ _____ _____ _____ _____

_____ _____ _____ _____ _____

Completed by: _____ Date: _____

Figure 9.2 *(Continued)*

Following are two useful Web sites:

- AutoResponders.COM at www.autoresponders.com

  More information on mailbots, including a list of AutoResponder Service Providers, should you be interested in setting up your own

- ReadyInfo AutoResponder Directory at www.readyinfo.com

  A group of directories which list documents that may be instantly retrieved via e-mail autoresponders

Newsgroups

The majority of newsgroups contain opinion and discussion between individuals, a combination of personal and professional Internet users. A few contain news releases. Many newsgroups contain messages with references to information elsewhere online. Newsgroups are accessible immediately, so you can dial right in and download whatever you see. Check out the following:

- Talkway at www.talkway.com

  Talkway lets you search for information in over 35,000 active groups, which include Usenet newsgroups and publicly accessible e-mail discussion lists.

- Deja at www.deja.com (formerly known as Deja News)

  Deja.com helps you locate discussions in thousands of newsgroups by keyword, e-mail address, and newsgroup. Besides providing archives for online discussions, Deja.com also features "people-powered ratings of approximately 9,000 products, services and topics in more than 400 categories."

Mailing Lists

There are two main mailing lists that will interest you for your Internet marketing plan: e-mail discussion lists and company announcement lists. E-mail discussion groups usually contain opinion and discussion. Companies operate a few for the express purpose of encouraging product users to exchange information. A few contain news releases. Many lists contain messages with references to information found elsewhere. Compared to retrieving information on the Web, there is a delay in receiving messages from lists, subject to the nature of the list. Many list owners archive back issues and digests. Some list archives may be searched by keyword.

- Kim Bayne's Marketing Lists on the Internet at wolfBayne.com/lists

  This is a Web-based directory and a printed newsletter. The Web version includes links to over 125 lists, newsgroups, and forums on a variety of marketing-related topics. If you are looking for your online marketing colleagues, you'll find where they hang out by visiting this site.

- Email Discussion Groups/Lists and Resources at www.webcom .com/impulse/list.html

  Promoted as a "one-stop information resource about email discussion groups," it includes a section on where to find discussion lists and list archives.

- Publicly Accessible Mailing Lists by Stephanie da Silva at www.neosoft .com/internet/paml

  An extensive compendium of mailing lists, which is updated regularly. The list is posted monthly to two Usenet newsgroups: news.lists.misc and news.answers.

FTP

- FAST FTP Search at ftpsearch.lycos.com

  Lycos provides a search engine to retrieve listings for over 100 million files on the Internet. I was curious to see if the wolfBayne FTP directory was cataloged. I entered "wolfBayne" and found a link to ftp://ftp.iex .net/users/wolfBayne/, which allows users to retrieve archived copies of selected conference presentations. Enter your competitor's name or product to see what you retrieve.

World Wide Web

The World Wide Web currently has the easiest-to-locate information. There are literally thousands of searching sources on the Web. If that isn't enough, some sites even search the search engines. Not all these resources are free. Some have a minimal fee that is well worth the cost.

Consolidated News

- NewsHound at newshound.com

  This is Knight Ridder's personalized news delivery service, which is available via e-mail subscription and on the Web. The company's Mail Call service lets you retrieve NewsHound articles by telephone. Subscribe to the plain text service for e-mail delivery, subscribe to Mail Call and dial a toll-free number to listen to NewsHound headlines or entire articles.

Consolidated Search Engines

NOTE These sites search or point to other sites, such as search engines, manually compiled Web directories, reference resources on the Internet, and a host of business indexes.

- SavvySearch at savvysearch.com

  This site was listed as a CNET Editors' Choice for Metasearch on the Web. If you're looking for trends, the SavvySnoop page tells you what other users of this site are researching.

- StartHere at www.starthere.com

  StartHere looks through search engines, white pages, yellow pages, databases, directories, and so on.

- Search Engine Forms by Beaucoup! at www.beaucoup.com/formengs .html

  Beaucoup.com contains "Search-All Forms for General Engines," which includes about 2,500 plus search sites. Stop here to look for plain links to computers, software, employment, and media sites, as well.

Business Directories

- AT&T Toll-Free Internet Directory at www.tollfree.att.net/forms/tf.html

  Stop here to look for a business by location or category.

- The Better Business Bureau at www.bbb.org

  The BBB provides access to business and consumer alerts and other useful business resources.

News

- Business Wire at businesswire.com

  Primarily a resource for journalists, you can search by keyword to find recent news releases on companies in your industry here.

- PR Newswire at prnewswire.com

  Another leading resource for company information, including such topics as multimedia and investor relations information.

- CNN Interactive at cnn.com

  Create a personalized news page to track stocks, weather, and news on one page. Log in each day to check out what's happening in your industry.

Market Research

- Computer Economics at computereconomics.com
- Forrester Research at forrester.com
- Jupiter Communications at jup.com
- The Yankee Group at yankeegroup.com

Financial Information

- Dun & Bradstreet at dnb.com

  Compiler of business credit and background information.

- Hoover's Online/IPO Central at ipocentral.hoovers.com

  A subsite of the Hoover's financial market portal, used for locating business contacts, investment information, and competitive intelligence.

- Northern Light Investext Search at northernlight.com/investext.html

  Search for company information by industry and keywords. You can browse industries by clicking on associated links.

- Yahoo! Finance at finance.yahoo.com

  Includes current stock quotes, investment and loan information. You can register to track your own portfolio or track your competitor's stocks.

Federal Resources

- GPO Access Databases at www.access.gpo.gov/su_docs/aces/aaces002 .html

  Connect to Databases Online via this Web-based GPO Access. Find information in the Federal Register, Congressional Record, or Code of Federal Regulations, for example.

- usgovsearch at usgovsearch.com

  Search government and military Web sites, NTIS documents, and the Northern Light special collection.

Legal Research

- Meta-Index for U.S. Legal Research at gsulaw.gsu.edu/metaindex/

  This is recognized as a top 5 percent site by Lycos.com, contains resources on judicial opinions, legislation, federal regulation, other legal sources, and people in law.

Patents

- IBM Intellectual Property Network at www.patents.ibm.com

  The IPN lets you search and research patent documents from the United States, Europe, and Japan as well as patent applications published by the World Intellectual Property Organization (WIPO).

Miscellaneous

- The Lawrence Livermore National Laboratory (LLNL) List of Lists at www.llnl.gov/llnl/lists/listsc.html

  This site includes links segmented by a variety of topics, including science lists, government lists, research laboratories lists, World Wide Web lists, publication lists, educational lists, computer lists, and commercial lists.

Conducting Customer Surveys by E-mail

If you wish to gather your own market research by using internal customer surveys, you may have thought about using e-mail for this purpose. Many Internet market researchers use e-mail to bulk-distribute surveys. Problems with this approach include the following:

It used to be that e-mail would get someone's attention quickly because it was so rare, but now e-mail is easier to ignore. Recipients are using filters in their e-mail programs to sort incoming mail by the various header fields and message text. Finally, if the recipient is not interested, there is no paper sitting around after the message has been deleted.

You can't include a monetary incentive to reply in e-mail. Some surveys include dollar bills or an inexpensive gift as a pre–thank you for participating. For example, I recently received an opinion survey from a manufacturer that contained a dollar bill as a "small token of our appreciation." Companies who include money with a survey feel that the recipients will be more inclined to answer questions if they've already been "paid" to do so. Marketers rely on a recipient's guilt or sense of obligation for this strategy to work. A market researcher can always include an offer of a special report in an e-mail survey, but it's still not as good as having something in your hand. If you think this approach works for you, offer to snail mail something to participants after the survey is completed.

E-mail surveys exclude everyone who is not online or doesn't want to respond via e-mail. This can eliminate responses by a good portion of your audience. If you are trying to survey only individuals who actually use the Internet, you avoid having a control group with which to compare answers.

Results from e-mail surveys may be skewed by false, forged, and anonymous responses. However, this problem is not restricted to just Internet surveys. Some surveyors feel that anonymous responses yield more honest results. Others feel that anonymous responses can yield more false results, since anonymous responders have nothing to lose by lying, and often do. When questions are too intrusive, but your participant wants the free gift you're offering, that person will still respond, but not with truthful answers.

Often, e-mail surveyors use addresses gathered from special-interest lists or newsgroups. The addresses are compiled using software packages that allow keyword searches. There are more youngsters on the Internet than ever before, and it is often impossible to determine whether an e-mail address belongs to a working professional or a young high school student. E-mail surveyors often forget that students are less likely to subscribe to professional print journals, which produce a more accurate demographic mix.

E-mail responses are not necessarily completed in a timely manner. For some reason, people allow e-mail surveys to accumulate and then send in the response whenever they have time. Surveyors often forget to include a deadline on these e-mail surveys, thinking that everyone will respond immediately since it's on the Internet. It just isn't so.

There are many marketing novices who think that e-mail surveys will answer all their questions. When you interview someone on the telephone, you have an opportunity to ask that person to qualify his or her statements, which can give you additional information for this and future surveys.

Surveyors may believe that the results from e-mail surveys are easier to compile. E-mail surveys, like other types of surveys, have their percentage of incomplete answers. This forces the surveyor to either ignore the response, compile inaccurate results based on half answers, or reconnect with the respondent for complete data. Surveyors should state that incomplete surveys are not accepted. However, without the aid of a software program to read and sort incoming surveys and calculate results, each e-mail message must be manually handled.

For those marketers who still wish to conduct surveys via e-mail, there are turnkey software packages that make the job easier. Here are some resources to check out.

- Decisive Surveys at www.decisive.com
- The Survey System's E-mail Module at www.surveysystem.com/e-mail.htm
- SumQuest at www.sumquest.com/
- SurveySolutions at www.perseus.com/index2.htm
- StatPac survey and statistics software at www.statpac.com

Web sites with survey forms that have required fields have a better chance for accuracy than e-mail surveys for two reasons.

1. Surveyors will receive complete information from a motivated individual who has taken the time to visit a Web site. If someone has chosen to visit a site, complete a form, and register an opinion, he or she is motivated.

2. Web developers can program Web-based forms to reject forms that are incomplete or improperly completed. Also, once the deadline for the survey has passed, late responses are eliminated from the mix by removing the form from the Web site.

CHAPTER 10

Executing Public Relations and Promotional Programs

**A lot of the contacts are impossible to reach by email.
There is just too much news in their in-boxes.**
*Michelle Gillett, Director of PR, Brooklyn North,
in a June 1999 post to the Internet Public Relations Discussion List*

This chapter discusses how you can use the Internet to enhance your public relations activities. If you are responsible for media relations for your company, you are no doubt already using the Internet for this purpose. You have developed a custom in-house list of editorial contacts used to disseminate company and product information on a regular basis, whether through e-mail or regular postal delivery. You have a list of bookmarks pointing you to appropriate places to announce activities throughout the Web. You contact reporters and editors via e-mail and follow up with telephone, voice mail, faxes, regular mail, and in person at industry trade shows.

In Chapter 9, Conducting Market Research, you learned to develop your own online search strategy off-line, to save time and energy. You also read about some excellent Web-based resources for gathering competitive intelligence.

In Chapter 10, Executing Public Relations and Promotional Programs, you will continue to strengthen your marketing mix with the addition of Internet-based public relations. This chapter will contribute to the further development of your Internet marketing plan.

Effective Supporting Materials for the Plan

Including data that reinforces your decision to market on the Internet best supports your Internet marketing plan. This section of your Internet marketing plan can be expanded by including any combination of the following:

- Plan of action for teaming portions of selected public relations activities with the Internet

- Recommendations for cost savings in traditional public relations

- Reviews of different online publicity tools, including chat, streaming audio and video, whiteboards, and online slide presentations

- A comparison of costs for posting news releases on your Web site, through traditional news distribution services and through free or inexpensive Internet-only news distribution services

- A summary of how incorporating the Internet into public relations will improve your marketing communications program efficiency

Getting the Most out of This Chapter

This chapter discusses using online resources to distribute news and information about your company to the public. This can be accomplished a number of ways. Regardless of the other tools you embrace, it is best to use e-mail selectively in this capacity. Editors' addresses are published everywhere online, in such places as Web site directories, in e-mail discussion lists, in newsgroups, and in free downloadable files posted by well-meaning folks. Just because you can easily find an e-mail address for a reporter or journalist doesn't mean that this person prefers to be contacted in this manner. Use the Internet as you would use any other form of contact, with informed discretion.

Know Your Audience: The Press

Knowing the communications preferences of the individuals on your press list is always the first rule of conducting media relations. If you haven't established an in-house press list, you'll need to do so, whether it's painstakingly compiled one editor at a time or supplemented by purchasing an external list from a reputable PR media company. Use the accompanying form (Figure 10.1) to interview editors when they first call and to update your database with information from various off-line and online sources.

Remember that the boilerplate approach to PR rarely works, if at all. For example, I prefer e-mail, because it's easy to cut and paste information into documents. It's also easier to delete if the pitch doesn't fit my editorial needs. I'm not too keen on receiving faxes for text, since faxes can be hard to read and I can't capture text to move to other applications. Finally, I can't stand e-mail attachments. I resent having to constantly download the latest virus data for protection (which I do often) just so I can avoid having my computer system hosed by a nasty intruder. If you send me an attached file and I don't know who you are, I'll delete it without looking at it. My outgoing inquiries for interviewees often state that I don't want e-mail attachments, but I can't count how many times that's ignored. In a nutshell, it's a good idea to catalog how reporters would like to receive your online PR communiqués and then distribute your information accordingly.

Internet Communications and the Changing Face of Public Relations

Internet companies have come a long way since those fated few days in 1995 when trade publications pointed an accusing finger at Intel's Pentium PR fiasco. *Business Marketing* magazine's front page carried the headline: "Intel Wipes Out Surfing the 'Net: Few Master Online PR Wave." The story was but one of several on Intel and its Pentium problems. The *Business Marketing* article pointed out that Intel also had problems with its Internet public relations. Intel received a tremendous amount of coverage, but it was not alone. An *Electronic Engineering Times* story around the same time reported that an engineer from LSI Logic of Canada posted his condemning opinion about Viewlogic's ASIC design tools to a newsgroup. His company responded on the Internet with an apology and the promise that this type of post would never happen again. On CompuServe, a user was posting bad reviews of a certain company's products in a variety of forums. Reportedly, the user was the employee of a competitor.

Risks and Opportunities

Companies no longer evaluate whether they should take advantage of the Internet as part of their public relations program. It's a given. But in spite of the amount of progress PR has made online, the Internet can be a very dangerous place for your reputation when it comes to marketing. It doesn't have to be. Companies often fail because they are blind to what is happening online. They don't recognize that the Internet has taken on so much clout and they waste time by not dealing with problems as they occur. By failing to act appropriately, such companies as Intel have secured an embarrassing place in Internet history. Your company doesn't have to make the same mistakes.

Marketing communications and public relations staff must monitor and respond to online communications and not stick their heads in the sand. I'm always amazed when I meet communications specialists who aren't online or who are online once a month or less. Yes, scheduling regular time to observe Internet discussions and news requires dedication. Sometimes it can even be boring. Think about how bored you'd be if you were out of work because your company went under . . . all because of bad press on the Internet.

Instructions

- If you have an external PR agency, use this form to update them on editors who contact your company directly.

- If you do not employ a PR agency, subscribe to a press-list service. Many include editors' e-mail addresses and preferences for communication.

- Use this form to build, update, and/or enhance your in-house list.

- This form can be e-mailed, mailed, and faxed.

- You can convert this form to HTML and post it at your Web site in the press area.

- You can use this form to interview editors while you already have them on the phone.

- Follow up personally with individuals who do not respond.

Editor's name: _____

Job title: _____

Publication: _____

Publishing company: _____

Address: _____

_____

City: _____ State: _____ Zip: _____

Telephone: ( ) _____ Extension: _____

Fax: ( ) _____

E-mail: _____ @ _____

Figure 10.1 Editorial contact database update.

Publication's URL: http:// _____

Other: _____

Which topics do you cover for this publication?

❑ _____ ❑ _____ ❑ _____
❑ _____ ❑ _____ ❑ _____
❑ _____ ❑ _____ ❑ _____
❑ _____ ❑ _____ ❑ _____
❑ _____ ❑ _____ ❑ _____
❑ _____ ❑ _____ ❑ _____

Name two other editorial contacts at this publication who cover these topics.

Editor's name: _____

Job title: _____

Telephone: (   ) _____ Extension: _____

Editor's name: _____

Job title: _____

Telephone: (   ) _____ Extension: _____

What is your contact preference? (Number in order of preference for standard news releases.)

_____ Mail

_____ Telephone

_____ Facsimile

_____ Electronic mail

_____ Newswire

Figure 10.1 *(Continued)*

_____ ASCII text on disk

_____ FTP site ❑ Password-protected ❑ Open access

_____ E-mail autosponder

_____ Internet mailing list

_____ Web site ❑ Password-protected ❑ Open access

_____ Other (specify): _____

Circle the method you most prefer for breaking news.

Our company would like to include news releases at its Web site. If our news appears at our Web site, how likely is it that you will still consider it for publication?

Highly unlikely **1   2   3   4   5   6   7   8   9   10** Highly likely

Comments: _____

_____

_____

_____

If you preferred an embargo period prior to posting news on the Web, what would that be?

❑ Do not post on the Web   ❑ One month   ❑ Three weeks

❑ Two weeks   ❑ One week   ❑ 48-hours   ❑ One day

❑ Other _____

Please return this form to: _____

E-mail: _____ Address: _____

Figure 10.1 *(Continued)*

Like everything else, Internet PR has its advantages and disadvantages. By using the Internet to disseminate information directly to the public, you eliminate the middleman, those publishers and editors who sift through the news and decide what their audiences should read and see. The news is distributed exactly in the manner you meant for it to be. In this way, there's less chance that a publication will misinterpret what you have to say or even insert its own editorial opinion, which may be mistaken for fact.

The risk you take by relying entirely on the Internet for news dissemination is that you now lose the third-party endorsement of the press. The public knows there's no filtering process in place, which means that your message may have less credibility than traditional editorial coverage. Furthermore, anything that you do online, you do for keeps. Take the Intel incident. All you have to do is visit Dejanews at www.dejanews.com and search old newsgroup discussions for the keywords "Pentium" and "Intel" (Figure 10.2). You'll be treated to a menu of endless Pentium jokes and tirades. Working with the press and the public online can be a humbling experience.

Working Tips for Internet Public Relations

Many Internet marketers feel that the Internet will replace traditional public relations. Everything will be done electronically, without the need to build relationships. Yet it's even more important that Internet marketers build relationships now because of the volume of Internet marketers operating under that same misconception. If you thought your finely crafted news release was good enough to get that reporter's attention a year ago, remember this. That

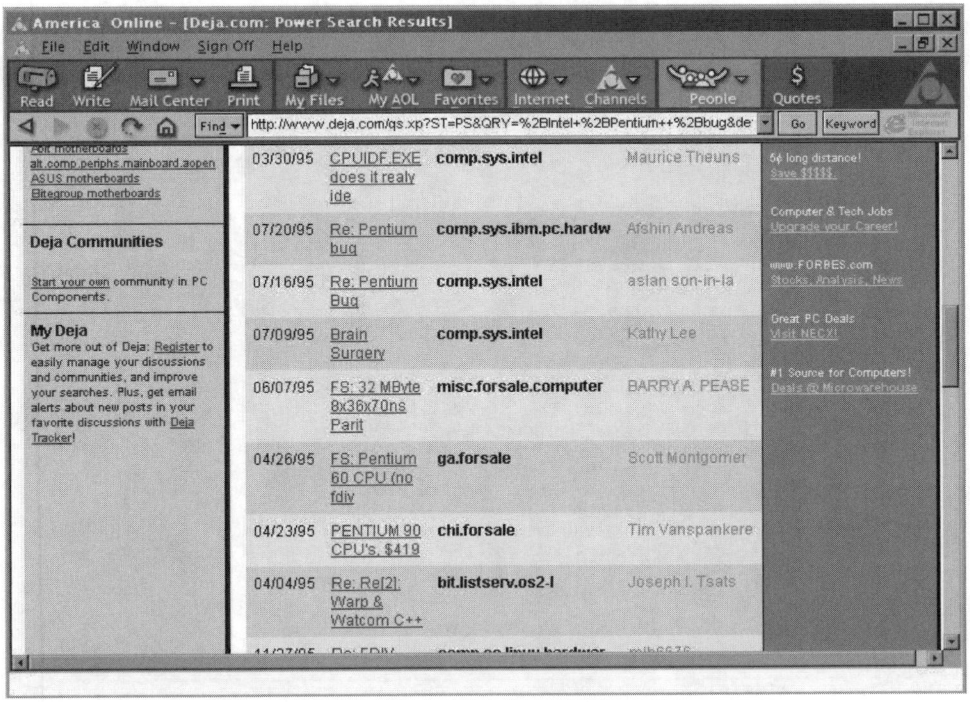

Figure 10.2   Intel secured a place in digital history with its Internet PR mistakes.

reporter now has 500 other finely crafted (some not so finely crafted) electronic news releases to sift through each day.

The rules for building relationships with the press are the same whether you use the Internet, the telephone, a facsimile machine, or a traditionally mailed press kit. Take your time to become familiar with the publication *and* the editor who covers your industry and products. Whichever method you use to contact the press, be as helpful as possible to help them do their job. Provide as much background material as possible and bring your editorial contact up to date. Contact the editor on a regular basis to share news and get news. Nothing substitutes for relationships, not even the Internet. If you can't do this personally, find someone who can.

Use the Internet to Enhance External Communications

Continue using the same modes of communication you have used before, using the Internet as an adjunct or complement to your off-line PR activities. Distribute news via e-mail only to those editors who prefer e-mail, *and* post news at your Web site for those who don't (Figure 10.3).

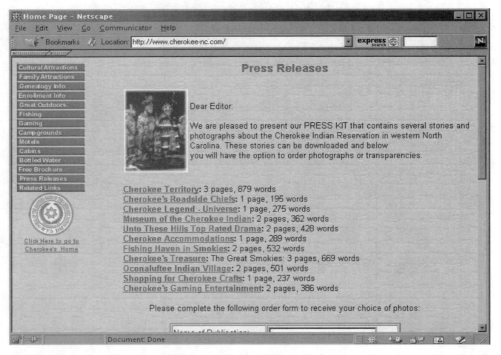

Figure 10.3 The Cherokee Nation's Eastern Band of Cherokee Indians in Western North Carolina offers stories and photographs through an online press kit.

If you don't know where to start and you're going to do Internet PR yourself, you need good resources. One supplier of detailed media information is MediaMap at www.mediamap.com. It has compiled "dossiers" on more than 20,000 media contacts, including information on personal preferences and pet peeves. If you're new to PR or even new to just one editor, this is a good place to start to ensure you meet the media's needs for information. You'll know immediately if a reporter is open to receiving your news release in e-mail. MediaMap updates its database monthly, so if you don't have the resources to build or maintain a press list of your own, here's your answer.

While we're on the subject, news releases on the Web are not just for editors. You want your customers to read this information as well. Provide unrestricted access to news at your Web site. Allow customers to see the news and don't require registration. You can always provide additional information to the press that the public can't reach, if you prefer. The main news should be available to anyone who asks.

To simplify the use of your online news library, consider installing a search engine at your site. This will allow reporters who are researching a background piece to immediately find what they are looking for without having to track you down and wait for a response.

The History of Web Embargoes

In the early days of Web marketing, public relations professionals, Internet experts, and the media warned you to avoid using the Web to disseminate news. I was one of these. We said that editors who found your news on your Web site would avoid covering your company and products, since most publications don't want to reprint "old" information. I talked to a few editors back then and each confirmed they would look elsewhere for hot news. So the need to honor Web embargoes *was* there . . . once upon a time. Today, it's not. You can publish your news immediately at your Web site or anywhere else on the Web, if you choose.

All this concern about offending the press is overblown. Any online user can read the news the day it's distributed. Once you remind yourself that journalists never reprinted your news releases verbatim anyway, you'll see why it's ridiculous to require a Web embargo. Journalists have always sought out interviews with senior-level executives and industry analysts, just to add objective insight to the news and avoid promoting a company's "party line" or "spin."

If your Web site makes it easy for reporters to perform research for an upcoming feature article, they just might call you for a quick sound bite before going to press. Journalists have become so accustomed to seeing news on the Web that if you don't have an easy-to-find press area, they get annoyed at not seeing this information on demand.

DIRECT CONTACT PUBLISHING

Paul Krupin, president of Direct Contact Publishing at www.owt.com/dircon, emphasizes the need for "precision (in) writing and professionalism" in all online communications. As publisher of *The US All Media E-Mail Directory,* Paul offers these "Ten Tips For Using E-mail To Get News Coverage."

1. Think, think, think before you write.

2. Target narrowly and carefully.

3. Keep it short.

4. Keep the subject and content of your message relevant to your target.

5. Use a two-step approach—query with a hook and news angle before transmitting a news release.

6. Tailor the submittal to the media editorial style or content.

7. Address each e-mail message separately to an individual media target.

8. Reread, reread, and reread and rewrite, rewrite, rewrite before you click to send.

9. Be brutally honest with yourself and with your media contacts.

10. Follow-up in a timely manner.

Remember, there are real people at the receiving end. Your success with the media depends on you respecting the media and being courteous, plus your credibility, reputation, and performance.

In the editor's notes of your next news release, include the direct URL of your Web-based press library (Figure 10.4). Tell editors you'll also provide announcements in any form that they prefer. If you distribute your news through e-mail, ask for permission to add a reporter to an e-mail distribution list. Use the Internet News Dissemination PR Checklist included with this book to brainstorm about all the ways you can distribute company news (Figure 10.5).

One more tip: Show your appreciation to publications that cover your company. Include a detailed bibliography of editorial coverage at your site with links to these publications. And don't forget to e-mail the reporter or editor a brief thank you.

How Much Are You Going to Put Online?

Before converting your news releases to online use, make a master document list (Figure 10.6). You'll need these details so you can get accurate bids from

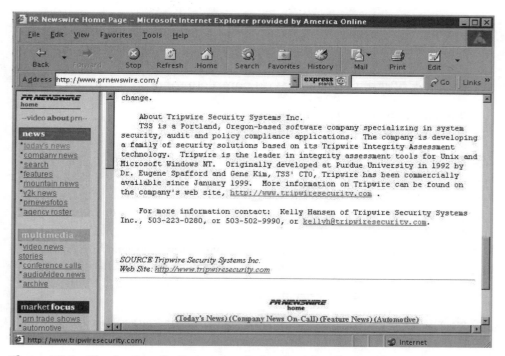

Figure 10.4 Tripwire Security Systems reminds editorial contacts of its Internet presence by including a URL and e-mail address in news releases distributed via PR Newswire.

outside services. If you don't use an outside firm, you'll still want to know how much work you're considering. Keep track of where the files reside, in both off-line and online form, even after you upload them to the Internet. Include the various options for distributing your news release, in both online and off-line forms.

Resources

Some of these companies charge for their services and products, while others are free due to online advertiser support. As you gather cost information, include it in your Internet marketing budget.

Media Directories

American College Media Directory at www.webcom.com/shambhu/acmd/home.html. Includes contact information on 3,000 college newspapers, radio stations, and television stations that deliver news and information to 12.8 million college students in campuses across the nation.

Instructions

- ◆ Use this list as a reminder of the different ways to distribute your news.
- ◆ Check off all activities as you complete them.

❑ Distribute your news by regular mail.

❑ Distribute your news by fax to editors who prefer it.

❑ Distribute your news through the newswire services for thorough coverage in print and online.

❑ Distribute your news by e-mail to editors who prefer it.

❑ Post rewritten and brief excerpts of your announcement to *appropriate* newsgroups.

❑ Distribute your news to individuals who have *voluntarily* signed up for a company-managed Internet mailing list. Cost to manage mailing list:

Setup fee _____ Monthly maintenance _____

Contact your local Internet service provider or your computing services department for costs to add to your budget.

❑ Upload your news in HTML to your Web site.

❑ Upload your news in ASCII text to an FTP directory.

❑ Upload your news in ASCII text for use by mailbots.

❑ Provide your news in ASCII text on diskettes.

❑ Include all Internet addresses in your news releases, either preprinted on letterhead or included in the body of the release.

❑ Include all traditional contact information, such as telephone, address, and fax, in all news releases regardless of their format.

❑ Participate frequently in online discussion groups by providing answers from your news that directly addresses users' concerns.

❑ Refresh your online files by removing old news or archiving it.

❑ Distribute news via other traditional methods to reach those editors who prefer it.

Figure 10.5 Internet news distribution PR checklist.

❏ Follow up with editors by telephone or in person to provide them with additional or new information.

❏ Other: _____

❏ Other: _____

❏ Other: _____

❏ Other: _____

Figure 10.5   *(Continued)*

Gebbie Press at www.gebbieinc.com. Publishers of the All-In-One Media Directory, Gebbie offers contact information on radio and TV stations, daily and weekly newspapers, trade and consumer magazines, black and Hispanic media, which includes fax and e-mail information when available. This Web site offers free databases on TV and weekly newspapers.

MediaMap at www.mediamap.com. Subscriptions include the computer industry editorial calendars online, PR report service, software and data service, trade show report, and the electronics trade press service (Figure 10.7).

Press Access at www.pressaccess.com. Offers an editors directory and databases in the high-tech arena, North American computer trade, and business press.

SRDS at www.srds.com. Publisher of printed media directories for many years, SRDS continues to offer press information in many forms, including CD ROM.

Clipping Service and Monitoring Bureaus

Bacon's Media Directories at www.baconsinfo.com. Directories include newspapers, magazines, radio, TV, and cable contacts in all industries.

Burrelle's Media Directories at www.burrelles.com. Media directories are available in print, on disk, on CD-ROM, and on the Internet.

eWatch at www.ewatch.com. eWatch provides online press monitoring services.

Luce Press Clippings at www.lucepress.com

News Distribution and Wire Services

Business Wire at www.businesswire.com

Internet Media Fax at www.imediafax.com

Internet News Bureau at www.newsbureau.com

Press Release	Release Date(s)	Internet Distribution
wolfBayne announces CyberSleuth 2000 Internet PR Tracking Software	Press—January 1, 1999; Web site— January 14, 1999	E-mail, HTML—Web; ASCII text—FTP and mailbot; HTMARCOM list

Other Distribution	Total Text	Graphics No., Types, Sizes
ASCII diskette in product announcement kit, mail, fax, newswire	Pages = 2; word count = 652	One screen capture opening screen, *.GIF format for Web

Conversion Costs	Archive Location	Online Location
To HTML and ASCII— none, complete in-house	c:\wb\sleuth.htm plus disk #24	../nash/music.htm

Uploaded	Updated	Initials
7/25/96	8/25/96	

Figure 10.6 Master PR document list.

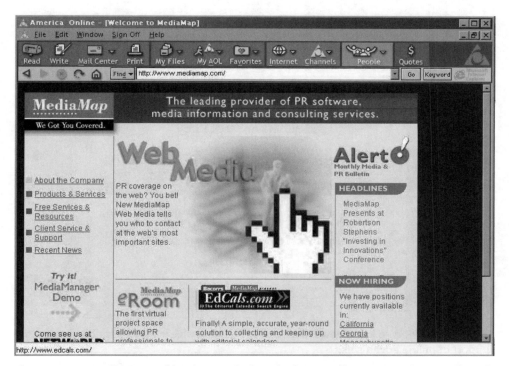

Figure 10.7 MediaMap and its sister Web site EdCals.com offer an easy way to track trade publications, editors, and upcoming editorial opportunities.

InternetWire at www.internetwire.com

Newsbytes News Network at www.nbnn.com

Newspage at www.newspage.com

North American Precis Syndicate at www.napsnet.com

PR Newswire at www.prnewswire.com

PR Net at www.prnet.net

PR Web at www.prweb.com (Figure 10.8)

PIMS' MultiFax Broadcast FAX Service at www.pimsinc.com

URLwire at www.urlwire.com

Virtual Press Office at www.virtualpressoffice.com (Figure 10.9)

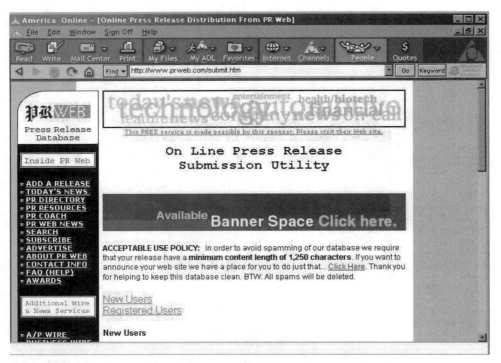

Figure 10.8 PR Web's free news release distribution service is made possible through the support of online advertisers.

Figure 10.9 VPO offers access to thousands of press kits from trade shows around the world.

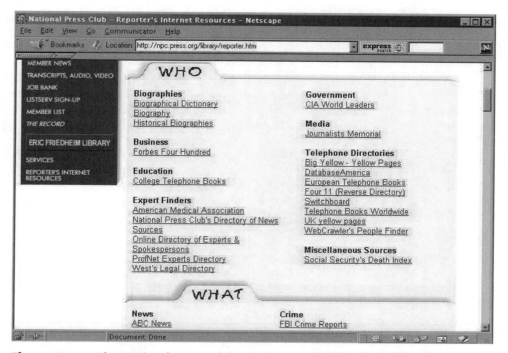

Figure 10.10 The National Press Club site links to numerous journalism resources through the Web.

Miscellaneous PR Resources

Editor and Publisher at www.mediainfo.com

National Press Club at npc.press.org (Figure 10.10)

CHAPTER 11

Incorporating Sales Support Functions

One of our competitive advantages is our extensive back-end fulfillment system.
Susan Heywood, PR Manager, Insight.com

This chapter discusses how you can use the Internet to enhance your sales support activities. Sales support is a mixed bag of tricks at most companies. These activities may simply include customer care and service, such as a telephone/Web bank of individuals who handle incoming inquiries from various marketing and sales activities. If you have sales support responsibilities for your company, your duties could include anything from developing distributor and reseller incentive programs to scheduling and arranging all the activities for a company-wide sales meeting. As diverse as this area appears to be, there are a few activities without which your Internet marketing presence would not be complete: order processing and leads management. This chapter will focus on those two.

In Chapter 10, Executing Public Relations and Promotional Programs, you continued to strengthen your marketing mix with the addition of public relations. You reviewed examples of how you could use the Internet for media relations and promotion. You located Internet resources for press directories, clipping services, and news distribution.

In Chapter 11, Incorporating Sales Support Functions, you will continue to strengthen your Internet marketing mix with the addition of sales support and customer care. This chapter will contribute to the further development of your Internet marketing plan.

Effective Supporting Materials for the Plan

Including data that reinforces your decision to market on the Internet best supports your Internet marketing plan. This section of your Internet marketing plan can be augmented by including any combination of the following:

- Plan of action for teaming portions of selected sales support activities with the Internet
- Recommendations for cost savings in traditional sales support
- Evaluations of outside services for leads management activities
- Evaluations of outside services for customer support
- A summary of how incorporating the Internet into sales support will improve your marketing communications program efficiency

Applying the Internet to Sales Support

As in all other activities associated with your company's marketing communications, use your Web and e-mail addresses in all the materials you distribute or display for your sales support activities (Figure 11.1). This simple inclusion is essential to publicizing your Internet marketing presence in a cost-effective manner. Internet marketers are teaming the technology of the Internet with other technologies as well. Provide your Internet address on product demonstration diskettes, telephone cards (Figure 11.2), and browsers configured to open to your Web page. Reinforce both your traditional and Internet marketing message in multiple ways.

Include technical support literature, such as product specifications, in your Internet promotional campaign. By duplicating this content on the Web, you may more than double the reach of your traditional literature-fulfillment activities (Figure 11.3).

Infobots, Autoresponders, and Mailbots Again!

In Chapter 9, Conducting Market Research, I told you about gathering competitive information by e-mail through different companies' mailbot or autoresponder addresses. As a review, the term *autoresponder* refers to an e-mail account, such as info@wolfBayne.com, or the software or script used to filter that account. The user usually sends a blank e-mail to the mailbot address and quickly (one would hope) receives a form letter or canned response. Some mail-

SCUDDER

Scudder Canada Investor Services Ltd.
BCE Place
161 Bay Street
P.O. Box 712
Toronto, Ontario M5J 2S1
416 943 8665
Fax 416 350 2018
www.scudder.ca

With Compliments

Shabina Bahl
Marketing Assistant

Figure 11.1 Scudder Funds of Canada takes full advantage of opportunities to include its URL on sales materials, including this "with compliments" package insert. (Source: Scudder Canada Investor Services at *www.scudder.ca*.)

Figure 11.2 Customers of Prairie Systems enjoy the convenience of using a collectable TeleCard displaying a Web address and toll-free telephone number.

(Source: Prairie Systems at *www.prairiesys.com*.)

News Release

The Gates Rubber Company
P.O. Box 5887 • Denver, Colo. 80217
(303) – 744-1911

Release: IMMEDIATELY

Contact: Jerry Donovan
Publicity Manager
303-744-5520; jdonovan@gates.com

October 24, 1995

**Hose, Belt Technical Tips
On Gates Internet Page**

An Internet home page, containing technical tips on coolant hoses and serpentine belts, has been created by The Gates Rubber Company.

The World Wide Web site is accessible from any computer connected to an Internet service provider or gateway such as Compuserve, America Online or Prodigy. A Web browser (Netscape or Mosaic) is required.

Gates Internet WWW site has information on selecting, installing and maintaining engine hoses, and recommendations for reducing noise from belt drives. Headlines are "Give a good squeeze to detect a bad hose," "Troubleshooting cooling system hoses," "Hot news about coolant hose failure," "Replacing small molded coolant hoses," and " Troubleshooting V-ribbed belt noise." Each of the five tips has several illustrations.

The home page also includes various news items under the headings of "What's new at Gates" and "Special Offers." The items have an email address for obtaining product literature that will be mailed to the inquirer within 24 hours. Gates also has set up several links for reaching other automotive aftermarket WWW sites.

Gates Internet page can be found at http://www.gates.com/gates/

\# \# \#

intnetpr

Figure 11.3 Gates Rubber Company points its customers to the technical support literature now available on Gates' Web site.
(Source: Gates Rubber Company at *www.gates.com*.)

bots work with a master e-mail address, filtering incoming queries by specific keywords found in the Subject Field of the e-mail. All mailbots (one would hope) work 24 hours a day, 7 days a week.

If you did your homework, you have already experienced retrieving literature through someone else's mailbot. Now it's your turn to think about how you can enhance your customer service with a little more icing on the cake—automatic response. By using these neat little doo-dads yourself, you can process a ton of questions requiring pretty much the same answer. But don't fool yourself into thinking that every routine request for information can be delegated to a mailbot. Human beings are involved on an ongoing basis, especially since e-mail filters are tricky and don't always do what you expect. Of course, human beings are involved. They have to put autoresponders in place to begin with. They also have to decide on file content. Finally, the human being, or Internet marketer responsible for autoresponder content, must decide when and how often to update these files regularly.

Autoresponders are a nice feature and creating content to handle their outgoing needs isn't rocket science. If you've written a piece of literature in a word processing program, it's not hard at all to convert it to ASCII text for use in an autoresponse file. If you're concerned at all about keeping track of who requested your materials this way, most, if not all, mailbot programs track the e-mail addresses of the leads for you. You can use these e-mail addresses selectively to contact prospects at a later date to inquire about continued interest, but don't overdo it. Many mailbot users don't expect to be added to a direct e-mail list without their permission.

You can use your mailbot records to spot in an instant if your competitor is raiding your library. By the way, a reverse e-mail directory is available through the Internet Address Finder at www.iaf.net, if you feel like checking out exactly who's retrieving your autoresponder content.

Autoresponder content is a great tool for live customer-service staff, as well. Staff should keep handy a copy of every boilerplate document used for automatic response. When providing live assistance to online customers, it speeds customer care sessions along to be able to cut and paste prewritten answers for run-of-the-mill questions, saving actual typing for that personalized extra bit of information.

Remember: All autoresponder files should include direct e-mail addresses of key personnel along with all traditional contact information, just in case your form letter or automated answer generates more interest. Publicize your e-mail autoresponder address on your product literature and take advantage of it as much as possible. You can use autoresponders for as many applications as you need and/or you wish to track.

A Quick List of Autoresponder Applications

Advertising. Use mailbots for ads that run in different media in order to track the origination of your sales leads. Companies often use initials or abbreviations for user names to designate different publications or radio programs where their ads appear (e.g., IMTR@wolfBayne.com, BusMktg @wolfBayne.com, mc@wolfBayne.com, NewMedia@wolfBayne.com).

Collateral materials. Use mailbots for each corporate brochure, direct-mail piece, newsletter, or product flier. You can provide updated accessories, discount pricing, or product-specific price lists. You allow readers to request updated information at will (e.g., IMP2e@wolfBayne.com, WebTips@wolfBayne.com, or IMP2e-bookmarks@wolfBayne.com).

Market research. Use mailbots for incoming e-mail responses to an online or print survey. Allow interested parties to retrieve a questionnaire on demand (e.g., survey-wiley@wolfBayne.com, e-commerce-survey@wolfBayne.com, or AdAge-survey@wolfBayne.com).

Public relations. Use mailbots for requests by journalists and editors to provide news releases in text format (e.g., WeeklyNews@wolfBayne.com, update@wolfBayne.com, or pressbot@wolfBayne.com).

Sales support. Use mailbots to publish updated lists of your products' distributors or resellers network. Encourage customers to e-mail your sales mailbot for a special coupon (e.g., sales@wolfBayne.com, resellers@wolfBayne.com, distributors@wolfBayne.com).

Trade shows. Use mailbots to distribute copies of your exhibit or conference schedule, complete with booth numbers and links to trade show Web sites. Provide special e-mail addresses to audience members who've heard you speak at a recent event, allowing them to receive copies of your presentation notes (e.g., tradeshows@wolfBayne.com, conference@wolfBayne.com, or Chicago99@wolfBayne.com).

Creating a Mailbot

You can create a mailbot or autoresponder of your own, if you are ambitious enough and/or have some basic programming skills. At the system level, sometimes it's a matter of defining a script, filter rules, and files. You can include lines of instructions to accompany your online files, telling it what and where to sort, and what to send. If it doesn't understand the incoming e-mail, it just puts it into your general mailbox for processing the normal hands-on way.

But if you don't have, don't want to develop, or don't want to pay for the programming skills needed to create a mailbot, look into an outsourcing service on the Web. Costs for this service range from a $25.00 set-up fee and $9.95 monthly to paying per item e-mailed. A list of such providers can be found through AutoResponders.com.

With a handful of files to distribute, I wanted to test the Web-based mailbot waters. I found an easy place to do it at www.sendfree.com. SendFree.com is a "cooperative network of autoresponder owners who receive free promotion by exchanging ads." If it doesn't bother you that you have little control over the ad headers put in your mailbot messages, then this is the place for you. Send-

Free.com offers statistical reports, such as how many times your content was retrieved. You can update the text of your message at any time (Figure 11.4).

Taking Orders on the Internet

The Internet allows you to automate the sales order process in a very dramatic way. Companies that offer order entry, order tracking, and additional product information in one location on the Web do it best. One of the reasons Internet commerce stalled for so long was because there wasn't a secure way to handle transactions online. Sometimes your browser can tell you if you are accessing a secure server on the Internet. Sometimes the customer still prefers to pick up the phone and call someone, rather than risk putting his or her credit card number online. Still, many companies continue to host their Web pages on unsecured servers, mainly because they haven't yet decided to incorporate direct sales into their site design.

If you decide to incorporate order processing at your site, discuss this with your computing services department and/or your Internet service provider.

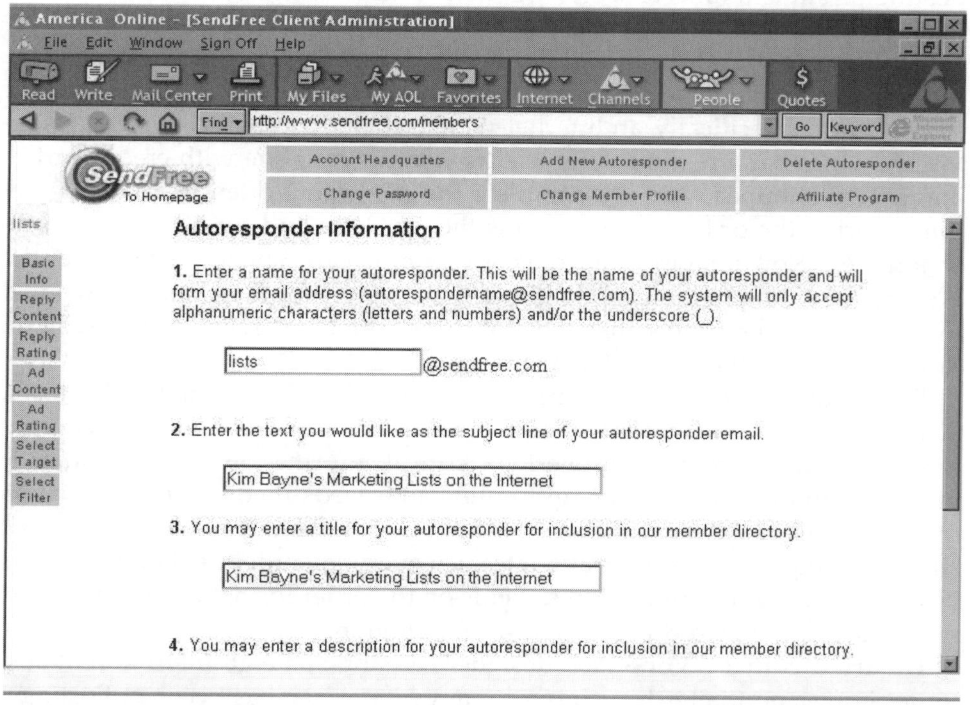

Figure 11.4 SendFree.com allows users to choose a mailbot address and include a subject line, title, and description for its member directory.

Some service providers design different, more secure Internet servers for their business customers. For in-house Web servers, upgrading your server may impact your budget. They may have a cost-effective solution for you already in place.

Converting Browsers to Buyers

In August 1999, Net Effect Systems, at www.neteffect.com, announced the completion of its survey on online shopper expectations, part of a series of studies on e-commerce. The survey found that 94 percent of users make use of the Internet for prepurchase activities, such as product research and price comparison, while only 10 percent actually buy these same products online. The conclusions of this study run contrary to the concerns of bricks-and-mortar retailers who have been intimidated by the Internet's potential impact on local store sales. Net Effect's survey also found that most respondents noted two primary reasons for not buying online: 74 percent cited ongoing security concerns while 73 percent cited weak fulfillment policies. Online merchants who tap into these concerns and address them adequately will be able to overcome the barriers to online buying. Merchants can address these issues initially by posting prominent links to security policies and procedures, as well as an estimate of delivery times associated with representative online purchases.

Net Effect 's president and CEO Julie Schoenfeld finds that the most common dysfunctional aspect of e-commerce-driven Web sites is poor customer service, more specifically, an Internet-wide lack of *live customer support*. Imagine knowing that a ready-to-buy user is visiting your site with credit card in hand. That shopper wants to complete the sale. More often than not, something during the order process derails the purchase and the shopping cart is abandoned. Now imagine hundreds of shopping carts abandoned all over the Web, representing millions of dollars in lost revenue for merchants who failed to close sales. And all because most of these merchants relied too heavily on technology to do the selling for them.

The problem could be as commonplace as a badly designed order form. Schoenfeld mentions that many online order forms are too long and complicated, causing customers to overlook critical information. If a customer is interested in buying a holiday gift online and needs it shipped to a location other than his credit card billing address, he could be out of luck. Some Web sites aren't equipped to accommodate such everyday order deviations. Others include separate shipping address fields on the order form, but the customers miss it because they didn't scroll down far enough.

The truth is that no one Web designer can anticipate all the different customer issues, no matter how Internet-savvy he or she has become. Posting a FAQ (frequently asked questions) document doesn't work, because it requires the site visitor to hunt for the answer. The real solution to completing online sales lies in providing a mechanism for live customer support on the Web.

The ability to click on an easy-to-see button, no matter where the customer is in the purchasing process, is crucial to completing the sales transaction. It's as if the customer were in the aisle of a real store and had a quick question on the size, color, style, or price of any given product. On the Web, the customer stops filling out the order form because she wants to know if the gift will make it to her mother in time for the holidays. She clicks on a live help button and ta-da!, she asks a real live warm body (a.k.a. customer service rep) if the product is in stock now and if it will arrive in time. The customer is satisfied, enters her credit card number, and completes the sale. It can't get any simpler than that.

Outsourcing Customer Support Functions

Providing live Web-based customer care can be a full-time job, and not all e-merchants are ready for the commitment. Such companies as PeopleSupport.com offer a solution to Webmasters interested in testing the need for such a service. A pay-by-use agreement allows Web sites to save money, when compared to traditional customer support programs. PeopleSupport.com's president and chairman Lance Rosenzweig observes that many companies build a customer service or technical support team only to have employees sit around unoccupied during nonpeak hours. By outsourcing live customer support to another company, such as PeopleSupport, many Web-based retailers stay focused on their core businesses.

Often outside teams work in tandem with an in-house team, and since the service is supplied via the Web, the activity is transparent to the user. Visitors rarely know that another company might employ the representative answering the questions. Web technology makes it easy to service more than one customer at a time, so while one online customer is looking at a new Web page pushed through the browser, the support person can provide a quick answer to someone else seeking help. Try doing that with a customer service representative on the telephone.

If providing 24 by 7 customer support seems too daunting a task, either technically or financially, think about establishing online office hours anyway. Train your staff members to use one of the freely available online applications to touch base with customers during business hours. For small companies with limited budgets, there are several chat providers who allow businesses to use sites and software for little to no cost. Just make sure you post your office hours and access information in a prominent place so customers know when your employees are available to answer questions.

Resources

Here is a short list of chat-hosting providers for your use in establishing a live customer support function for your Web site.

- Beseen.com
- Chatspace.com
- LiveUniverse.com
- Nerd World Media at chat.machine.net

If a formal chat room isn't your style, think about publicizing a new buddy list or screen name for live questions. On a business-to-business basis, I find that being able to chat quickly online is very helpful for those two-second questions about guest booking arrangements for my syndicated radio program (Figure 11.5). If you haven't started using this application, here's a short list of instant-messaging software providers.

- AOL Instant Messenger at aim.aol.com
- ICQ at www.icq.com
- PowWow at www.tribalvoice.com
- Yahoo! Messenger at messenger.yahoo.com

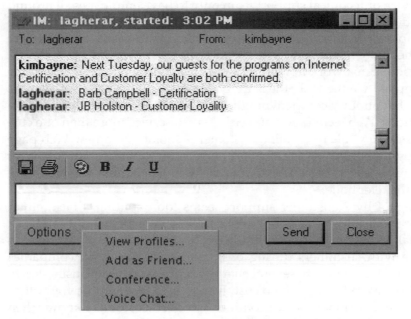

Figure 11.5 Yahoo! Messenger allows the user to type comments in real time, plus invite online colleagues to a group conference or voice chat.

EXPERTCITY.COM

Providing customer support on the Web for your own or your clients' products is one thing, but how about providing real-time customer support for anything that happens to knock on your digital door? That's exactly what Expertcity.com had in mind when it launched its Web site for "expert services" in August 1999. For help, the user types any question into a field on the home page and waits a maximum of two minutes for experts to respond with an offer of assistance.

If unfamiliar with the technology, visitors can take a free 10-minute personal tour of Expertcity, getting first-hand experience in using the screen-sharing software and whiteboard (on-screen drawing) application. Expertcity's proprietary DesktopStreaming technology allows a support person to share screens, controlling the mouse and keyboard of the other user (Figure 11.6). To maintain visitor comfort levels during the session, the support person asks for permission before taking control of the screen.

The enabling application is available for quick download from Expertcity.com before each help session. It was so easy to use that I returned the next day to conduct a chat interview with Sharon Lum, manager/supervisor of the experts. By way of introduction, I opened my e-mail software to show her my signature block, which avoided an extra step in cutting and pasting information for her to read. Seeing my screen on her computer, Sharon could virtually look over my shoulder while I edited portions of this chapter in Word.

Expertcity's BuddyHelp, available from buddyhelp.com, is a scaled-down version of the main application. I have used BuddyHelp to show a colleague a new Web site and point her to other related resources. With features similar to Expertcity's main application, BuddyHelp offers drawing capabilities for circling and emphasizing areas of the screen. After the session ended, my browser was redirected to a survey page. As a recent customer, I could provide immediate feedback to Expertcity for its use in upgrading its product on an ongoing basis.

The Santa Barbara, California-based company provides person-to-person expertise on a variety of technical topics, such as help in operating Excel, PowerPoint, Word, and Windows. Expertcity plans to expand by offering visitors "personalized expertise from professionals on a wide range of topics." In addition, management is looking at providing outsourcing services to other companies, to either supplement preexisting customer and technical support activities or replace them entirely.

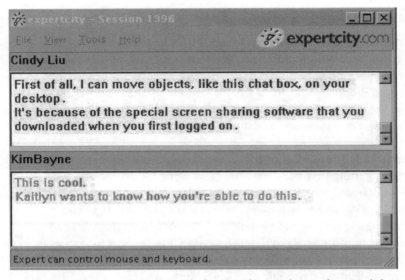

Figure 11.6 Expertcity.com's Cindy Liu shows the author and her daughter how the expert help software works.

Going That Extra Mile: After-the-Sale Service

It's amazing how many businesses forget to follow-up with customers after ringing up a sale. If more online businesses would provide quality reminder services by way of e-mail, more customers would return for a second purchase.

I had almost forgotten that I had registered my car on MSN CarPoint at carpoint.msn.com, that is, until I received an e-mail with my CarPoint Service Reminder (Figure 11.7). If my auto dealer had provided this e-mail service, I might still consider buying there when I'm ready for my next automobile.

I love making crafts, so getting a coupon for my favorite hobby store is a great way to encourage me to drive over to spend my money. Each week, Hobby Lobby Creative Centers at hobbylobby.com sends me a different Internet coupon, linked within the body of an HTML e-mail message (Figure 11.8). If I don't want to receive the coupon in my e-mail, I can still go to this site and print out the Internet coupon of the week. I take it with me to the store when I'm ready to replenish or add to my crafts supplies. Hobby Lobby doesn't have to worry that I'll forget it's in town and I get to buy products at a discount. Of course, the next step for Hobby Lobby would be to allow needle workers like myself to specify that I'd like to receive only those coupons related to cross-stitch and needlepoint. I'll cross my fingers for luck.

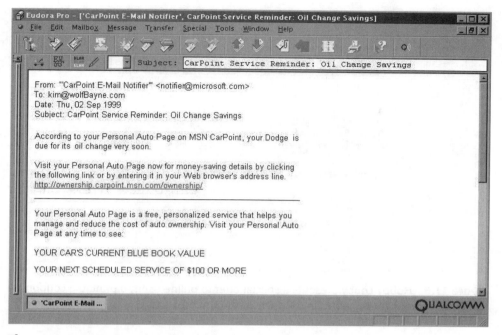

Figure 11.7 MSN CarPoint allows users to register to receive a regular e-mail update on needed automobile maintenance.

Sales Lead Management

Market studies show that sales personnel contact only a small percentage of total sales leads generated by a company's marketing. On the Internet, the problem is even more widespread, due to the sheer volume of e-mail transmitted daily. During an on-site visit at a high-tech company, I watched while the vice president of sales inadvertently deleted the directory that contained his Internet e-mail inquiries. Rather than recover the file, he responded with indifference. "They're only e-mail leads," he chuckled. "If they were serious leads, they would have called us."

E-mail inquiries have fast become the "bingo" lead of the 1990s. *Bingos,* or reader service cards, are those postcards that trade publication subscribers use to request additional information. Reader service cards, like Rodney Dangerfield, don't get "no respect." Readers indicate product interests by circling numbers on a postcard, and then mailing it to the publishing company. Most of the time, readers circle a group of numbers, whether or not they are interested in every single vendor's offerings. As the leads come in, the publishing company processes them and generates a report for the advertiser. Many companies mail out literature packets to these leads, using the prepasted labels provided by the magazine, but that's about it. High-tech publications, such as those on comput-

Figure 11.8 Hobby Lobby presents a special offer to online users, a printable coupon for use at any one of its 196 stores in 19 states in the United States.

ers and electronics, provide access to these leads through the Web, allowing companies to download reader inquiries on demand. This allows the marketer to import leads into a database, sorting them for better and quicker processing.

Marketing and sales managers often feel that magazine-generated sales leads are hardly worth the trouble. Many companies don't even bother to follow up on these leads at all. They treat them as "tire kickers" or trade show trick-or-treaters, cherry-picking the whole batch for recognizable company names.

Companies spend hundreds of thousands of dollars to generate leads through magazine advertising and now through their Web sites. Most of these companies process leads either poorly or not at all. Remember, your presence on the Internet may be the first time a prospect has heard about your company. If you disregard an Internet user's interest, how do you know that user won't go to your competitors? You've lost a sale, all because you discounted the seriousness or credentials of the inquirer at the other end of the Internet connection.

If you're discounting Internet leads, revamp your leads-management system, as well as your attitude. If you're trying to demonstrate that your Internet marketing presence is worthwhile, you'll need to take advantage of every lead the Internet generates for you. If you are short-staffed or unable to develop an effective in-house leads-management system, evaluate outside firms (Figure 11.9). Outside leads-management firms, such as Saligent at www.saligent.com (Figure 11.10), provide outsourced services in just about every aspect of sales lead and inquiry management. Many outside firms will generate detailed analysis reports to support your Internet marketing program.

Instructions

- ◆ Check off all services that you need for your Internet marketing program.
- ◆ Note those services that you are able to handle in-house by filling in that department or manager.
- ◆ Obtain competitive bids on remaining services from outside vendors.
- ◆ Insert the top three companies in each category and the costs.
- ◆ Weigh these costs against hiring additional personnel in-house.
- ◆ Include cost information in your Internet marketing budget.

Services Needed/ Description	In-House/ Assigned To	Outside Service Bureau	Cost
❑ Consulting services		1. _____	_____
		2. _____	_____
		3. _____	_____
❑ Data entry		1. _____	_____
		2. _____	_____
		3. _____	_____
❑ Database development		1. _____	_____
		2. _____	_____
		3. _____	_____
❑ Inquiry tracking		1. _____	_____
		2. _____	_____
		3. _____	_____
❑ Inbound telequalification		1. _____	_____
		2. _____	_____
		3. _____	_____
❑ Lead generation		1. _____	_____
		2. _____	_____
		3. _____	_____

Figure 11.9 Checklist for sales lead management services.

❑ Literature fulfillment

1. _____ _____
2. _____ _____
3. _____ _____

❑ Outbound telemarketing

1. _____ _____
2. _____ _____
3. _____ _____

❑ Product shipping

1. _____ _____
2. _____ _____
3. _____ _____

❑ Sales lead distribution

1. _____ _____
2. _____ _____
3. _____ _____

❑ Staff training

1. _____ _____
2. _____ _____
3. _____ _____

❑ Other: _____

1. _____ _____
2. _____ _____
3. _____ _____

❑ Other: _____

1. _____ _____
2. _____ _____
3. _____ _____

❑ Other: _____

1. _____ _____
2. _____ _____
3. _____ _____

❑ Other: _____

1. _____ _____
2. _____ _____
3. _____ _____

❑ Other: _____

1. _____ _____
2. _____ _____
3. _____ _____

Figure 11.9 *(Continued)*

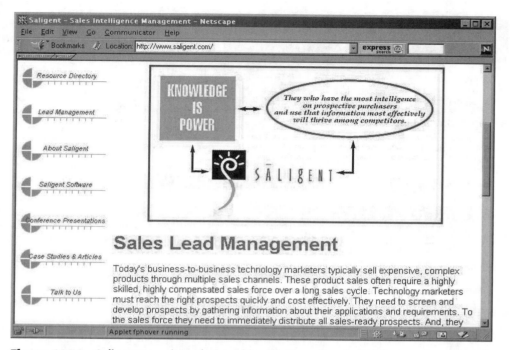

Figure 11.10 Saligent taps into the wealth of information found in a variety of leads generated by both traditional and online sources.

Fun with Frames

One of the biggest complaints about directing customers to place orders online has been the navigational problem associated with Web sites. The bare minimum Web approach to sales includes making sure that every page contains a menu bar and every menu bar contains a link to the online order form. Repetitive menu bars at the tops and bottoms of Web pages still require the user to scroll up or down to find them. If your document is long, this can be one more barrier to getting that online sale.

Webmasters have started to solve this problem by using Web features designed to keep the "order button" visible at all times. Frames, the most frequently used design feature, divide up one Web page into two or more adjacent "windowpanes" within the browser window. Frames allow you to keep a selected portion of your Web page, such as an order button, visible at all times. For example, on NetGrocer's Web site, items added to your shopping cart are displayed at the bottom of the screen in a separate frame (Figure 11.11). Frames allow users to browse freely yet maintain the ability to jump to any page at any time. For more information on frames, search the Web with the keywords "frames," "Web page layout," or "Web design."

Figure 11.11 NetGrocer's Shop Fast section allows users to create and save personalized shopping lists then add preselected items to the shopping cart.

Resources

The following companies offer a variety of electronic order-processing, billing, and payment systems for both online consumers and businesses.

CheckFree Corporation at www.checkfree.com. Provider of electronic commerce services, software, and related products. CheckFree designs, develops, and markets services that enable its customers to make electronic payments and conduct secure transactions.

CyberCash at www.cybercash.com. Provides secure financial transactions services over the Internet, including secure credit card transactions, electronic checks, and microtransactions.

DigiCash at www.digicash.com. Recently acquired by eCash Technologies, DigiCash is a developer of electronic payment mechanisms for open, closed, and network systems that provide security and privacy.

E-commerce solution and software providers can provide you with fee-based credit card processing and automated shopping cart functions. Some include the ability to build an e-store right on their servers or will guide you in creating one

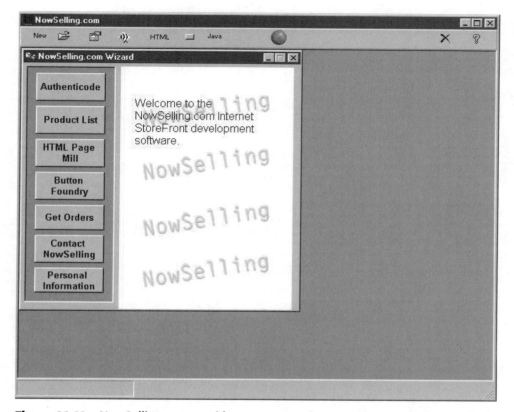

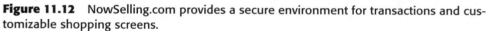

Figure 11.12 NowSelling.com provides a secure environment for transactions and customizable shopping screens.

on yours (Figure 11.12). Prices for installing a back-end solution for order processing range from very inexpensive Web-based service providers (iCat at www.icat.com charges $9.95 per month for up to 10 products) to very expensive high-end solutions ($50,000 or more). The best solutions allow the merchant to integrate inventory checking into the order-processing function.

CHAPTER 12

Planning Trade Shows

It's easier for a prospect to keep clicking than to stop at your virtual trade show and if you don't deliver the information your online prospects need, they're gone.
Mark S. A. Smith, Partner, The Guerrilla Group, Inc.

This chapter will discuss the different elements of trade shows, conventions, and event planning as they relate to Internet marketing. After completing this chapter, you will better understand how the execution of your exhibit and meeting duties are made easier through use of the Internet.

Many activities in this chapter involve little to no expenditures, barely impacting your Internet marketing budget. Incorporating the Internet into your trade show programs often involves nothing more than adding an action item or two to a list of traditional activities. When contacting the different suppliers, conference organizers, and sales personnel, just change your mode of communications from telephone and fax to e-mail and Web sites. If you are updating your real-world show floor image, such as adding furnishings to reflect your new online presence, you will need to research and budget for these items.

In Chapter 11, Incorporating Sales Support Functions, you reviewed and enhanced traditional sales support operations, such as customer service, reseller programs, field sales activities, and technical support, with the addition of the Internet into the marketing mix.

In Chapter 12, Planning Trade Shows, you will continue to strengthen your marketing mix by using the Internet to streamline trade show and event-planning activities. This chapter contributes to the further development of section six of your Internet marketing plan.

Effective Supporting Materials for the Plan

Including data that reinforces your decision to market on the Internet best supports your Internet marketing plan. Section six of your Internet marketing plan can be expanded by including any combination of the following:

- Plan of action for converting selected trade show activities to the Internet
- Plan of action for teaming portions of selected trade show activities with Internet activities
- Suggestions for incorporating Internet addresses and your Web presence into displays
- Recommendations for outside service firms that conduct business on the Internet
- Recommendations for participating in virtual trade shows
- A list of equipment needed for demonstrating your online presence to booth visitors
- A summary of how incorporating the Internet into the trade show function will improve the marketing communications program efficiency

Getting the Most out of This Chapter

The activities in this chapter include contrasting and comparing one or more options for enhancing your trade show activities. Throughout this chapter, I use the words *trade shows, conferences, expositions, seminars,* and *meetings* interchangeably. That does not mean that I am specifically referring to only those types of events when discussing any of the resources mentioned here. During your reading, please assume that I mean any type of special event that involves advance planning, trade shows notwithstanding. Should you find a resource or approach that meets your needs, take advantage of it. For example, if you are interested in booking your company executives at industry conferences as part of your public relations campaign, use online conference and exhibit directories to request information on applicable shows by e-mail or Web-based forms from the speaker or program coordinator.

The suggestions in this chapter are not all-inclusive. You will discover many other uses not covered here. I recommend that you keep a checklist of trade show functions and make notes of how each can be enhanced through use of the Internet. Ask your colleagues how they are using the Internet to enhance their trade show functions. Visit trade show booths to observe how prominent industry players and competitors are taking advantage of the Internet's offerings. As you specify cost-related Internet activities for incorporation into your

Internet marketing plan and budget, obtain bids from outside vendors. The Internet is perfect for requesting bids via e-mail and you can use boilerplate or duplicate e-mail messages to submit requests for bids from multiple companies at the same time.

Applying the Internet to the Trade Show Function

The Internet's impact on the trade show industry has been nothing short of phenomenal. Trade shows have taken on a new life online, and marketers are flocking to take advantage of it. If your job responsibilities include scheduling, planning, and post-show follow-up on any or all of your company's trade shows, conferences, and seminars, you will be pleased at the variety of planning functions that can be completed online. In addition, as part of your marketing promotional activities, you can also include the Internet as one more tool to help draw visitors to your booth.

Dressing for Success

You know your company is exhibiting at an upcoming trade show. You've just launched your Web site and you need a unique way to get the word out about your Internet presence. You have several weeks remaining before the show's opening day and you want to order something special for your exhibit participation. How about establishing a new dress code for your booth staff? Nothing gets an attendee's attention faster than booth personnel dressed in matching garb. Print your Web address on the back of brightly colored T-shirts or golf shirts so visitors to your booth will have a constant reminder of your online presence (Figure 12.1). An added bonus to clothing your staff in imprinted sportswear is the free publicity as they walk around the show floor. Some trade shows restrict company activities to within the confines of your booth space, so this is a subtle and legal way to get more attention in the aisles, possibly drawing in those visitors who otherwise might not have noticed you were at the show. Train staff members to read the badges of approaching attendees and invite selected individuals to your hospitality suite that evening.

If your Web page address is long and difficult to remember, provide the booth visitor with your URL in print. (Of course, that's only a temporary solution, as the real answer lies in using a better Web address.) Along with your distributed product literature, distribute a reminder (Figure 12.2), such as an advertising reprint or small business card. Better yet, your Web address will remain longer in the visitor's mind if you preprint your Web address on liter-

Figure 12.1　Synergex employees sport casual wear emblazoned with the company's Web page URL.

(Photo courtesy of Synergex at www.synergex.com.)

ature or add a brightly colored URL sticker to the fronts of folders and brochures. Some companies distribute a printed coupon to be used only for online purchases. If attendees request that you mail literature to them after the show, include your Web site information in the literature packet, too.

There are several other ways to bring attention to your Internet presence during exhibits and conferences. Neon signs shaped like the letters that make up your company domain name are effective, as are scrolling electronic message boards that state, "Visit our Web page at www.our-company-domain .com." Include your URL on portable signs that can be taken from trade show to trade show, regardless of your booth configuration. Small, inexpensive desktop signs are useful in this regard, and if you're short on time, a plastic 8 by 10 sign holder can be picked up at your local office supply store.

Why Ordering A Molded Heater Hose Isn't The Run Around It Used To Be.

Before, when you needed a molded heater hose, you went to a new car dealer. Now it's as close as your nearest jobber, which means you'll get higher quality at a competitive price. And with our Hose Locator Guide, finding the location and routing of a hose will be easier than ever before. For details, talk to your Gates jobber or call 1-800-788-2358.

THE WORLD'S MOST TRUSTED NAME IN BELTS AND HOSE.

The Gates Rubber Company, Denver CO 80217   Gates internet home page: http:// www.gates.com/gates/

Ad code: 313
Job #: GAU-41801
Ad size: 1/2 PG 4C Hort.
Description: Molded Coolant Hose
Date prepared: 5/95
Prepared by: Bozell/Omaha

With their abrasive rocks, the mines of central Wyoming used to chew up a good hose in about a month -- until the Terminator™ hose arrived. With its rugged synthetic rubber cover and resilient polyester reinforcement, the Terminator hose will outperform any multi-purpose hose on the market today. If you work in a tough environment, the Terminator hose makes sense. It can handle intense heat, and covers hundreds of applications, including oil, water, air, chemicals, grease sprays, paraffin wax and salt solutions, so practically anyone can use it. The Terminator hose will take more punishment and cause less downtime than any other leading hose.

So call your Gates distributor and place your order today. Because while the Terminator hose may be tough, the decision to buy one shouldn't be.

THE WORLD'S MOST TRUSTED NAME IN BELTS, HOSE AND HYDRAULICS.

The Gates Rubber Company, Denver CO 80217 (800) 788-2358 FAX (303) 744-5771 Gates internet home page: http://www.gates.com/gates/

Figure 12.2 Ad reprints can be distributed at trade shows and included in literature packets as a reminder that a company is online.

(Source: Gates Rubber Company at www.gate.com.)

Booth furniture provides you with yet another opportunity to tout your Internet pride. If live presentations are part of your exhibit, order custom imprinted chairs to accommodate the weary trade show visitor. Canvas director chairs are great for this purpose, because the removable fabric backs are easy to silk-screen. Imagine the reinforced message you send your guests if, during the course of a 5- to -10-minute entertaining presentation, they glance at the seat backs (and your URL) several times.

Hand out a visitor registration card to help prequalify serious buyers—while they answer a brief questionnaire in exchange for booth goodies, they'll notice your Web address printed at the top of the form. When the presentation is over, registered attendees will stand in line to pick up a free beanbag animal, complete with your URL embroidered across its cute little chest.

If you're in the habit of renting carpet for booth installation, think about the convenience of purchasing your own. By purchasing, you guarantee that the color will match your booth decor and will not change from show to show. This would allow you the option of ordering carpet with your domain name dyed or woven into the threads. Of course, since specialty carpeting is cost-prohibitive, try another, equally as effective, solution to decorating your booth. Order a small area rug or counter placemats with a color picture of your Web site's home page for placement in strategic locations throughout the booth.

That's It? I Just Reproduce My Web URL on Everything?

Well, not exactly. Those examples are the easiest to implement. If you're looking for something less passive and more impressive, think about getting the booth visitor involved with your Web site. After all, the Internet is supposed to be interactive, isn't it? It would be a shame not to take advantage of it while you've got a live, warm body in your temporary place of business.

If you have computers in your trade show booth, or if you can rent them, it's always a good idea to let visitors test-drive your Web site on the spot. You're right there to answer any questions they may have, and you can point them precisely to the best material. Or, if you're concerned about show floor connections or bandwidth sluggishness, bring a selection of your Web pages along and let visitors tour your Web site from the hard drive.

Demonstrating your Web site on the show floor can reinforce your product information as well. Perhaps your exhibit received more visitors than you previously planned. You've run out of literature. Pull up your Web site and you've got a temporary solution while the folks back home ship more data sheets to you overnight.

Another neat application uses your Web site to register show floor leads. Arm registration desk staff members with direct connections and links to your Web site registration pages. They'll enter visitor information right into the Web page, sending it right back to the home office in real time. If your Web site has the middleware in place to process customer inquiries for database import, you've got it made. No extra step is needed for leads processing.

Sharing Trade Show Calendars with Off-Site Personnel

If you're looking for a free and easy way to publish and distribute your company's exhibit schedule, register at one of the many Web-based calendar sites. At Yahoo! Calendar, you can create a public marketing calendar to inform your sales staff on demand. No more printing out updated booth number lists and distributing them. You just point personnel to the Web so they can check company events or activities anytime without having to talk to you directly.

Your public calendar might have an address such as calendar.yahoo .com/public/your-company-name (Figure 12.3). The calendar-sharing func-

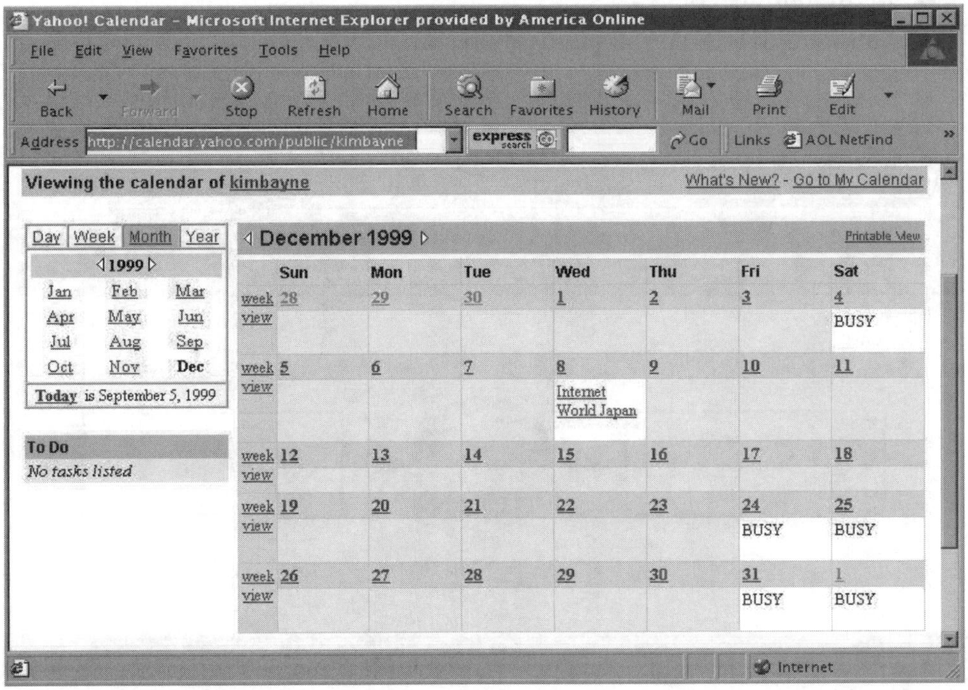

Figure 12.3 Yahoo! offers a public calendar function that can be used to quickly upload your trade show calendar to the Web.

tion at Yahoo! publishes a read-only version of your calendar that you can publicize through company e-mail or link to from your company intranet. You can also publish a group calendar for updating by anyone. The Yahoo! calendar allows you to program it to send out e-mail reminders or invitations to a select group of people, as well. The best feature of all is synchronization. If you're using a supported application or device, such as Microsoft Outlook or a Palm Pilot, you enter the information just once and use downloadable software to update your Web calendar (Figure 12.4). No HTML programming is needed and you don't have to rely on someone else to upload the new page to the Web.

Resources

You can register for a Web-based calendar at any one of these sites.

- Appoint.Net
- CalendarServer.com
- Calendars.net
- Evite.com
- JointPlanning.com
- Yahoo! Calendar at calendar.yahoo.com

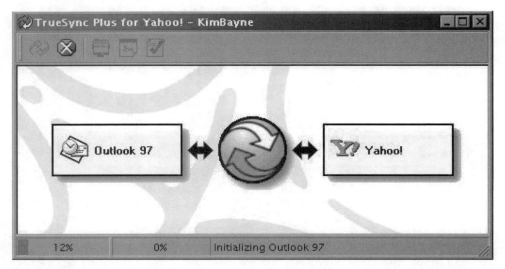

Figure 12.4 TrueSync client software allows users to synchronize applications and devices anytime.

Show Selection

Let's think back a moment. Weeks, months, or even a year before this date, you selected this show for your company. How did you do it? Did an exhibit-space sales representative call you on the telephone and discuss the show's opportunities? Did a colleague tell you about this show? Did you see a competitor at this show last year and decide you needed to be there? Just how did you get enough information to make your decision to exhibit?

Prior to the use of the Internet for marketing purposes, trade show coordinators, administrators, and exhibit managers compiled show information manually. They read trade and business publications and gathered conference brochures from various sources. The conference ads run in industry publications reminded marketing professionals of an upcoming event and they would call for information. If they needed information on multiple shows, they would, in turn, make several telephone calls. In response, conference brochures would either be faxed to the office or would arrive in the mail. Many times, brochures would arrive on their own, only to be stacked on the floor in the corner of an office cubicle or crammed into the back of a file cabinet.

Eventually, the marketer required another, more consolidated resource for keeping track of all the possible exhibit opportunities. The printed trade show directory, a compilation of show listings by industry and geography, was the perfect solution. As a reference tool, it was a handy yet bulky reminder of the overabundant choices available to the exhibitor. The trade show companion quickly became outdated, a built-in obsolescence only the publishing company could appreciate. Quarterly updates were published to update subscribers but the updates just weren't timely enough. Each year the exhibit manager would subscribe to this paperbound resource and each year he or she would reevaluate whether the expenditure was actually worth it.

Today, there is an alternative that takes up no shelf space and is easily accessible from anywhere in the world, including the computer in your office. On the World Wide Web, there reside several dozen free and easily searchable directories of conferences and expositions that a marketer can use to assist in the planning process. For example, Trade Show Central at www.tscentral.com (Figure 12.5) was created to help marketers quickly find information on thousands of different trade shows in a frequently updated online database. An exhibit services directory, show profiles, and information for trade show organizers can be found here as well. Another Internet exhibitor resource, EXPOguide at www.expoguide.com, is a directory of trade shows, conferences, exhibition halls, show services, and show-related classifieds (Figure 12.6). EXPOguide also allows you to search by location, date, or general keywords. Once you locate an appropriate show, you can

Figure 12.5 Trade Show Central offers exhibit managers an extensive online database.

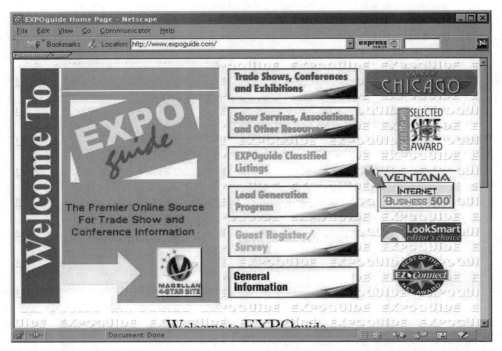

Figure 12.6 EXPOguide offers searching capabilities to speed the process of locating targeted shows.

request additional information through an e-mail form at the Web site (Figure 12.7). Trade show research has come a long way—locating contact and show management information, reviewing show locations and dates, surveying exhibitor profiles, and contacting show management has been simplified. Still, this is the tip of the iceberg. The trade show manager still has much work to do.

Once the trade show manager has reviewed the choices, made the selections, and compiled the annual show schedule (which is always updated throughout the year), the process of arranging show services begins. If you are this manager and your company participates in 20-plus shows per year, you are well aware of the amount of paperwork, including service orders and invoices, that is involved. You could choose to have an exhibitor management firm handle these details, hire or assign someone in-house to fill out all the paperwork for you, or complete these activities through the Internet.

Figure 12.7 EXPOguide's show request form allows users to request information from a variety of events.

Resources

- ExpoWeb at www.expoweb.com
- MeetingsNet at www.meetingsnet.com
- Trade Show Central at www.tscentral.com
- Trade Show News Network at www.tsnn.com

Exhibitor Services Firms

If you're in charge of exhibit design and logistics, your job has been made easier by exhibitor services companies on the Internet. Turnkey exhibitor service firms, such as Condit Exhibits at www.condit.com, will handle every aspect of your display.

If you're looking for a consolidated Web-based resource for services, check out Convention Central Information Services at www.conventioncentral.com and Convention Planner at www.conventionplanner.com. You'll find links to a variety of exhibit-related companies, including suppliers and service companies in audio-visual, computer rental, destination and event management, education, entertainment, facilities, graphic design, hotel booking, and marketing and public relations. If you travel frequently and want portable information to reference on the airplane, Convention Planner Hotline offers a fax-back list of suppliers for your destination city.

Displays for Rent

If you haven't yet ordered that pop-up exhibit for that 10 by 10 booth next month, there is still time to locate an exhibit design house. The Internet has its share of companies who manufacture pop-up displays, tabletop displays, and modular units. Some vendors will also allow you to reserve a rental exhibit at their sites if you're not yet in the market to buy one. Don't forget to order those custom booth graphics online, too.

Accommodations and Travel

Nothing is worse than waiting until the last minute to book hotel reservations. Sometimes, your frantic request to a busy travel agent is nothing more than another item on his or her list of last-minute requests. Since you have to find a place to stay while you're in that out-of-town location, why not research and/or book it through one of the various travel sites? (See Figure 12.8.)

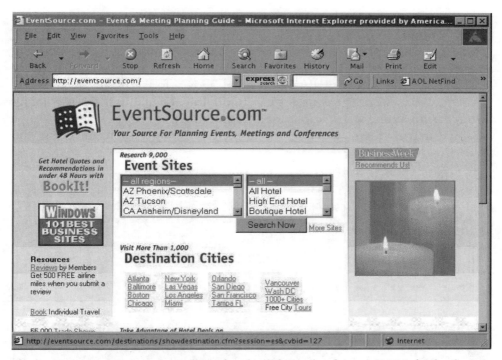

Figure 12.8 EventSource.com offers planning information for over 1,000 destinations.

Many Internet travel Web sites serve as a turnkey solution for your convention planning needs, but you may still not have the time to book travel yourself. If you already have an established relationship with a responsive travel agent, ask for his or her e-mail address to which you can send in travel requests. Think about how much easier it will be to receive e-mail responses than to play telephone tag or wait on hold.

On the Internet, you'll find traditional, independent travel agents with years of experience who have recently developed an Internet presence. You will also find those who service only online customers. Some Internet travel agents provide an incentive to those who take advantage of their online services, such as airline bonus miles when travelers purchase a ticket through the company's site. Last-minute business travelers can save on airline expenses by taking advantage of low prices on last-minute deals as well.

You can find out about the best deals for airline tickets through several different sites, and most will e-mail you with specials on your targeted cities. Travelocity's Best Fair Finder allows you to check fares right at its Web site.

If you're someone who prefers to book directly with the airlines, commercial airline sites such as America West at www.americawest.com allow you to enter departure city, destination city, travel dates, and preferred time of day. You'll receive a listing of flights from which to choose and you can buy your tickets directly online.

Meeting planners can view hotel rooms on the Web through a cooperative arrangement between MadSearch, a Web site for meeting planners at www .madsearch.com, and HotelView, a hotel video tour producer at www .hotelview.com. Visitors to this site can find a travel agent and site-see online through a streaming video application (Figure 12.9).

Most Internet travel sites offer extensive hotel information, including the following:

Figure 12.9 Hotelview.com plays a narrated video describing hotel amenities for the Miami Airport Hilton and Towers.

- Addresses
- Telephone numbers
- Facsimile numbers
- Number of rooms
- Available meeting space
- Nearby airports
- Courtesy car
- Room rates

These detailed listings can save the company much more in the long run than the cost savings realized through Web-based trade show planning. Finding a hotel's facsimile number at its Web site can be a big help when you need to send that time-sensitive document to the company president. Reminding your sales force of the hotel's courtesy car can cut down on the number of multiple-taxi fares from the airport to the hotel.

Occasionally, hotels will offer packages and promotions to Internet users who book reservations through their Web sites. Larger chain hotels supplement traditional advertising and promotional programs by including descriptions of special packages that are often only available through the Web. While current members of frequent-guest clubs may already be aware of these specials, your visit to your favorite hotel Web site will save your company travel budget. Fully aware of the dangers of relying solely on the Internet for customer feedback, most companies prominently display toll-free reservation numbers on their Web pages.

If you plan to exhibit internationally, Hotels on the Net at www.asiahotels.com catalogs hotels in the Asia-Pacific region, in such locations as Australia, China, Hong Kong, Guam, India, Indonesia, Japan, Korea, Malaysia, Philippines, Singapore, Taiwan, and Vietnam. This site includes detailed information on conference facilities, health clubs, and restaurants.

Convention Facilities and Amenities

Aside from telling your visitors that your company will exhibit at a show, the Internet allows you to connect to other helpful information as well. The GWCC, Georgia Dome and Centennial Olympic Park Home Page at www.gwcc.com, includes information on the city of Atlanta and how to get around. GWCC provides directions to its facility, traffic information through the Georgia Department of Transportation, links to the Atlanta area, and weather information.

While just about any conference facility will run a telephone line to your booth, the quality of the connections leaves something to be desired. Many convention centers make a special effort to inform you through their Web sites that they offer T-1 line connections and computer and software rental. Arkansas Meeting and Convention Facilities' site at www.arkansasmeetings .com can tell you in an instant about rates and reservations in Little Rock or show you a floor plan for review.

Graphics Creation

PosterWorks for Windows is a useful PC software tool for creating very large trade show display images. More information is available at www.poster-works.com. Use it to create a booth-size version of your Web site that users can walk through. For your reference, the PosterWorks site points you to large-format service bureaus.

Booking Entertainment

Many sites offer one-stop indexes for planning professionals interested in booking special event performers or presenters. Stop by these sites to find consultants, entertainers, and related entertainment services for your next event.

Resources

- Canadian Association of Professional Speakers at www.canadianspeakers.org

- Directory of Experts Worldwide, Authors, Consultants, Spokespersons, and Expert Witnesses at www.experts.com

- KeynotePage.com

- National Speakers Association at www.nsaspeaker.org

  If you're interested in live presentations in your trade show booth, investigate this company. It provides services from one-person gigs to multi-faceted stage performances.

- Live Marketing at www.livemarketing.com

Keep Current on Trade Show Developments

Check out *Exhibitor* magazine's site, The Exhibitor Network at www .exhibitornet.com, for the latest issue, tips on exhibiting, new show information, and a resource center of trade show suppliers. Another good source of exhibiting information is the Trade Show Exhibitors Association, located at www.ieabbs.org.

Getting the Word out about Your Event

Adding your trade show schedule to your Web site will inform users of your presence at a show they plan to attend. Online trade show producers often list exhibiting companies and point to exhibitors' sites, so don't forget to ask for your free link. Consider providing reciprocal links from your Web-based trade show schedule to show attendee information so visitors can register online. Show management might offer exhibitors the use of mailing lists of preregistered attendees. Take advantage of this service and mail potential customers a printed color postcard announcing both your Web site and your booth location. If the mailing list contains e-mail addresses, ask the list supplier if this is an opt-in list, that is, users have indicated an interest in receiving show-related information by e-mail. Don't e-mail attendees unless you've had previous contact or you're sure they've given permission, otherwise your attempt to publicize your exhibit will backfire.

Another way to get the word out about your exhibit is to tap into your existing database of customer e-mail addresses, either from previous shows or other marketing activities. Use this database to send a digital Internet postcard or greeting to your preferred customers (Figure 12.10). Some digital greeting sites provide a URL for retrieval by the recipients while others embed the card directly into the e-mail. If you use this digital approach to sending graphically pleasing online invitations, include a comment about bringing the invitation to the booth for a special gift. You'll be able to track the effectiveness of this online promotional activity.

Resources

- Always Free Virtual Greeting Cards at www.prismweb.com.
- Send-A-Card at www.media-magic.com/digital.
- Pacific Products Gallery Free Greeting Cards at www.prismweb.com allows you to use an image on your hard drive, such as your logo, a nice option for online branding activities.

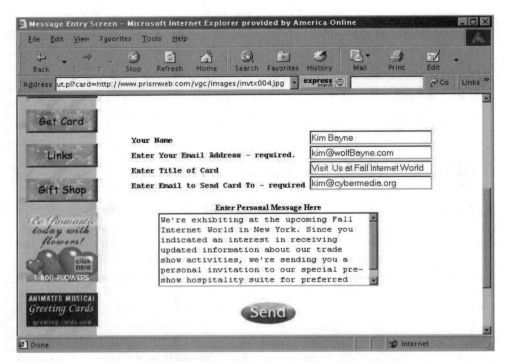

Figure 12.10 PrismWeb visitors can send a free digital postcard inviting customers to a trade show booth or hospitality suite.

These Web-based event planners allow you to send out virtual invitations and collect RSVPs online, which is very important for estimating catering needs for that upcoming hospitality suite in Las Vegas (Figure 12.11).

- Easy RSVP at easyrsvp.com
- PleaseRSVP.com

Virtual Trade Shows and Other Ideas

You can take advantage of the way in which trade shows have materialized in other forms online. Producers of the long-running computer and electronics shows now employ full-motion video and real-time audio telecasts on the Internet as part of their show. Some larger conferences have dedicated television channels that run in hotel rooms and on large video screens throughout the multiple exhibit halls. These channels are also telecast to the Web in streaming audio and video, and offer the Web site visitor updated conference news, reviews, and interviews with exhibitors. If you are exhibiting at such an

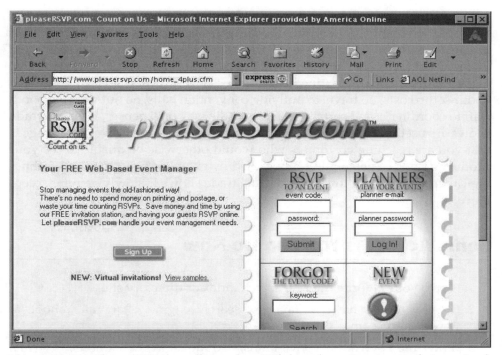

Figure 12.11 PleaseRSVP.com offers a free Web-based event manager that can track RSVPs for special events.

exposition, you can get your message out on the Internet at the same time. Online with the Comdex trade show, found through www.zdevents .com/comdex, you'd be able to listen to events through ZDTV Radio, requiring you to download Windows Media Player.

Finally, this brings us to the idea of virtual trade shows. *Virtual trade show* is a concept that has many definitions. A virtual trade show is "almost" a trade show, which means that the Internet is used to simulate the activities that would normally take place on the exhibit floor. Virtual trade shows consist of interactive product demonstrations and three-dimensional "booths." Attendees are invited to download the beta version of a new software package, play online games to win a prize, and enter a chat room to talk to a company representative. An interactive pavilion allows visitors to roam the aisles and click on links to products and demonstrations. Like their traditional counterparts, virtual trade show producers target an industry, technology, or theme for the event, and invite various companies to exhibit online. For virtual trade shows, product literature can be published online, just as it is at your company's real Web site. Sometimes a few of these shows coincide with the actual off-line event of the same name held simultaneously.

The virtual trade show concept was born out of necessity. With costs for show participation climbing, small companies lacked the resources to exhibit at multiple shows. Regardless of the show size, smaller firms are often dwarfed by bigger ones and see fewer online visitors as a result. The advantage to the exhibitor in participating in one of these virtual events is that there are no booth-setup costs, no travel to outlying convention halls, no out-of-town booth staff to coordinate, and certainly far less in the way of expenses. If virtual trade shows are used in conjunction with the actual physical event, the advantage is that you are reaching customers who would otherwise be unable to see your product demos in person. Initially stalled by exhibitor resistance and technological limitations, the concept of virtual trade shows is slowly gaining acceptance.

Some Activities You Can Do Now

1. Go to your favorite Internet search index or directory site.
2. If you don't have a favorite search engine, start at Yahoo! at www.yahoo.com.
3. Enter the keywords "conventions," "trade shows," "exhibits," "virtual trade show," "conferences."
4. Take notes on the different virtual trade show options and examples.
5. If you don't get enough results from your search here, click on the other directory links found at the bottom of the page. Yahoo! will send your search with you to the next location.
6. Read the services offered by companies at the various Web sites.
7. Bookmark any applicable sites for use in writing your Internet marketing plan.

Additional Activities You Can Do Now

1. Review some simple ways you can quickly marry your trade show programs with your Internet marketing programs (Figure 12.12).
2. Once you've decided on your programs and plans, list and check off all the associated activities (Figure 12.13).
3. Look into stretching your trade show budget through the use of virtual trade shows. Investigate whether they can supplement your national shows by reaching buyers unable to attend your real-world exhibit (Figure 12.14).

❑ Update all print ads, including those that run in show dailies, to reflect both exhibit locations: "See us at Comdex Fall, Booth 1234" and "Visit us on the Web at http://www.comdex.com/."

❑ Hand out T-shirts with a silk-screened copy of your Web page to qualified booth visitors.

❑ Ask booth visitors if they would like to receive product information via e-mail. Include an extra line for Internet addresses on your show leads' qualification forms or in your leads database.

❑ Offer a free gift to booth visitors who register online before the show.

❑ Offer a free gift to booth visitors who download a designated page from your site and bring it to the show.

❑ Create a password-protected Web page with a clickable schedule where editors can register for a show-site meeting with company executives based on currently available time slots.

❑ Investigate virtual trade shows as a way to complement your physical trade show exhibits (Figure 12.14).

❑ Use the Internet to send booth staff updated schedules for booth-duty assignments.

❑ Use the Internet to order food and beverages for your show's hospitality suite.

❑ Set up a touch-screen kiosk in your booth containing your complete Web site.

❑ Connect computers in your booth to the Internet and display your Web pages in real time from the show floor.

❑ Process trade show leads on the spot via computer; then upload the sorted leads by region to your company's FTP site for downloading by sales personnel.

❑ Encourage visitors to request product literature during their visit to your booth by having them fill in a page at your Web site. This serves two purposes: They visited the site and they filled out your leads form.

❑ Get the word out about your Web site without leaving your booth by giving away attractive tote bags with your URL in large type. Note: This works well in shows with large venues.

❑ Keep company employees and customers posted on activities from the show floor. Use a digital camera to take photos during show hours, and upload them to your company's Internet site daily.

Figure 12.12 Brainstorming ideas for fitting the Internet into your trade show mix.

❑ Include a disk in your preshow mailing that contains a browser preset to visit your site.

❑ Forward leads as attached files or text pasted into e-mail messages directly to resellers and distributors.

❑ Put files containing the layout for booth graphics online and allow your international offices to save shipping expenses by having signage produced in their own countries.

❑ Take a look at the exhibitor kit and notebook for your next show. Pull out all the forms for services that contain an Internet address. Do business with these companies first. Complete these forms now.

❑ Before a show, make sure you personally inform every booth staffer that your company is now on the Internet. Hand them a card with the addresses.

❑ Instruct all booth personnel to mention your new Web site to all booth visitors.

❑ Contact your graphics designer at least six months prior to your next show to request unique ways to incorporate your domain name into the booth.

❑ If your ad materials are already at the publication's offices, remind the art production staff to strip in your Internet address on the negatives for the next ad you run.

❑ Make sure all trade show press releases contain a reference to your Internet presence.

❑ Create a sticker for the front of the press-kit folders that you plan to put in the show press-kit room.

Figure 12.12 (*Continued*)

❏ Include a color printout of your home page, along with bullets listing your site's features, in your show press kit.

❏ Wait to reprint your sales literature until just before the next trade show so you can add your URL.

❏ Use online freight and overnight courier Web sites to track the arrival of your packages and exhibits to and from the show floor.

❏ Sell your old trade show booth online by putting pictures, specifications, and price at your Web site.

❏ Upload conference presentations made by your executives on the Web immediately afterward for downloading by customers who could not attend the show.

❏ Order custom lanyards with your Internet addresses to wear with your trade show badges.

❏ Conduct preshow staff training during Internet chat sessions.

❏ Invite special customers to a hospitality suite debut of your Web site.

❏ Subscribe to the TRADESHOW mailing list (e-mail discussion group). Send a message to listproc@nevada.edu. In the body of the message type: *subscribe tradeshow your_full_name.*

❏ _____

❏ _____

❏ _____

❏ _____

Figure 12.12 (*Continued*)

Instructions

- ◆ Check off any of the following trade show activities you wish to implement for your trade show program.
- ◆ Search the Internet for trade show service firms that conduct business online.
- ◆ Bookmark their Web sites for future reference.
- ◆ Make notes on this form next to the trade show activity that needs enhancement.
- ◆ Begin gathering costs for incorporating the Internet into your trade show program.
- ◆ Use this data to create the next portion of your Internet marketing budget.

Exhibit Design

❑ Display   ❑ Signage   ❑ Carpeting   ❑ Furniture

❑ Exhibit crates   ❑ Photography   ❑ Other: _____

_____

_____

_____

_____

Show Activities

❑ Live talent   ❑ Presentation scripts   ❑ Booth giveaways

❑ Staff training   ❑ Leads forms   ❑ Telephone lines

❑ Equipment   ❑ Hospitality suites

_____

_____

_____

_____

Completed by: _____ Date: _____

Figure 12.13 Trade show functions checklist.

Show title: _____

Dates: _____ Contact person: _____

Web URL: _____ E-mail address: _____

Sponsor or show management: _____

Show description: _____

_____

_____

_____

_____

Check one:

❏ This is a new show.   ❏ This show was last held on (date): _____

❏ Last show: Total exhibitors: _____   Total attendees: _____

❏ Next show: Anticipated exhibitors: _____

Anticipated attendees: _____

How will the number of visitors be tallied?

❏ Hits   ❏ Registered visitors   ❏ Other: _____

If other, please explain: _____

_____

_____

_____

_____

Figure 12.14 Virtual trade show evaluation form.

How is the show being promoted? ❑ Internet ❑ Advertising ❑ Direct mail

❑ Other: _____

_____

_____

_____

_____

Notable companies exhibiting at this show: _____

_____

_____

_____

_____

List the technologies, such as software and programs, available for visitors during the show: _____

_____

_____

_____

_____

Costs to participate: _____

Payment terms: _____

Is this a true virtual trade show or just a Web site designed to look like a convention center? In other words, will this event be an interactive experience for attendees?

❑ Yes   ❑ No   ❑ Unsure

Completed by: _____ Date: _____

Figure 12.14   (*Continued*)

CHAPTER 13

Measuring Internet Marketing Results

Web measurement (and) the whole Web revolves around the user's experience.
Greg Neal, Director of Online Measurement, for MatchLogic, Inc., on an edition of
"The Cyber Media Show with Kim Bayne"

Why did I include measurement in the implementation phase of your Internet marketing plan? Because measurement must be a forethought to marketing communications activities rather than an afterthought. Proper measurement is the only activity that demonstrates the effectiveness of your Internet marketing program.

Your measurement focus is driven by your original goals—what do you want your Internet marketing presence to accomplish? There are many different types of measurements, all over the Net. Some forms of measurement are directly related to increasing site traffic while others are related to generating online sales. Some are related to verifying a site's ranking within high-profile Web directories and search engines. Still other forms of measurement are related to positive third-party mentions in selected online forums. Regardless of what you measure, consider how you'll measure long before you undertake any form on Internet marketing activity. Your business objectives for your online presence will lead you in choosing which measurement activities will work best for you. This chapter discusses different options for measuring your Internet marketing presence.

In Chapter 12, Planning Trade Shows, you learned about the different Internet resources now available to aid in your trade show planning. You were introduced to virtual trade shows and compared them to the traditional kind. You found out about online resources designed to keep you current on conferences and events for your exhibit schedule planning.

In Chapter 13, Measuring Internet Marketing Results, you will continue to strengthen your marketing communications program by finalizing plans for your Internet marketing program launch. This chapter will contribute to the further development of your Internet marketing plan.

Effective Supporting Materials for the Plan

Including data that reinforces your decision to market on the Internet best supports your Internet marketing plan. Any combination of the following will expand this section of your Internet marketing plan:

- Comparisons of and recommendations for different measurement and analysis tools
- An analysis of how selected measurement activities will demonstrate that your online presence is meeting certain Internet marketing plan objectives
- An analysis of how your Internet presence supports your traditional marketing activities
- A checklist of what can be measured on both online and off-line programs

Getting the Most out of This Chapter

For this section of your plan, you'll decide how to measure your Internet marketing program against the goals you previously established. Measurement will help you justify a continuation of your program in the next fiscal year.

Review the different options for Internet marketing measurement for applicability to your Internet marketing program. Select those activities that will accurately demonstrate Internet marketing's effectiveness and impact on your overall marketing communications program. Research Internet and marketing publications for up-to-date reviews of software packages and measurement firms.

What Is Marketing Measurement?

Measurement always seems to be the poor forgotten relative when it comes time for action. A word of warning: *Don't, don't, don't* ignore this part of your program. In many cases, putting a measurement function into place after the fact is more difficult than you think. ("Hey, Bob, how many people visited our site after the press conference yesterday? What do you mean you don't know?")

If you forget measurement on traditional programs, you can always reconstruct the data later—somehow. Perhaps your public relations program will benefit by a retroactive analysis of press clippings done by an outside firm. You just don't have that option when it comes to the Internet. To put it bluntly, if you ignore measurement and its associated software programs, adding it in later, you may have no way to recover any of the lost data. Not unless you somehow invent a time machine and manage to travel back to correct your mistake. (If you do, let me know. There are several lottery number combinations I'd like to buy tickets for.)

Just the Facts, Ma'am

Measurement is the closed loop of marketing. It gives you a sense of accomplishment and a sense of closure. Without it, you're operating in the dark. Marketers often implement and continue operating marketing programs based on instinct. Instinct is fine, especially if you've cut your marketing teeth in the trenches, because you have hands-on experience to support your views. Of course, "marketing instinct" is nothing more than educated guessing. Sometimes instinct is not enough. You need proof in the form of hard numbers and expert analysis. In traditional marketing, this analysis can take any number of forms. In just about every aspect of marketing communications you have the choice of measuring the quantity of your results, measuring the quality of your results, or measuring both. Often, you need to measure both for your reports to be useful in revising your marketing strategies and tactics. The same holds true for traditional *and* Internet marketing.

Before you implement a measurement program, review your marketing objectives. For example, your overall objectives might include improving brand identification. A subset of that might be directly related to editorial coverage. Many companies analyze press clippings to indicate success from many different angles.

Editorial Coverage

In public relations, one way to measure the effectiveness of your media relations program is through an analysis of the final result: press clippings. First, you clip coverage and start looking at the trends, then your coverage grows and analysis becomes more complicated. Often you hire an outside firm to gather clippings for you. Service bureaus such as Burrelle's Information Services, Bacon's Clipping Bureau, and Luce Press Clippings track coverage in print and broadcast media for a fee. These companies provide their individual clients with copies of press clippings so they can see the results firsthand. Customers select coverage on company names, divisions, and parent companies. Clipping and tracking firms can track both editorial coverage and advertising for competitors as well. If you contract to an outside firm to track your editorial coverage, design a set of criteria for analyzing your coverage. Is it good? Is it bad? Who wrote it? What's the best way to report results to management?

How to report is equally as important as knowing *what* to report. You can tell management that you received 15 clips in May and 20 in June, but that would barely demonstrate that you are doing your job as a public relations practitioner. If press clippings are lukewarm reviews of your company and products, your report of the *number* of clippings didn't amount to much.

Advertising Equivalency

If your marketing goals include showing that public relations is producing as much interest in your products as advertising, you may wish to equate editorial mentions with advertising expenditures. This is one way to show a return on your PR investment. It's not a very scientific way to demonstrate effectiveness of a program and it's a quantitative rather than qualitative measure of success. Compared to demonstrating Web marketing success through sales reports, advertising equivalency is a poor second cousin.

Editorial Slant

Bad press can adversely affect sales. You'll want to recognize mediocre or bad press coverage early so you can proactively adjust. Effective public relations campaigns manage a company's identity in the marketplace. Presenting your company in the best light is a business marketing expectation. By analyzing your press coverage for fairness and tone, you'll understand how your market is forming its opinion of your services and products. Remember: There are hundreds of little places around the Internet, in the form of online-only publications and forums, which count for editorial coverage, so don't overlook them.

Key Message

Your company's image is governed by the primary messages it presents to the public. If you want the public to identify your company with a certain product or technology, you've got to create key messages. Getting your key messages out to the public is part of your job. Analyzing your press coverage for key messages demonstrates whether the public is receiving your messages at all and to what degree.

In the marketing communications area of advertising, you might measure readership retention to determine whether your current advertising campaign is gaining recognition.

What to Measure

My favorite Internet marketing advertisement is one that appeared in the December 11, 1995, issue of *Brandweek* magazine. The full-page ad was placed by *Penthouse* magazine. It showed two bars side by side on a chart with the head-line, "Ours is bigger than theirs." The first bar represented the number of hits that the *Playboy* Internet site was receiving. It was 800,000 Internet hits daily. The second bar represented the number of hits the *Penthouse* site was receiving. It was 2.9 million Internet hits daily. *Penthouse* wanted you to know that its site was worth exploring for advertising placement.

Webmasters look at their log-analysis reports on a daily or weekly basis to see how many hits were registered for a particular page. This is how they know whether a page is generating interest. When it comes time to reevaluate the content at their sites, the pages with low hit reports will either be renamed, revamped, archived off-line, or deleted entirely. Pages with high hit counts will be evaluated to determine what additional and similar content can be created to include in the site. In other words, if your visitors prefer one type of product or service information to another, you'll know immediately. You'll be able to compensate and mold your site to suit your market.

If you're counting hits at your site, you are roughly demonstrating activity level. Your measurement program won't be complete if that is your only yardstick. Hits show only quantity not quality. Programs that count only the number of hits miss the overall picture and don't answer the following questions:

- Who is visiting this site and are we reaching the right customers?

- How did the visitor learn about this site, that is, which site referred him or her to this site?

- Which pages are visitors viewing the most and should we create more similar pages?

- How long do visitors stay in one particular section of the site and, if not very long, should we eliminate or redesign that section?

- How has the design of this site either helped or hindered the visitor's access to important information?

There are dozens of other questions about your Web site and its visitors you will want answered. Programs that measure hits alone won't give you these answers. Hits are nice to look at and can provide an immediate ego boost but you need more than hits if you're a Web marketer trying to demonstrate a return on your investment.

Where Did They Go and How Did They Get There?

Clickstream-analysis reports can show you a visitor's path through your site. This can be helpful, especially if you're trying to determine why that page announcing your new services isn't getting any play. You could analyze clickstream reports to determine whether your site organization needs review. You can also use this data to determine how certain types of visitors navigate your site. If your site requires registration by company, job title, and/or industry, clickstream analysis will be worthwhile for you to review.

Knock, Knock. Who's There?

Are you trying to show management that your site has increased your company's international reach? Tracking the domain names and countries of your visitors will help. Again, this measurement by itself won't show quality. There might be quite a few students in that foreign country who are visiting your site. You may not have any way of knowing until you analyze a few more details. I wouldn't open up a sales office in another location based on this Internet measurement alone.

How Many Browsers Does it Take To . . .

Browsers come in many different flavors, although some Web monoliths would have you believe otherwise. Internet users have a choice in how they view the Web and latch onto a favorite browser soon after joining the world of online users. Meanwhile, Webmasters like to experiment. The latest and greatest HTML code extension, graphics trick, or applet can be incorporated into your site to make it look and feel great. It does look and feel great—to everyone *inside* your company. Too bad your customers are everywhere else.

Just what are visitors using to access your site? If you track the types of browsers that visitors are using to view your site, you can tell whether your market is seeing all your nifty work. You may find out that the majority of browsers out there are barfing every time they click on your hyperlink. If that's the case, think about providing an alternative version of your site for the browser-impaired.

Yes, I Saw Your Web Address in That Ad!

Did your recent advertising campaign or news release increase interest in your site? If you track how Web site activity has increased following a recent marketing launch, you'll know the impact of your programs. Of course, you have to be creative in how you track them, since there is no physical or technological connection between that print magazine and your Web pages.

Some companies create a special URL or Web address just to track the effectiveness of print advertising or media relations. This isn't foolproof, however, since many users truncate addresses when browsing the Web, but it's better than nothing at all. To ensure that more visitors put in the exact address used in your advertisements, add an incentive to the call to action. Rather than simply inviting or suggesting a site visit, offer magazine readers or editors something for their trouble. They're more likely to enter the entire address than disregard it, and you'll be closer to tracking how many users found out about your Web presence through another media.

Is it Sales Yet?

The easiest way to measure the success of your Internet marketing program includes tracking the sales generated by your Web site. If your sales lead management program is sophisticated enough to close the loop for you, then you're in good shape. If you don't have a good sales lead program in place, now's the time to think this one through. If your Internet marketing goals don't include sales, then you'll have to measure your program in other, less-tangible ways.

How Accurate Are Web Traffic Statistics?

The answer to this question could range from "excellent" to "not very accurate," depending on who you ask. Methodologies in tracking Web traffic differ drastically. By and large, Web marketers will tell you that Internet traffic statistics are far better than any tracking mechanism in place for traditional media.

Counting Beans and Other Pastimes

Log-analysis tools (Figure 13.1) allow you to track page hits, time of visit, domain names, IP addresses, sessions, geography, and so forth. In essence, these tools automate the tracking process by relieving you of the rigors of bean counting. Your ISP or Web hosting service providers may already have something in place that you can use (Figure 13.2). Evaluate what your needs are and compare. You may need something more detailed in order to create a thorough report on your Internet marketing progress (Figure 13.3).

Compiling data to support a return on your investment can be tricky. Downloadable shareware programs won't analyze the data for you, even if they do report it neatly. They certainly don't show the relationship of your hits to each other. Many shareware programs are inadequate for detailed marketing measurement purposes. Reports are impossible to use when trying to link your Web activity to your marketing communications objectives.

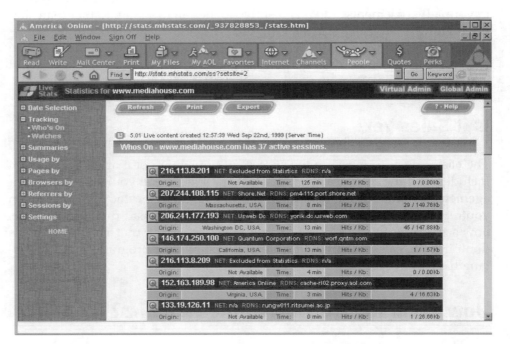

Figure 13.1 MediaHouse Software at mediahouse.com offers a "Who's On" report that details the "who" and "what" of visitor traffic.

World-Wide Web Access Statistics for the Site — Netscape

File Edit View Go Communicator Help

World-Wide Web Access Statistics for the Site

Last updated: Sun, 19 Sep 1999 02:08:18 (GMT-0600)

- Daily Transmission Statistics
- Hourly Transmission Statistics
- Total Transfers by Client Domain
- Total Transfers by Reversed Subdomain
- Total Transfers from each Archive Section
- Previous Full Summary Period

Totals for Summary Period: Sep 12 1999 to Sep 18 1999

```
Files Transmitted During Summary Period          37229
Bytes Transmitted During Summary Period      501947875
Average Files Transmitted Daily                   5318
Average Bytes Transmitted Daily               71706839
```

Daily Transmission Statistics

```
%Reqs %Byte  Bytes Sent   Requests   Date
----- -----  -----------  --------  |-----------
11.41 12.02     60347222      4246  | Sep 12 1999
11.27 11.21     56269595      4195  | Sep 13 1999
17.43 17.56     88154407      6488  | Sep 14 1999
18.77 18.24     91555290      6988  | Sep 15 1999
16.09 15.18     76177022      5991  | Sep 16 1999
14.51 13.92     69857419      5401  | Sep 17 1999
10.53 11.87     59586920      3920  | Sep 18 1999
```

Hourly Transmission Statistics

```
%Reqs %Byte  Bytes Sent   Requests    Time
----- -----  -----------  --------  |-----
 2.56  2.53     12677395       953  | 00
 2.03  1.79      8963658       757  | 01
 1.65  1.41      7097414       614  | 02
 1.85  1.64      8213775       688  | 03
 2.04  2.45     12274984       761  | 04
 2.34  2.54     12754299       870  | 05
 3.09  2.80     14073964      1152  | 06
 4.26  4.00     20058665      1585  | 07
 4.72  4.18     20983297      1757  | 08
 5.99  6.23     31281553      2231  | 09
 6.33  6.15     30887394      2355  | 10
 5.08  4.68     23489004      1892  | 11
 5.00  5.46     27410714      1862  | 12
 5.62  5.47     27441535      2093  | 13
 5.64  5.78     29024144      2099  | 14
 4.68  4.60     23096412      1743  | 15
 4.47  4.55     22836303      1665  | 16
 5.47  5.09     25558812      2037  | 17
 5.45  5.96     29914743      2029  | 18
 6.75  7.85     39412267      2512  | 19
 4.99  5.13     25758005      1857  | 20
 4.34  4.59     23063185      1617  | 21
 3.24  2.92     14652877      1207  | 22
 2.40  2.20     11023476       893  | 23
```

Total Transfers by Client Domain

```
%Reqs %Byte  Bytes Sent   Requests   Domain
----- -----  -----------  --------  |------------------------------------
 0.17  0.18       926761        63  | ae   United Arab Emirates
 0.06  0.05       275418        21  | ar   Argentina
 0.08  0.04       195267        30  | at   Austria
 2.73  3.07     15395777      1017  | au   Australia
 0.33  0.29      1447069       122  | be   Belgium
 0.12  0.05       235344        46  | br   Brazil
 0.04  0.03       152278        14  | bs   Bahamas
 2.88  2.77     13905221      1072  | ca   Canada
 0.11  0.24      1226393        40  | ch   Switzerland
 0.00  0.00         2267         1  | cl   Chile
 0.05  0.07       371953        19  | co   Colombia
 0.03  0.04       200382        13  | cy   Cyprus
```

Figure 13.2 The wwwstat HTTPd Logfile Analysis Software provides a summary of access statistics in HTML format.

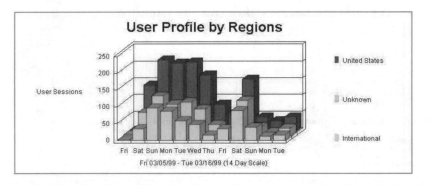

Figure 13.3 The WebTrends' User Profile by Regions report classifies the location of visitors to the measured Web site.

A commercial package might be a better solution for you. Commercial software packages have the added feature of customization for your unique requirements. If accuracy in reporting is important to you and you can't live with ballpark figures, don't rely on the free log-analysis tools. Investigate one of the commercial ones or look into contracting to an outside service firm for such services.

Measurement-Tracking Firms

Companies have been measuring marketing communications success since long before the Internet became a marketing issue (Figure 13.4). Outside agencies use a combination of software and/or individuals to track, verify, and audit your site. They analyze the data and report back with management-appropriate reports. Outside service firms can also offer an objective view of your Internet marketing traffic, which makes log tools and reports inaccurate by comparison. Many of these firms will save you time in compiling the results from your logs and do a better job of demonstrating how well your program is performing.

Outside service firms can be expensive. Some require minimum contracts that could run into the thousands of dollars. If you've spent thousands of dollars to launch an Internet marketing program, don't scrimp on this last part of your program. Before you hire an outside firm, make sure that you have an understanding of exactly what you're getting in return for your marketing dollar.

If you are interested only in showing independent verification of your site traffic, you can find a free measurement-tracking service on the Internet (Figure 13.5). These bureaus work by using a hyperlink inserted into your Web page and linked to their site. These bureaus may not be as useful as you'd like, but if you're limited in budget and time, they're a great place to start until you're ready to upgrade.

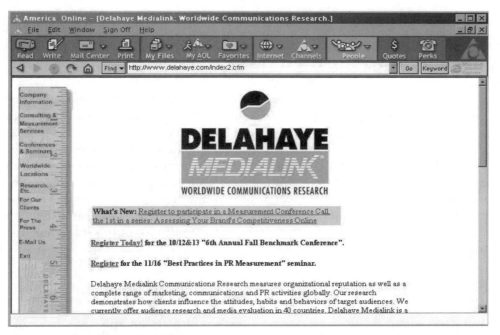

Figure 13.4 Delahaye Medialink Communications Research has been measuring marketing programs since 1964.

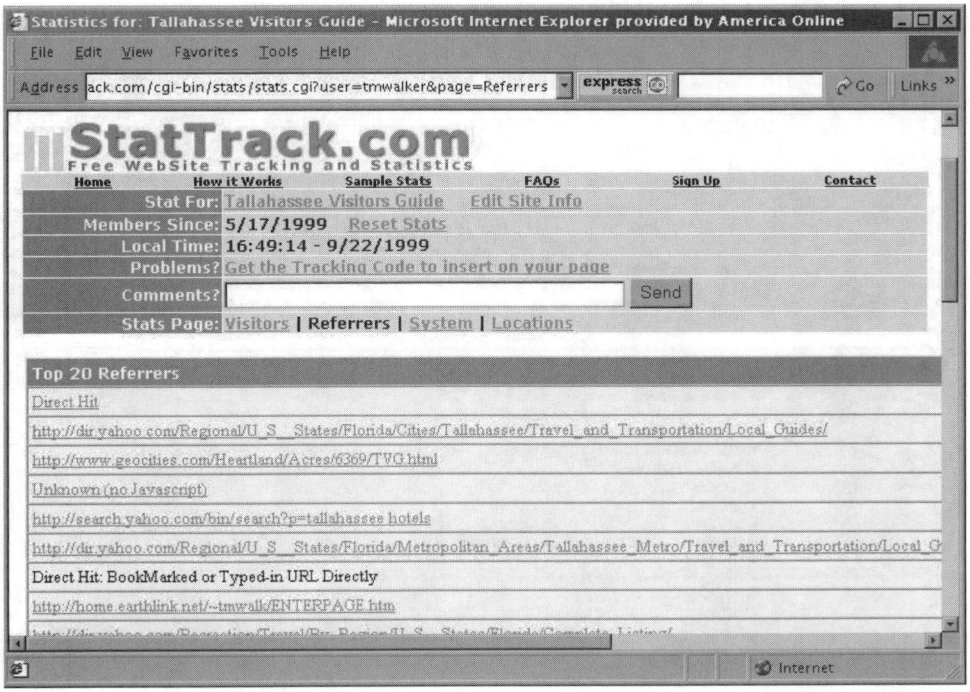

Figure 13.5 By pasting tracking HTML code on a Web page, Webmasters can use StatTrack.com, a free Web-tracking program that includes referral logs, visitors, and domain-by-country breakdowns.

Off-Line Tracking Methods

To track the effectiveness of your traditional marketing communications programs, assign different e-mail addresses or different Web page addresses to each activity. When I speak at trade shows and conferences, I provide a unique e-mail address for each event. This way, I know where my inquiries have originated. To keep track of reader inquiries from a particular magazine, assign a unique e-mail address to advertisements. This technique is similar to providing a toll-free number with an extension. Your automated switchboard can be programmed to track and route these calls, even if you don't have an extension with this number. As a marketer, this allows you to identify where the customer obtained your telephone number.

Summary

Your Internet marketing program can be as simple or as complex as you would like to make it. There are tons of possibilities for tracking the return on your Internet investment (Figure 13.6). Just remember that it's always difficult to estimate how well you've done on any size or type of marketing program unless you take steps to track your progress.

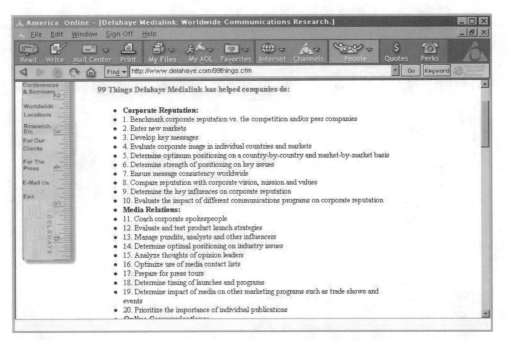

Figure 13.6 A few of the "99 Things Delahaye Medialink has helped companies do."

Instructions
- ◆ Review the various measurement options for applicability to your program goals and budget.
- ◆ Rate each option for its relevance to your current needs.
- ◆ Duplicate this form for each software or firm under consideration.

Software or outside firm   **Costs**

_____

_____

_____

_____

Features or services   **Ease of installation and use**

_____

_____

_____

_____

Relevance of services or reports to Internet marketing objectives:

    Irrelevant **1** **2** **3** **4** **5** **6** **7** **8** **9** **10** Relevant

Notes:  _____

_____

_____

_____

_____

_____

_____

Figure 13.7 Internet marketing measurement options.

Measurement is often an afterthought for many marketers. It shouldn't be. Measurement should be tied in from the very beginning as an essential part of your program. Take the time to evaluate a variety of measurement options and select one that meets your initial Internet marketing goals. (Figure 13.7) You can always upgrade later as your Web presence evolves. Remember, with measurement, you'll be able to ask for additional revenues to continue your program into the next year. With measurement, you'll be able to demonstrate to management how well you are creating awareness through your Internet marketing program. With measurement, you can accurately show how your Internet marketing program is a powerful complement to your complete marketing and sales activities.

CHAPTER 14

Launching Your Internet Marketing Program

I don't believe that traffic at a Web site is a function of money spent on that Web site. The content of a Web site is what generates the traffic.
Eric Ward, President, The Ward Group, on an edition of
"The Cyber Media Show with Kim Bayne

This chapter covers the steps needed to launch your Internet marketing program. The launch is one of the most fulfilling aspects of marketing communications. Its results can also be viewed as another form of Internet marketing measurement. Imagine the anticipation as you await feedback from industry analysts, reporters, and, the most important reviewers of all, the customers.

In advertising, the *launch* is the placement of ads in business and trade publications. It's the culmination of meetings with agency creatives, photographers, and copywriters. At trade shows, it's that moment on opening day when the exhibit hall bell rings signaling attendees to enter. When the doors open, you're exhausted after days of installing the booth and furnishings, but you're too excited to care. For public relations professionals, it's the climax of weeks spent interviewing company executives and product managers, days spent drafting releases for routing approval, and hours spent with a telephone receiver glued to their ears. The publications hit the stands and your company receives its due. A campaign launch is to marketers what opening night is to Broadway actors. Now get ready to begin scheduling and implementing activities in anticipation of a new launch—your Internet marketing program.

In Chapter 13, Measuring Internet Marketing Results, you read a brief overview of the different ways to measure the effectiveness of your Web marketing activities, including both manual and automated compilation of data. You used this information to plan for future improvements in your online programs.

In Chapter 14, Launching Your Internet Marketing Program, you continue to strengthen your marketing communications program by finalizing plans for your program launch. This chapter will contribute to the further development of your Internet marketing plan.

Effective Supporting Materials for the Plan

Including data that reinforces your decision to market on the Internet will best support your Internet marketing plan. Including any combination of the following can expand this section of your Internet marketing plan:

- Timeline charts showing Internet marketing activities alongside your traditional marketing activities
- Brief overview of each element in your online promotional plan
- A summary of your entire marketing communications program, including how traditional and Internet activities supplement each other

Getting the Most out of This Chapter

The activities in this chapter include summarizing your marketing communications program in its entirety and scheduling all activities in relationship to each other. You will consider what's reasonable to launch at what time as well as what's advantageous.

Some people will tell you that "A schedule is a schedule is a schedule." Forget the philosophical discussions about how deadlines are negotiable. You shouldn't take on an Internet marketing program half-heartedly. You must be serious about completing certain elements within a reasonable period. Creating a timeline for launching your Internet marketing program is essential. There's too much competition out there to let time get away from you.

If you don't know definitely, come up with your best guesstimate of when you'll get everything done. Of course, if you can afford to spend your days just surfing the Net and fit in your marketing whenever it occurs to you . . . more power to you. (Don't laugh. I know plenty of people who still operate in this mode . . . even today.)

Plan of Action: The Schedule

Now that you've decided what kinds of activities you'll include in your Internet marketing plan, schedule them. Presumably, you'll want to synchronize the announcement of your Web site with another noteworthy event on your marketing calendar. This allows you to use the editorial coverage from one event to attract interest to your Internet marketing activities.

Merely launching your Web site will not invite much press interest, unless your site is substantially different from the majority of sites already in existence. Even then, you'll need to get the media's attention in an unusual way. One caveat: Assess launch PR tactics with brutal honesty. Editors are inundated with Web site announcements on a daily basis, and they rarely cover one as an event in itself.

Let's assume you're planning to exhibit at a major industry trade show six months in the future. During that show you also plan to announce a major extension of your product line. Announcing your Web site at the same time will allow you to use the Web to further enhance your public relations activities. In this case, your timing is scheduled strategically to take advantage of efforts already under way. Taking that six-month time frame into account, let's look at a sample schedule showing only the Internet marketing portion of the plan (Figure 14.1).

This sample Internet marketing plan format is not going to work for everyone. You will have different elements in your Internet marketing program. You may already have a company domain name, but not a Web site. Registering a domain name and waiting for its approval won't be in your plans. You may already have a Web site, but it's not residing on your own Web server. You won't have to sign up for Internet access, but you will have to review it for changes.

You'll notice several repetitive activities in the sample schedule. They are as follows:

- Continue market and competitive research.
- Review Web tracking or measurement logs.
- Review mailbot/autoresponder filter logs.
- Respond to Internet sales leads.
- Update online documents.

Once your program is under way, you must check on your progress. Aside from paying attention to incoming e-mail inquiries, reviewing logs is the only way to verify that activity is actually occurring at your site. Your logs will alert you to potential problems from a number of angles.

Responding to Internet sales leads should be done within 24 hours or less of receiving a message. Inquiry turnaround within a few hours is quickly becoming the Internet norm. Those sites with live Web-based customer support, available at the click of a button, have the best response time of all. The Internet is a fast-moving world. If you're fast to implement technology, but slow at maintaining customer service standards, your online reputation suffers. Remember: Word-of-mouse fells the best launch intentions.

Finally, the Internet requires a regular commitment to updating online documents. If you don't plan and execute updates, your site becomes static and stale. This makes you fair game to those who would honor your site with one of the Internet's dubious distinctions—a Ghost Site, a site that has become "abandoned and derelict" (Figure 14.2).

One Year Before

Establish Internet service account.

Register domain name.

Begin competitive research.

Nine Months Before

Upgrade Internet access.

Research feasibility of Web server installation.

Six Months Before

Install Web server.

Compile first draft of Internet marketing program budget.

Form Internet marketing task force.

Five Months Before

Flowchart or outline Web site content and navigational aspects of your Web site.

Obtain bids from outside suppliers and vendors.

Test Web site access.

Purchase press directory, enhance in-house directory, or consult with PR firm.

Four Months Before

Create Internet style manual.

Hire interactive agency or Web design firm.

Begin document conversion to HTML.

Begin developing new documents in HTML.

Alias domain name.

Test aliased Web site access.

Consult with outside inquiry management firm.

Consult with outside Internet measurement firm.

Three Months Before

Inventory stock of print marketing literature.

Plan for reprints to include e-mail and Web addresses.

Add URL and e-mail to all trade show ads.

Compile list of Web sites as targets for exchanging reciprocal links.

Update sales lead database with fields to accommodate customer e-mail addresses.

Figure 14.1   Sample Internet marketing program schedule.

Two Months Before

Install and test Web site search engine.

Research and join appropriate industry- and technology-specific mailing lists.

Design, test, and install HTML–to–e-mail forms.

One Month Before

Install Web tracking or measurement software.

Continue market and competitive research.

Design standard company signature block for all outgoing e-mail.

Register Web site in multiple search engines and directories.

Prepare traditional news release or press advisory outlining key features of Web site.

Install mailbot/autoresponder.

Upload completed Web pages and test download times and other problems.

Launch Week

Enable Web site access for off-site users.

Distribute news release or press advisory through traditional and electronic media.

Continue market and competitive research.

Review Web tracking or measurement logs.

Review mailbot/autoresponder filter logs.

Respond to Internet sales leads.

Update online documents.

One Month After

Revisit search engines and directories to verify listings.

Review editorial coverage in key publications.

Continue market and competitive research.

Review Web tracking or measurement logs.

Review mailbot/autoresponder filter logs.

Respond to Internet sales leads.

Update online documents.

Two Months After

Plan for site evaluation and next revision schedule.

Continue market and competitive research.

Review Web tracking or measurement logs.

Figure 14.1 *(Continued)*

Two Months After *(Continued)*

   Review mailbot/autoresponder filter logs.

   Respond to Internet sales leads.

   Update online documents.

Three Months After

   Continue market and competitive research.

   Review Web tracking or measurement logs.

   Review mailbot/autoresponder filter logs.

   Respond to Internet sales leads.

   Update online documents.

   Plan for site relaunch.

Figure 14.1   *(Continued)*

Figure 14.2   Steve Baldwin Associates at www.disobey.com/ghostsites critiques sites that haven't been updated in a while, earning them various ratings on a ghost-o-meter scale.

How will your final schedule look after you combine it with your traditional program? That choice is up to you. You may wish to include only the Internet portion in your marketing plan. Conversely, you may decide to highlight only those activities directly affected by the Internet. Perhaps you'll show your entire marketing communications program, with the Internet marketing elements highlighted, to give management a better overall concept of how all the pieces fit together. Figure 14.3 shows another schedule variation.

In-house personnel should give you their best estimate of when they can complete certain activities. Outside agencies must do the same. You will need this information when you put together your own schedule. Take into account other projects currently in the queue that may take priority, and plan accordingly.

Online Promotional Plan

Eventually, you must let the world know you're open for business. The key areas of focus for online promotional activities follow.

Read Relevant Newsgroups

Perform keyword searches with a newsreader or at Deja at www.dejanews .com (Figure 14.4) to locate appropriate groups for your promotional efforts. Before posting your first message, read Frequently Asked Questions (FAQs)

	January	February	March	April	May	June
Advertising and Direct Mail		Create and update advertising materials, insertion orders.				Run ads.
Collateral			Order literature reprints.		Update fulfillment services.	
Public Relations	Update press list, begin ongoing editorial contact program.					
		Place feature stories.			Draft news releases.	
Trade Shows	Review shows.	Book shows.	Update booth graphics.		Order giveaways.	
Internet Marketing		Develop Web site.		Test Web site access and navigation.		

Figure 14.3 Sample combined marketing plan.

and if one doesn't exist, contact the newsgroup moderators for guidance. FAQs are documents regularly posted to newsgroups to educate new users. FAQs will tell you whether you can post announcements or news releases to selected newsgroups. Plan your participation in each newsgroup accordingly. If a Web site forbids formal announcements, find another more appropriate way to get the word out. Participate in discussions and include your Web URL in your signature block. Some newsgroups do not allow commercial posts, while others consist entirely of them (Figure 14.5). For more information, go to www.faqs.org/faqs/usenet/ to read various FAQs on Usenet newsgroups, including one on advertising posts (Figure 14.6).

Join Relevant Mailing Lists

If you're looking for lists or e-mail discussion groups that cater to select individuals, find a Web directory that catalogs mailing lists. Look for "lists of lists" such as Publicly Accessible Mailing Lists at www.neosoft.com/internet/paml/ (Figure 14.7) and Kim Bayne's Marketing Lists on the Internet at www .wolfBayne.com/lists/.

Figure 14.4 Deja.com offers a quick search of more than 40,000 online discussion forums.

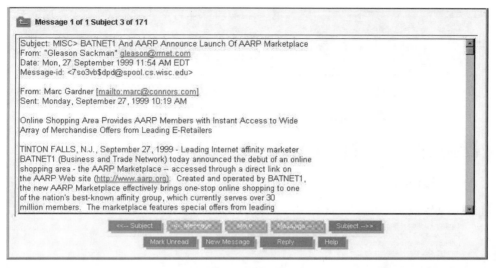

Subject: MISC> BATNET1 And AARP Announce Launch Of AARP Marketplace
From: "Gleason Sackman" gleason@rrnet.com
Date: Mon, 27 September 1999 11:54 AM EDT
Message-id: <7so3vb$dpd@spool.cs.wisc.edu>

From: Marc Gardner [mailto:marc@connors.com]
Sent: Monday, September 27, 1999 10:19 AM

Online Shopping Area Provides AARP Members with Instant Access to Wide
Array of Merchandise Offers from Leading E-Retailers

TINTON FALLS, N.J., September 27, 1999 - Leading Internet affinity marketer
BATNET1 (Business and Trade Network) today announced the debut of an online
shopping area - the AARP Marketplace -- accessed through a direct link on
the AARP Web site (http://www.aarp.org). Created and operated by BATNET1,
the new AARP Marketplace effectively brings one-stop online shopping to one
of the nation's best-known affinity group, which currently serves over 30
million members. The marketplace features special offers from leading

Figure 14.5 Comp.internet.net-happenings allows commercial posts on Web launches.

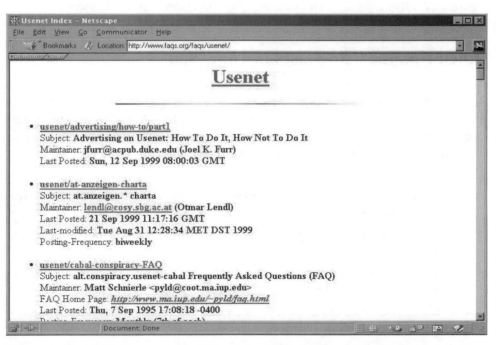

Figure 14.6 A FAQ document on "Advertising on Usenet" is available for conscientious Internet marketers.

Figure 14.7 Stephanie and Peter da Silva's PAML Directory catalogs thousands of e-mail discussion lists on a variety of topics.

Quick Tips for Using Lists in Your Plan

Once you locate several appropriate lists for your Internet marketing plan, read the INFO and/or WELCOME files associated with each. These documents are available by e-mail and/or posted on the Web. These e-mail versions of the newsgroup FAQs will help you determine whether each list is a fit for your activities. After familiarizing yourself with the style and culture of each list, do the following:

1. Join only relevant lists. You may wish to select digest version, since traffic on these lists can clog your in-box.

2. Before posting any message, lurk for a while. *Lurker marketing* refers to reading content before participating.

3. When you see an opportunity to join in discussions, do so in an informative and educational manner. Resist the urge to self-promote.

4. Include your Web address in your signature block so interested users can drop by for more information.

5. If the list allows it, post your announcement. Keep it brief and try to follow the style of other approved posts.

Submit Your URL to Search Engines and Indexes

You can register your Web site in various locations on the Web in one of several ways.

1. Visit individual directories, such as Lycos at www.lycos.com or WebCrawler at www.webcrawler.com (Figure 14.8), and submit your URL to each site.

2. Visit a consolidated submission site, such as Submit It! at www.submit-it.com/ (Figure 14.9) or Net Creations' PostMaster at www.netcreations.com/postmaster/.

3. Hire a commercial Web site promoter.

Figure 14.8   WebCrawler allows you to submit the URL of your Web site for inclusion in its search engine index.

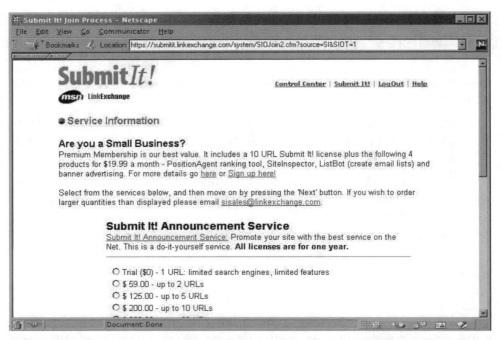

Figure 14.9 Submit It! offers a free trial to Webmasters for publicizing a URL to search engines and directories.

Include Commercial Online Services

If your account is with an Internet service provider, don't forget to include commercial online services, such as America Online, CompuServe, and Prodigy in your promotional plans. These sites have separate forums dedicated to a variety of topics, and you can't access many of them from the Web. If you don't have an account, establish one. Many services offer free hours (Figure 14.10) which can either stretch that marketing budget and/or help you determine whether there exists a reason to maintain an account for the long term.

If you're using an outside promotion firm to announce your site, ask your account representative if the firm subscribes to these commercial online services. If not, ask the firm to sign up or arrange with a colleague to trade promotional duties.

Trade Reciprocal Links

Locate sites in your industry that would be willing to trade hyperlinks with you. Search for similar sites in your favorite search directory. Ivan Levison,

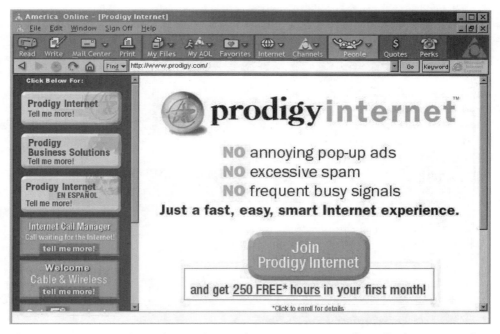

Figure 14.10 As an incentive to sign up for an account, Prodigy offers users 250 free hours in the first month.

editor of *The Levison Letter,* provides this tip to marketers who want to find out which sites are offering links to another site. You'd be amazed at how many Web sites out there are pointing people in your direction.

> For a complete list of links to your home page (excluding your own site), just follow these simple instructions. The whole process takes only a minute. No kidding!
>
> 1. Go to www.altavista.com.
> 2. Enter the following in the empty search box. (Obviously, you have to substitute your own Web site address in both places. I've used mine [www.levison.com] as an example.)
>   +link:www.levison.com/ -url:www.levison.com
> 3. Press "submit" and in no time at all you'll get a complete list of sites that link to yours!

Check your competitors' links and ask to be linked to the same general industry sites as well (Figure 14.11).

Distribute the News

Along with all your extensive Web promotional activities (Figure 14.12), don't forget to send out a traditional news release. Keep your release short and sim-

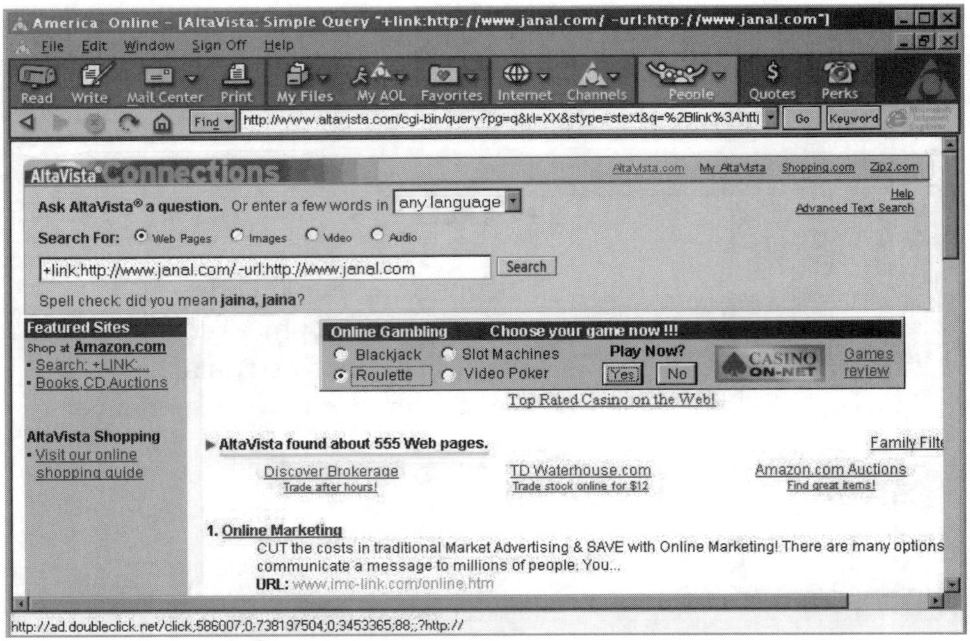

Figure 14.11 AltaVista provides access to over 140 million pages on the Internet.

ple, highlighting its key features. Distribute the release through a variety of media, including it with any other announcements your company may be sending out that week. Include your URL and e-mail address in the editor's notes on your other releases as well. If you decide to follow up with editors to encourage coverage of your site, please don't call them up and say, "Did you get my release?" Thousands of companies are announcing Web sites at the same time. Editors need to know how your announcement is unique, interesting, and fits into their current focus. Weave your Web site discussion into something else you're doing, and gear it toward whatever the editor happens to be writing about at the moment.

In the Future Everyone Will Be Famous for 15 Minutes

No better example of that famous forecast of fleeting fame exists than in those sites that promote the hottest and coolest: Cool Site of the Week, Cool Site of the Millennium, Hot Site of the Nanosecond, or Cool Site During the Bottom of My Manic-Depressive Cycle. In exchange for several hours of time surfing the Web, a cute logo, and a willingness to review just about anything, anyone can become a bona fide site reviewer. And they most certainly do.

Instructions

- ◆ Research appropriate places to publicize your Web site.
- ◆ Write down or bookmark these Internet addresses.
- ◆ Submit your announcement to each online resource.
- ◆ Check back periodically to confirm that your site has been listed. Each list, newsgroup, and Web site has its own schedule.

Relevant Newsgroups   **Date Appeared**

_____   _____

_____   _____

_____   _____

_____   _____

Relevant Mailing Lists   **Date Appeared**

_____   _____

_____   _____

_____   _____

_____   _____

Search Engines and Indexes (choose one)

❑ Individual directories, indexes, and robots.

URL   **Date Appeared**

_____   _____

_____   _____

_____   _____

_____   _____

❑ Consolidated announcement site. Specify: _____

❑ Commercial Web site promoter. Cost: _____

Figure 14.12 Web promotion checklist.

Commercial Online Services (name appropriate forums)

America Online	Date Appeared
_____	_____
_____	_____
_____	_____
_____	_____

CompuServe	Date Appeared
_____	_____
_____	_____
_____	_____
_____	_____

Prodigy	Date Appeared
_____	_____
_____	_____
_____	_____
_____	_____

Other	Date Appeared
_____	_____
_____	_____
_____	_____
_____	_____

Reciprocal Links	Date Appeared
_____	_____
_____	_____
_____	_____
_____	_____

Figure 14.12 *(Continued)*

Hot and Cool Sites   Date Appeared

_____   _____

_____   _____

_____   _____

_____   _____

News Release

❑ Draft copy.

❑ Route for approval.

❑ Distribute. Date distributed: _____

Distributed by: _____

_____

❑ Include follow-up with other editorial contact activities.

Publication   Date Appeared

_____   _____

_____   _____

_____   _____

_____   _____

Figure 14.12   _(Continued)_

Whatever happens to suit someone's fancy that week, that day, or even that minute can suddenly become _the_ site to visit. Users love these rating sites. They love them so much that Yahoo! has even dedicated a category to them. I love them so much that I made a big deal out of receiving one when my daughter's Web site, Kaitlyn's Knock Knock Jokes and Riddles, was selected as the Safe for Kids Site of the Week for July. That was fun. Now for business.

How do cool and hot ratings apply to your Internet marketing program's bottom line? Well, they really don't. That's the point. Ratings are one of those Web elements that have nothing to do with why your competitor is online or why anyone at all is marketing on the Internet. At least, I hope not. Some Webcrafters live for this type of recognition and will do anything short of selling their souls to attain cool or hot status. These rewards are nice to get as secondary kudos for all your hard work.

These Web site awards won't convince people to buy your product or service. They might convince people to visit your site and look around. I don't mean that you shouldn't pursue Web site ratings. In some cases, being singled out as a cutting-edge site can enhance your Internet promotion. Just remember to be selective about the ones you pursue. You're judged by the company you keep.

CHAPTER 15

Planning Your Internet Marketing Budget

**You may decide that your objectives need to be tightened up
if you have something less than the optimum budget. This isn't science.**
Jim Houck in ClickZ.com article "The Interactive Media Budget: How High Is Up?"

This chapter will help you become familiar with budgeting for activities associated with bringing your company online. Before you claim that you don't need, use, or even want a budget, remember that marketing on the Internet is not as cheap as *they* say. Sure, you can always get good deals—free Internet access, free Web site hosting, and a host of other so-called free services. While these might be good for the short term, eventually you'll have to come up with the money to do it right. To keep these costs from getting away from you, you must at least define the initial financial parameters for creating your Internet marketing presence, no matter how modest. You'll find that it's the little things that add up—making your presence on the World Wide Web not so cheap after all. This chapter contains a brief overview of the options, along with tips for developing your budget.

As part of your budget responsibilities, you may need to include preliminary estimates for new or upgraded computer equipment and software. If you are in charge of actually purchasing and configuring your own Web server, there is a wealth of books on the market to help you. This isn't one of them. For marketers, the less time spent on assuming the role of a systems operator, LAN administrator, or MIS manager, the better.

You'll notice that I've placed the chapter on budget-planning activities at the end of this book. That isn't a definitive statement of priority. Budgeting will no doubt be decided throughout your entire formation of an Internet marketing plan. You may not know what the numbers are until you read the other chapters, so I hope you didn't jump ahead to this section. Completing this chapter alone will not give you all the numbers you need on which to base an Internet marketing decision. Previous chapters in this book will provide you with the insight into most of the costs involved. Whether you hire an outside agency, use in-house staff, or just create your presence all by yourself, you need to know how this impacts your Internet marketing budget.

In Chapter 14, Launching Your Internet Marketing Program, your program activities were integrated and then scheduled for the eventual launch or announcement of your online presence.

In Chapter 15, Planning Your Internet Marketing Budget, you'll review the different ways dollars are allocated for marketing budgets. In previous chapters you looked at different aspects of an Internet marketing program and how they each contributed to your budget. You will now aggregate this information, enhance it with additional knowledge gained from completing this chapter, and finally compile a comprehensive budget plan on which to build an online program. This is the final chapter in developing your Internet marketing plan.

Planning Your Internet Marketing Budget

Including data that reinforces your decision to market on the Internet best supports your Internet marketing plan. This Section of your Internet marketing plan may include any combination of the following:

- Estimates on Internet service and development costs, including upgrade expenses
- Estimates of purchasing, configuring, and operating an in-house server
- A budget spreadsheet with cost breakouts for each Internet marketing plan element
- An assessment of the impact of your Internet marketing program on other traditional media expenditures

Why You Need an Internet Marketing Budget

Management likes to know where it has spent its money. It's just that simple. If you operate a small business, you want to know, as well. Of course, *needing* an Internet marketing budget and *getting* one are two different things. How do you allocate or obtain funds for your program? There are several choices as follows:

- Wait for your company to come around and provide you with working funds.

- Wait for increased sales to justify an expenditure in that area and siphon off a small percentage.

- Pick a number out of the air.

- Drive that action right now by gathering, analyzing, and presenting the facts.

Ways to Determine a Budget: A Look at Methods

You never have enough money to do everything you'd like to do when it comes to marketing. The Internet is no exception. If you don't have an endless supply of funds, you'll have to come up with an approach. Of course, if you work for someone else, management may just walk up to you and say, "Here. What can you do with this?" As the owner of a small business you may look at the current balance in your company checkbook and decide from there. In which case you have to employ the best methods you can for the money you have. Yeah, I know. That's pretty much an intangible and useless guideline.

By the end of this book, you will have quite a bit of ammunition needed to either win or budget for those coveted Internet marketing budget dollars. That doesn't mean that you'll get what you ask for or need, but it's certainly worth a try. For example, if you're planning to attract outside investors and your Internet presence is a visible part of the pitch, a good plan will increase the chances that you'll obtain enough financial backing to succeed online. You can improve your chances if you understand a little bit about how companies determine budgets. If you're not part of that peculiar decision-making process, it can sometimes appear to be magical and mysterious. Some companies are better at budgeting decisions than others. Let's look at some of the options.

The Internet Marketing Budget Is Based on Last Year's Internet Marketing Budget

Of course, I'm assuming that you've already developed an Internet marketing presence and you are reading this book to help you refine it. At the very least, you have a history on which to base a future budget. Assume you kept track of where your company spent the money, what worked, and what didn't. Now you have an even better concept of how to use your budget this year. When creating your budget, be sure to consider how costs have changed since the previous year, and whether any of your objectives include increasing your online visibility. In this case, you should propose an increase in budget to cover the additional programs you hope to implement.

The Internet Marketing Budget Is Based on a Percentage of Company Sales

When it comes to marketing, I believe in the separation of church and state. Editorial and advertising departments of reputable trade publications operate independently. Company marketing and sales departments should operate independently also—related only in that most marketing activities will hopefully bring in more revenue. It may take sales revenues several months to catch up with your Internet marketing efforts. If you look *only* to your sales dollars for guidance in determining marketing dollars, your programs could suffer. If it doesn't bother you that this sounds like the tail wagging the dog, then you could use this approach until you've proven the worthiness of your Internet marketing program.

What should the percentage be? That's not an easy question to answer, but there are helpful resources out there if the decision is yours. Look for industry-specific almanacs, such as *The Computer Industry Almanac* by Karen Petska Juliussen and Egil Juliussen, that contain information on the marketplace, trends, and market forecasts. Talk to Internet consultants, gurus, and experts. Interview analysts. Read trade magazines for clues. Use these guides as a beginning for determining a reasonable percentage on which to base your budget. Industry market and financial almanacs will also be useful for gathering facts on which to base Internet marketing strategies and for Internet marketing plan data that supports your market analysis.

Under this method, your budget may not necessarily remain a fixed dollar amount. You may or may not be able to count on it from one sales period to the next. In this case, you will want to make an effort to show a direct return on your investment upon which the company can base future budgeting decisions. If allocating a percentage of sales is your only choice, you can still work with it, just not as effectively.

The Internet Marketing Budget Is Based on a Percentage of the Total Marketing Budget

This approach assumes that Internet marketing is not a complementary or equal partner in the marketing mix. It is merely a subset. That's the bad news. In many companies, Internet marketing is merely the icing on the cake. The company has already established a very strong presence independent of online media. That's the good news. With this type of budget, you appropriate or allocate new dollars. You will be able to continue other established marketing programs without a financial impact.

The Internet Marketing Budget Is Based on a Reallocation of Marketing Dollars

This approach assumes that you will either decrease or eliminate certain activities in traditional media, while Internet marketing takes up the slack. If you already know that some programs aren't working and you are eliminating them in favor of the Internet, then you're shifting dollars to more effective marketing tools. That's perfectly acceptable.

If you reallocate marketing dollars because you hope that your Internet marketing presence will automatically decrease a need for other media, then you're shifting dollars away from tried-and-true methods in favor of something new. This approach is extremely risky. If your Internet marketing program fails to meet projections, then you have lost on two fronts: on the Internet and in the programs from which you have siphoned funds.

The Internet Marketing Budget Is Based on What Other Companies in Your Industry Are Spending

In traditional marketing, companies such as AdScope report advertising dollar expenditures by industry and company (Figure 15.1). Reports are emerging on estimated Web expenditures, but not nearly enough to cover every industry and possible configuration. On the Internet, it's nearly impossible to make these guesses by yourself. There are just too many variables for this method to be 100 percent accurate, including the costs of Web development and Internet access, which appear to change regularly.

Let's imagine for a moment that you have all the competitive spending information you need. You know exactly how much your competitor spent to put together its Web site. Your competitor is spending a relative fortune to make itself known online. You plan to position your company in the same manner. Yet you have decided to create an effective marketing presence without selling the farm. Good for you.

Take a good look at the objectives of your competitor's Internet marketing presence before you assume that you have to "up the ante." It's fairly easy to uncover your competitor's marketing objectives, since most PR practitioners make a habit of quoting or creating such quotes for inclusion in company news

Figure 15.1 AdScope.com provides a free sample competitive ad spending report to interested marketers.

releases. You can also hypothesize about certain objectives by the functions of a competitor's Web site. Notice a conspicuous absence of e-commerce activities? That's a big clue! If your competitor uses its Web site only for public relations purposes, and you plan to take orders online, then your approaches to allocating budget dollars are driven by different objectives.

The Internet Marketing Budget Is Based on Creating an Effective Online Presence

How much does it cost you to get what you need to succeed? Answer this question and you'll take the best approach to creating an Internet marketing budget. This type of budgeting method looks at the actual activities associated with creating an Internet marketing presence and tailors them to your unique needs. It allocates the funds accordingly. The primary focus of your Internet marketing program is to meet your company's marketing needs. This budgeting method is also the one used least often, especially by those companies needing it most.

The Internet Marketing Budget Is Based on a Graduated Plan Tied into Measurable Results

This budgeting method assumes that you will continue to operate your program from year to year. Of course, this budgeting method also assumes that you will be able to continually demonstrate either a return on your investment or some type of positive effect. Provided you allocate enough time and dollars to measurement programs, this is a good approach to budgeting for Internet marketing.

If your Web site takes direct orders online, then you have little to worry about . . . at least as far as total sales dollars generated. If your site has been established for other reasons, including those related to image management, then you will have to apply more stringent formulas for demonstrating success.

The Internet Marketing Budget Is Based on a Combination of Several Factors

In many ways, both traditional and new media marketing success is so intangible that you can't rely on just one approach to budgeting. How should you present your Internet marketing plan budget? The best approach may include a combination of all the previously mentioned methods. If part of your Internet marketing proposal includes asking for new dollars to implement it, you will want to provide management with some options.

- Prepare three budgets—one low, one medium, and one high—in terms of total program dollars.
- Include whatever information you have to support each of these approaches, such as the following:

    Competitive advertising expenditures, if you are able to obtain this elusive cost data

    Highlights of budget changes from one version to the next

    A subjective assessment of how each budget version may impact your overall marketing program

By being fully prepared, you will be more effective in influencing managerial decisions. At the very least, you will have provided your executives with additional insight into what they can reasonably expect for the available dollars.

Dialing for Dollars: How Much Does Everything Cost?

Now that you've become familiar with the reasoning behind budget allocations, it's time to start evaluating the size of the budget we are talking about. Here are just a few of the areas that you will need to cover in your Internet marketing plan.

Internet Service Options

Chances are that you already have access to the Internet. If so, and if you work for a big company, discuss options with your computing services or IT department for upgrading your existing account to meet Internet marketing goals. This may include finding a better or bigger service provider (Figure 15.2). Even though these costs may come out of the computing services budget, it's still a good idea to include this information in any Internet marketing budget request (Figure 15.3).

Figure 15.2 Used as a resource for individuals seeking an Internet service provider, Internet.com catalogs rates and services for ISPs around the world.

Instructions

- Ask your computing services department for details on the current configuration and costs for your company's Internet account.

- Ask for computing services' assistance in completing this form, if possible.

- Visit various ISP Web sites for preliminary information on costs and services.

- E-mail the Internet service provider for additional information.

- E-mail or telephone the ISP's customer-service department for additional clarification.

- Duplicate this form as needed for each Internet service provider.

- Check off choices and fill in the blanks with costs where applicable.

Name of Internet service provider: _____

Contact person: _____

Telephone or e-mail: _____

1. Account setup or activation fee _____

2. Monthly service plan or usage cost estimate
   _____

   a. Dial-up access _____

   b. High-speed access _____

3. Software (check one): ❑ Included ❑ Optional
   ❑ Not available

   a. Bundled Internet startup package _____

   b. Browser upgrade _____

Figure 15.3 Internet services costs worksheet.

4. Upgrades in access

    a. Dedicated/leased line _____

        (1) Number of additional company users _____

        (2) Estimated Web site traffic volume _____

    b. Toll-free line usage _____

    c. Wireless access _____

    d. Training (check one): ❑ Included   ❑ Optional ❑ Not available

        (1) Classes _____

        (2) Manuals _____

5. Miscellaneous Internet services

    a. Listserv operation (check one): ❑ Included ❑ Optional   ❑ Not available

        (1) List setup fee

        (2) Monthly maintenance and operation fees

    b. Anonymous FTP area (check one): ❑ Included ❑ Optional   ❑ Not available

    c. Gopher area (check one): ❑ Included   ❑ Optional ❑ Not available

    d. Newsgroup creation (check one): ❑ Included ❑ Optional   ❑ Not available

6. Web access (check one): ❑ Included   ❑ Optional ❑ Not available

    a. Hosting services

        (1) Basic _____

        (2) Premium _____

    b. Disk storage charges (check one): ❑ Included ❑ Extra _____ per _____ megabyte

    c. Domain name aliasing (check one): ❑ Included ❑ Extra _____ per _____

Figure 15.3 *(Continued)*

> d. Web log analysis (check one): ❏ Included
>   ❏ Extra _____ per _____
>
> e. HTML-to-mail function (check one): ❏ Included
>   ❏ Extra _____ per _____
>
> f. CGI scripting (check one): ❏ Included
>   ❏ Extra _____ per _____
>
> 7. Telephone company service (check one):
>   ❏ Not needed   ❏ Needed
>
>   a. Installation of additional telephone lines _____
>
>   b. Upgrade to better line _____

Figure 15.3   *(Continued)*

Internet Service Options: In-House Web Servers

If you anticipate that the user traffic to your Web site will either drain current in-house system resources or substantially increase costs for operation on your ISP's host machine, consider the purchase and installation of an in-house Web server (Figure 15.4). Remember that the decision to install an in-house server will demand that someone be responsible for its 24-hour operation, so budget for an extra staff person as well. System outages are intolerable on a round-the-clock network like the Internet's World Wide Web. If you do not have the personnel to assume dedicated responsibility for your server's operation, you're better off leaving your pages on an outside host.

Web Design Services

Many Internet service providers offer package services that include Web design in addition to access, hosting, and maintenance services. For example, FreeCart.com (Figure 15.5) and Signasoft.com (Figure 15.6) are examples of firms that provide turnkey solutions for small businesses. Whether you decide to have your Web pages designed in-house or outside, your budget will include costs associated with Web site design and development.

Instructions

- Ask your computing services department for details on the current configuration and costs for operating your company's Web servers, if applicable.
- Ask for computing services' assistance in completing this form, if possible.
- Visit various computer hardware Web sites for preliminary information on servers.
- E-mail individual Internet service providers for additional information.
- E-mail or telephone a local computer dealer for additional clarification.
- Contact your ISP for hardware advice on taking your Web pages in-house.
- Duplicate this form as needed.
- Check off choices and fill in the blanks with costs where applicable.

1. Hardware

    a. Additional workstations (check one): ❑ Not needed ❑ Needed
       _____

    b. Upgrade in hard-disk capacity (check one):
       ❑ Not needed ❑ Needed _____

    c. Increased memory (check one): ❑ Not needed
       ❑ Needed _____

    d. Higher-speed modems (check one): ❑ Not needed ❑ Needed
       _____

    e. Upgrade to 256-color monitor (check one):
       ❑ Not needed ❑ Needed _____

    f. CD-ROM drives (check one): ❑ Not needed
       ❑ Needed _____

Figure 15.4 Web server cost worksheet.

g. Other (specify)

_____

Cost: _____

2. Software

a. Web server (check one): ❑ Not needed
❑ Needed _____

b. List manager (check one): ❑ Not needed
❑ Needed _____

3. Additional personnel

a. Is someone in your company on call in case computer systems
go down? ❑ Yes   ❑ No

b. Do you have in-house technical personnel who can be dedicated to a Web server? ❑ Yes   ❑ No

c. If no, do you plan to hire someone? ❑ Yes   ❑ No
If yes, when? _____

4. Telephone company service (check one):
❑ Not needed   ❑ Needed _____

a. Installation of additional telephone lines

_____

b. Upgrade to better line _____

Completed by: _____ Date: _____

Figure 15.4   *(Continued)*

Additional Resources

For comparisons of features, pricing and services for Internet service
providers, hardware options for Web servers, and Web hosting and development services, visit these sites.

Internet Service Provider and Web Hosting Comparisons

- CNET's Ultimate ISP Guide at www.cnet.com/Content/Reports/Spe-
cial/ISP/index.html
- WorldWideWait.com (Figure 15.7)
- ISP Host Performance and Availability Rating at webperf.zeus.co.uk

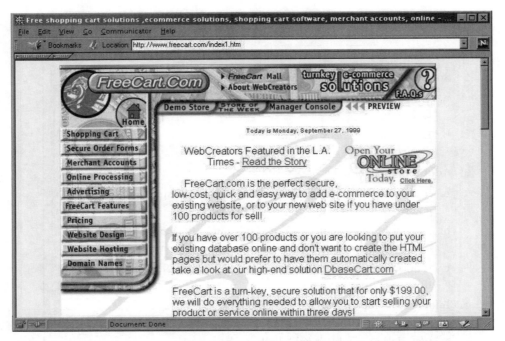

Figure 15.5 FreeCart.com provides an easy way for businesses to create an e-commerce-enabled Web presence.

Hardware Comparisons

- The Review Zone at www.review-zone.com
- MySimon.com

Web Server Product Reviews

- *PC* Magazine at www8.zdnet.com/pcmag/features/webserver/_open.htm
- Web Server Quick Compare at webcompare.internet.com/cgi-bin/quickcompare.pl (Figure 15.8)

Web Development Services and Costs

- NetMarketing Web Price Index at www.netb2b.com/wpi/index.html
- Web Developer Directory at www.businessmarketing.bsource.com

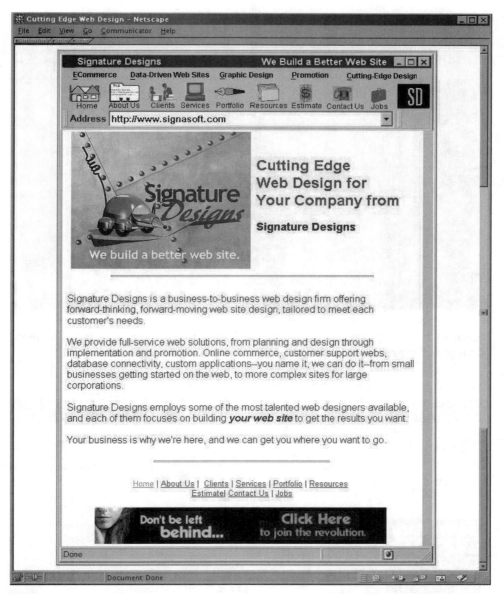

Figure 15.6 Signasoft.com offers full-service Web solutions, from design through promotion.

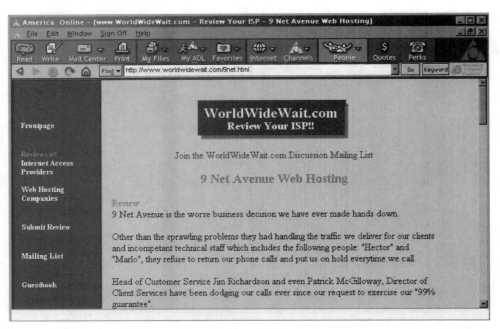

Figure 15.7 WorldWideWait.com provides a forum for users to post personal opinions about service providers.

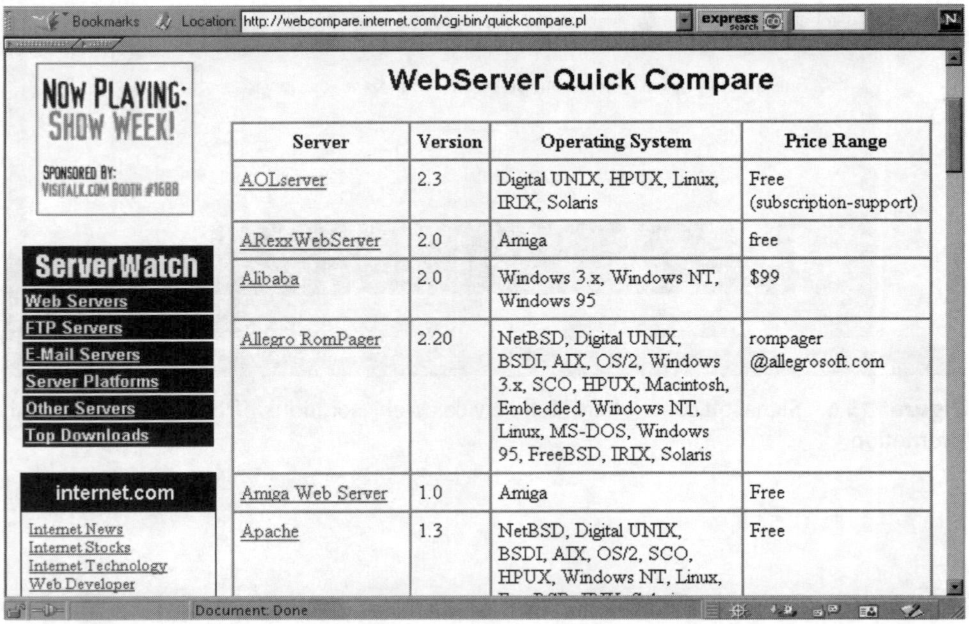

Figure 15.8 Web Server Quick Compare shows prices for a variety of server options.

Your Internet Marketing Plan Summary

As a final step in completing your Internet marketing plan, include a summary. Your summary should be brief. I can't tell you what to put in your summary because I haven't seen your plan. I'll leave that one up to you. After all, this plan is your baby. Perhaps the closing statements in your written proposal should resemble a toast. Here's one, made during a party to celebrate one company's Internet launch:

> *Our competitors are there. Our partners are there. Our customers are there, too. And now we're on the Internet, as well. At the very least, we have harnessed this phenomenon called Internet marketing before it took us by surprise. Here's hoping we can capitalize on it to make our company grow. With planning, dedication, and the work of many talented people, we will prosper by our Internet marketing presence. Maybe not today, maybe not tomorrow, but eventually. We'll be patient. We'll be realistic. But most of all, we'll have fun. After all, it's not worth doing if we don't enjoy it. L'Chaim.*

Internet Marketing Plan for (*Company Name, Division*) Submitted by (*Your Name*) (*Today's Date*)

This document is a basic template for your Internet marketing plan. To use this template, copy the disk file `inetplan.txt`. Use this duplicate to create your own written Internet marketing plan. Some sections of this plan may overlap, containing duplicate information from other sections. The examples provided are suggestions. The exact placement of Internet marketing plan data is up to you. You may reorganize the final document in any way that makes sense to you. You may wish to rearrange it to match the organization of your traditional marketing communications plan, in which case this document may change entirely.

Section One: Business Overview and Executive Summary

Instructions: Develop this section of your marketing plan from information you gathered while completing exercises in Chapter 2, Preparing the Business Overview and Executive Summary. Include answers from the completed worksheet(s) in this chapter as well as any supporting documentation you developed on your own. Emphasize any element of your company background and future that will be affected by or will affect your Internet marketing plan.

1. Internet marketing plan introduction
   a. Briefly explain why you are writing an Internet marketing plan

2. Company overview
   a. What are your company's goals, objectives, philosophies, and charter?
   b. Background and historical analysis
      (1) How long has your company been in existence?
      (2) State significant dates and events related to your company and its marketing programs
   c. Future outlook
      (1) Mergers
      (2) Acquisitions
      (3) Joint ventures
      (4) Strategic alliances or partnerships

3. Products and/or services overview: What type of business is your company engaged in?
   a. Products
      (1) Product line
      (2) Manufacturing capabilities
   b. Services
   c. Sales
      (1) Pricing
      (2) Volume
   d. Goals and objectives
   e. Future outlook
      (1) Research
      (2) Technology
      (3) Pricing

4. Market or industry
   a. Target definition
      (1) Customer
      (2) Industry

    b. Notable patterns or trends

    c. Competition

       (1) Primary competitors in your industry.

       (2) Products

       (3) Strengths and weaknesses

    d. Market share

       (1) Company

       (2) Competition

  5. Section summary

    a. Risks in relying solely on traditional marketing activities

Section Two: Applicable Internet Market Statistics

Instructions: Develop this section of your marketing plan from information you gathered while completing exercises in Chapter 3, Analyzing Internet Market Statistics. Include answers from the completed worksheet(s) in this chapter as well as any supporting documentation you developed on your own. Emphasize any elements of both general and specific Internet market reports that support your plans for an Internet marketing program.

  1. Online users: numbers and percentages

    a. General Internet studies overview

       (1) Overall estimate of worldwide users, host

         (a) Browser, platform, and connection speeds

       (2) Internet business usage trends

         (a) Breakdown of domain name registrations

         (b) Purchasing behavior and revenue

    b. Market or industry-specific studies

       (1) Growth of Internet use within your industry

       (2) Demographic breakdowns

         (a) Average age of selected users

         (b) Internet users by gender

(c) User profiles

—Purchasing influence and authority

—Computer and Internet proficiency among users

—Job titles

—Income

(d) Other

2. Section summary

a. How market reports advocate Internet marketing for your company

Section Three: Marketing Communications Strategies

Instructions: Develop this section of your marketing plan from information you gathered while completing exercises in Chapter 4, Formulating Marketing Communications Strategies. Include answers from the completed worksheet(s) in this chapter as well as any supporting documentation you developed on your own. Emphasize any marketing communications strategy that will be affected by or will affect your Internet marketing plan.

1. Objectives and goals

2. Specific strategies for achieving these objectives and goals

3. Section summary

a. Traditional and Internet marketing strategies, comparisons, and contrasts

b. How use of the Internet will strengthen your overall marketing goals

Section Four: The Internet Marketing Task Force

Instructions: Develop this section of your marketing plan from information you gathered while completing exercises in Chapter 5, Forming the Internet Marketing Task Force. Use your answers from the completed worksheet(s) and/or activities in this chapter. Emphasize any personnel or outside vendor issues that will be affected by or will affect your Internet marketing plan.

1. Task force overview

2. Details

a. Task force leadership

    b. Current staffing options

       (1) Marketing

       (2) Sales

       (3) Customer service

       (4) Technical support for Internet operations

       (5) Other

    c. Temporary personnel agency

    d. Outside vendors and services

       (1) Internet service provider

       (2) Web developers

       (3) Interactive agencies

       (4) Consultants

       (5) Other

3. Section summary

    a. How Internet marketing will affect staff and operations

       (1) Efficiency improvements

    b. In-house versus outsourcing considerations

       (1) Career opportunities for current employees

          (a) Training

          (b) Advancement/career paths

       (2) Talent and capabilities comparisons

          (a) Agency review

       (3) Other

Section Five: Internet Marketing Program Implementation

Instructions: Develop this section of your marketing plan from program implementation information you gathered while completing worksheet(s) and/or activities in the following chapters:

Chapter 6. Designing Advertising and Direct-Mail Campaigns

Chapter 7. Utilizing Collateral Materials/Sales Literature

Chapter 8. Developing a Corporate Identity

This section can also be supported by including data from any Chapter 3 market research report that includes references to the impact of the Internet on other media, Internet business usage trends, and purchasing behavior and revenue. Emphasize any element of your marketing communications program that will be affected by or will affect your Internet marketing plan.

1. Implementation overview

2. Marketing communications. Each of the marketing communications functions that follow can be described by including these items:

   a. Brief paragraphs on each Internet marketing communications activity

   b. Your rationale for individual program selection

   c. A discussion of how each Internet marketing activity complements and impacts your traditional program

   d. A plan of action for converting selected materials to the Internet

   e. Summary of activities that will include your Internet addresses for cross-promotional purposes

   f. Evaluations of outside vendors who might perform any or all of these functions

      (1) Advertising and direct-mail campaigns

      (2) Collateral materials/sales literature

      (3) Corporate identity

         (a) A preliminary draft of your corporate Internet style manual

      (4) Market research

      (5) Public relations and promotion

      (6) Sales support

      (7) Trade shows

      (8) Measurement

         (a) How selected measurement functions will demonstrate that you are meeting your Internet marketing plan objectives

      (9) Other

3. Program launch

    a. Launch summary

        (1) Brief overview of each element in your online promotional plan

    b. Month-by-month schedule

        (1) Timeline charts showing Internet marketing activities alongside traditional marketing activities

4. Section summary

    a. A summary of your entire marketing communications program, including how traditional and Internet activities will supplement each other

Section Six: Internet Marketing Budget

Instructions: Develop this section of your marketing plan from cost information you gathered while completing worksheet(s) and/or activities in each of these chapters.

Chapter 6. Designing Advertising and Direct-Mail Campaigns

Chapter 7. Utilizing Collateral Materials/Sales Literature

Chapter 8. Developing a Corporate Identity

Chapter 9. Conducting Market Research

Chapter 10. Executing Public Relations and Promotional Programs

Chapter 11. Incorporating Sales Support Functions

Chapter 12. Planning Trade Shows

Chapter 13. Measuring Internet Marketing Results

Chapter 14. Launching Your Internet Marketing Program

Do not go into too much detail in this section, other than to summarize budget line items. Remember, a complete description of each of these programs will be included in plan section five. Emphasize any element of your budget that will be affected by or will affect your Internet marketing plan.

1. Traditional marketing budget overview

    a. Insert your completed Internet marketing plan spreadsheet (disk file budget.xls) here.

2. Estimates on Internet marketing

    a. Internet service costs

        (1) Account setup or activation fee

        (2) Monthly service or usage

        (3) Upgrade expenses

           (a) Hardware

           (b) Software

  b. Purchasing, configuring, and operating an in-house Web server

        (1) Hardware

        (2) Software

        (3) Additional personnel

        (4) Telephone company service

  c. Internet marketing plan activity costs

        (1) Advertising and direct-mail campaigns

        (2) Collateral materials/sales literature

        (3) Corporate identity

        (4) Market research

        (5) Public relations and promotion

        (6) Sales support

        (7) Trade shows

        (8) Program launch

        (9) Measurement

           (a) Outside audit bureaus or agencies

           (b) Software tools

      (10) Other

3. Web development costs

4. Revenue opportunities

  a. Internet advertising placement/sponsorship

  b. Online sales

        (1) Products

        (2) Services and subscriptions

  c. Other

5. Section summary

  a. An assessment of the financial impact of your Internet marketing program on other traditional media expenditures

   b. Before and after charts: traditional and Internet marketing

     (1) Comparisons of marketing expenditures

     (2) Comparisons of sales revenue

   c. Recommendations for cost savings in traditional marketing communications functions

   d. Bids from outside vendors and suppliers

   e. Other recommendations and support for Internet marketing

Section Seven: Internet Marketing Plan Summary

Instructions: Develop this section of your marketing plan by reviewing your entire written Internet marketing plan. Summarize any element of your overall traditional marketing communications program that will be affected by or will affect your overall Internet marketing plan.

  1. Overall recommendations for action

   a. Why your company should execute a new or enhanced Internet marketing program

   b. Why your company should take action now: important timing considerations

Section Eight: Supporting Documents

Instructions: You may include supporting documents here or you may decide to weave them into your plan throughout as you discuss each section. The choice is up to you. Suggested materials for inclusion in this section are as follows:

  1. Press clippings

  2. Relevant sections from research reports

  3. Reference list of supporting works and Web sites

  4. Other

Glossary of Internet Marketing Terms

banner One form of online advertising, a banner is a rectangular graphic placed in selected positions of a Web page. The graphic is designed to advertise a company, product, or service. It can be a static advertisement such as a Web billboard, an animated advertisement with multiple rotating images, and/or an interactive advertisement that involves the Internet user. Most banners, if not all, are linked to the advertising Web site for more information or sales. Banners that provide functional drop-down menus may allow the user to choose which area of the new page to visit. Some banners are capable of processing a sales order without leaving the ad-hosting site.

clickthrough Clickthrough is the act or result of a user clicking on a banner ad and often leaving the current Web page to view a different Web page. The *CTR* or *click through rate* refers to the number of users actually clicking on the ad banner when compared to the total number of users viewing the ad banner. Clickthrough can also be used to describe *click on*, which refers to an interactive banner that does not necessarily cause the user's browser to view a new Web page. *Hover time*, the amount of time spent interacting with a banner, is another term included in this category.

cookies A cookie is a special computer file that is written to the user's computer, usually upon entering a new Web site or area of a site. Cookies may be used to track traffic through a site and are most often used to identify a returning visitor.

domain name   A domain name or Web site address is a designation for a unique area of the Internet. It is the alphanumeric and easy to remember substitute for a numeric server address. Domain names are directly related to a company's ability to create a recognizable online brand, since they often resemble a company's name or product. When a user types a domain name into the location field of the browser, he or she can view Web page files residing on a distant server connected to the World Wide Web.

filters   A filter is a script, software program, or file that allows the user to weed out unwanted Web sites or sort incoming e-mail into appropriate mailboxes. Some users have installed filters designed to recognize and ignore ad banners.

hits   An elementary and limited form of Web measurement, hits refer to the number of times users have displayed a Web page or graphic. This measurement can be misleading, especially at less-sophisticated Web sites with limited measurement programs. It is easy to inflate hits and mistakenly report them as representative of total visitors to a site. The measurement of Web page hits is unimportant unless it is combined with another form of measurement.

hyperlink   A hyperlink is a type of Hypertext Markup Language that surrounds a graphic or piece of text, allowing it to reference another Web location. Clicking on a hyperlink allows a user to display a different page or portion of a page.

impressions   A form of Web measurement, impressions refers to the number of times a banner is displayed. An impression may also be called a view, as in page view or banner view. The number of impressions is often used to calculate ad banner rates at hosting Web sites. This measurement can be misleading in that partial banner displays may be counted as full impressions.

ISPs   Internet Service Providers are companies that connect individual computers or networks to the rest of the Internet world. Services among ISPs differ greatly, so it's best to comparison shop for prices and service options.

META tags   The term *META tag* describes a type of Hypertext Markup Language used to index a Web page. Examples of META tags are TITLE, KEYWORDS, and DESCRIPTION. META tags are important to Internet marketing and promotion because they help search engines identify Web site pages and index them better. Proper use of META tags will increase a site's visibility.

PDF   PDF refers to Portable Document Format, one of the many options for Web publishing. PDF is often used for recreating annual reports and company brochures in a layout that closely resembles a company's printed literature.

search engine   Often confused with Web directories, search engines are consolidated sites that search the Web for new and existing pages to catalog. Search engines are often referred to as Web crawlers. Users visit a favorite search engine site to locate other sites. Search engines compile information through the use of automated programs that travel the Web collecting information. Search engines are very efficient at gathering Web page data and can take up to a few days to add new Web site listings. Search engines rely on technology to properly catalog Web pages and are often foiled in their attempts by a new site's poor design or lack of META tags.

Web directories   Often confused with search engines, Web directories are consolidated sites that catalog new and existing Web pages. Users visit a favorite Web directory to locate other sites. Web directories are compiled by human beings. Listings come from either individuals who travel the Web manually or Webmasters who voluntarily submit site descriptions. Web directory staff members can take up to a few months to add new listings. Web directories rely on human beings to properly catalog listings that are often subject to editorial interpretation.

Marketing Plan Software

If you still need additional help in preparing you Internet marketing plan after you complete this book, here are several software packages. These programs are designed to take you through the step-by-step process of building and/or enhancing your company's Internet marketing plans.

Marketing Plan Pro
Marketing Plus
Palo Alto Software, Inc.
144 E. 14th Ave.
Eugene, OR 97401 USA
Toll Free: 800-229-7526
Tel.: 541-683-6162
Fax: 541-683-6250
www.paloaltosoftware.com/marketingplanpro/index.htm

MarketingBuilder
JIAN Tools for Sales Inc.
127 Second Street
Los Altos, CA 94002 USA
Toll Free: 800-346-5426
Tel.: 415-254-5600
Fax: 415-941-9272
www.jianusa.com/

PlanMagic WebQuest Pro
PlanMagic Corporation
PMB 118, 3663 Lee Road
Jefferson Valley, NY 10535-0913 USA
Tel.: 914-737-7303
Fax (USA): 914-962-0149
E-mail (U.S. and International Sales): sales@planmagic.com
http://planmagic.com/webquest.html

Planned Marketing Software
1555 Pasqualito
Pasadena, CA 91108 USA
Toll Free: 800-799-0709
Fax: 626-799-7718
www.plannedmarketing.com/

Plan Write for Marketing
Business Resource Software, Inc
2013 Wells Branch Pkwy #305
Austin, Texas 78728 USA
Toll Free: 800-423-1228
Fax: 512-251-4401
www.brs-inc.com/

Index

CUSTOMER NOTE: IF THIS BOOK IS ACCOMPANIED BY SOFTWARE, PLEASE READ THE FOLLOWING BEFORE OPENING THE PACKAGE.

To use this CD-ROM, your system must meet the following requirements:

Platform/Processor/Operating System. IBM-compatible processor running Windows 95/98/NT 4.0.

RAM. 16 Mb minimum; 32 Mb recommended.

Hard Drive Space. 80 Kb.

Peripherals. Web Browser, Microsoft Word 95 or higher, Microsoft Excel 95 or higher.